In Plain Sight

by

Mo McCarthy

Copyright © 2025 Mo McCarthy

All rights reserved, including the right to reproduce this book, or portions thereof in any form. No part of this text may be reproduced, transmitted, downloaded, decompiled, reverse engineered, or stored, in any form or introduced into any information storage and retrieval system, in any form or by any means, whether electronic or mechanical without the express written permission of the author.

This is a work of fiction. Names and characters are the product of the author's imagination and any resemblance to actual persons, living or dead, is entirely coincidental.

ISBN: 978-1-918038-90-3

LETTERS

Ethel & Rose
The horrendous wail of the siren echoes in my brain, refusing to stop despite the arrival in A&E, as medical experts spill out to receive the most precious item known to me: I die, oh I die a thousand deaths, I am more dead at this moment than the woman laying on the gurney, eyes set and body frozen except for when the medics create a movement.

Who are you is bellowed at me by impatient staff, who am I ? Well, who am I, what do I say, who do I say it to, dare I say who and what I am in her life. I lamely mumble 'friend' of family as they shoot questions at me while I answer like the robot I have become.

Rose, my beautiful fair skinned beauty is dwarfed by the amount of people flitting around her, hooking things up, shoving lines into her body, calling for bloods, scans and all the while talking to Rose looking for a response.

I hold my position, frozen while inside my screams echo alongside the siren of other arriving ambulances. Tell us the last time she spoke, drank, ate, when! when! who, what, my head aches with the need to scream Rose back into consciousness who to call? what do you mean, I'm here and still being asked for next of kin. I am kin you couldn't get it more kin than me.

I despise you all, doctors, nurses, anyone with Rose that means I can't be with her. I am constantly shooed out of the room, out of the way, yet I am called back because they want to know if I remember anything, no she is not diabetic, no history of high blood pressure, not on repeat medication. Rose the gym and lettuce bunny is a health-conscious freak, at 57 she can pass for a 30-year-old while my wide untamed hips and bottom roll uncontrollable as I walk, 'scatter the room' is Rose's favourite tease as heads turn to watch my spectacle of a backside.

For the umpteenth time I repeat, we live alone, she was fine when I left around midday, I came back at four pm and found her slumped in the chair, no I don't know how long she's been like that, no she didn't feel cold to touch, no she hasn't been sick, no she has remained how I found her till now...no! no! no! no!

Rage is a funny thing, outwardly I am observing all social protocol but inside I know if anything happens to Rose, every single personnel here is in danger, I will hurt people so bad if Rose is not restored, I look around me and wonder what they see that makes them not see me, I try looking through their eyes and see an overweight very middle aged buxom woman, I also see their lack of patience for me as they wonder how much to share with me.

Jesus, Mary, Jane and the Apostles in full, we are finally on the ward, Rose is tucked up in a special ripple bed, attached to various that bleep gently, I am warned alarms will go off if there is any change, such as a drop in oxygen levels, I want to breathe for you woman, I will breathe for you Rose, I hold her hand gently, and rest my head next to her, the curtain is drawn so I should be okay.

Rose my love, where did the years go, how come we are 57, when I look at you I see and feel 13, the age we met, who are these two oldies all grey haired and laughter lined. I remember our first term in the boarding house, we were paired up as the late joiners. I had not really heard or paid mind to the word Valentine, but you became and stayed my valentine.

We weren't quite sure what to do when we were told to give a small gift and card, I saw the panic in your eyes, I knew you did not come from a rich household, so suggested we do something for each other. We agreed to decorate each other's bed area for Valentine.

I still have the card you made me Rose, you think I'm joking!

I'll bring it and read it to you tomorrow, my words are interrupted by the visiting over bell, my request to stay longer is brushed aside, dismissed like I hadn't spoken, this is the first person I will bash if anything happens to Rose, you are not family or next of kin she digs so we can't make an exception.

Back home, home, our love nest, created by us for us, I wander around aimlessly until I wrap your nightdress round my neck like a scarf enveloped in your scent my calm is restored. I finally drift off as dawn breaks. I came awake startled. It takes me a moment to identify what is wrong. Rose is not beside me and she has not made the tea we share like a religion.

No Rose, no soft flesh to sink into, no amber body to warm mine, no one spooning me gently caressing my voluptuous chest, touching me like I might break or disappear again, even in the thorns of lovemaking Rose remains gentle, attentive, totally giving. Surely my heart is going to break, I am going to die, I have to die because without Rose I am more paralysed than she is, I begin to dry heave as hot tears sting my eyes, what do I do ? What can I do, here we are, age fifty-seven plus retirement years creeping closer, we had both decided to get government posts in our late forties, secure and stress free guaranteed salaries we took pay cuts in exchange for a life together.

My Rose, my love, my woman, my passion, my need, please universe, the powers, whatever power please help me. I need Rose, in my foetal position I let the tears flow. I have three hours to kill before visiting. This is now a house not a home without Rose. Physically exhausted I drag myself across the hall, opening my wardrobe. I reach for the old biscuit tin, I put it by the door ready to pick up when I leave for the hospital. I can't tell you what I ate or how I got ready, not to talk of the drive there. I function robotically, if I kill a pedestrian or animal on the drive down, I have not noticed, noon finds me at my beloved's bedside.

Tubes remain everywhere, eyes taped shut, roll of crepe bandage in each palm to stop them clawing shut, MRI confirmed what we all know Rose has suffered a massive stroke and that thank you very much is all I need to know for now, no more bad news. Someone had tried to give her a clean, I know because the washcloth and small bowl are still by her bedside. I am grateful and angry at the same time; I should be the one or be involved.

Rose, clean, clever, tidy, articulate Rose lying unable to attend to her own needs, Rose who will step in the bathroom to wash my back many a times leading to the most gentle and beautiful love making or at the very least a long cuddle before heading out, now lies her expression frozen a mixture of horror, pain and surprise, still no movement, no reaction, no return of Rose.

I turn the tin upside down and take the first correspondent, that card sent to me from my lifelong Valentine, I lower my voice and read quietly to Rose.

Dear Ethel,
It is nice to meet you and be your friend. I am happy to be your Valentine.
Happy Valentine Day, I hope you like the hibiscus and little gift.
Love Rose Odi

With three hearts done in red biro long faded, a tiny plastic bag the remains of that long-dried hibiscus and unused yellow with age the first gift from Rose, a handkerchief, one from the pack of three she had. Her surname that never changed boldly signed. I nudged her gently, that was us, our hearts wide open to each other in trust, comfortable with the words 'you are my Valentine' I reached for the next letter in my pile.

Dear Elthel,
I wanted to say how proud I am of you coming top of your class. I will miss you, don't forget me when you are abroad doing whatever it is the rich do in far away Countries, can't wait to see you when we resume. Happy holidays.
Your friend forever
Rose Odi

Dear Elthel
Disaster, disaster, my period started, this is the rubbish I must put up with every month. I wish I was a boy; this is very inconvenient particularly the sudden swell to the chest. I wanted to share this moment with you even though you are away. I hope you are good; I am keeping a low profile just waiting the days out until it's time for boarding school. I feel too self conscious here, the boys are not even hiding their gaze to my chest, they make my skin crawl, apart from that I can't wait to give you a big hug. I will give this letter to you when I see you.
Your best better best friend
Rose Odi

Rose, you do make me laugh, your language and descriptions, if you can hear me move your arm against me? No, okay no worries. Thank you for all the gifts, I bet you didn't realise I kept every scrap you ever wrote to me, fill this, it's the handkerchief you gave me on our first valentine. I didn't have a name for it but I knew I wanted to spend time with you and preferred your company to anyone else. I feel alive when with you, enveloped with a sense of wellness, even just sitting side by side in silence was and remains fulfilling. Here Rose let me read you another one of your letters.

Dear Ethel
I wanted to say thank you for being my friend.
I love you
Rose Odi

I think this was the note you left for me under my pillow when my parents turned up without notice and took me home. They didn't want to tell me my brother had passed in school. When I returned you were in class, but I found the note in my bed when I tucked my hands under my pillow, you knew my facedown hands under pillow manner. It was the first thing I felt, I have never felt so connected to anyone as I felt connected to you in a moment.

That day we shared our first kiss after lights out. Maybe more of a nose and teeth clash. I had tied sheets round our bottom bunk, located in a corner that gave us maximum privacy. Everything felt right, the gentle touches and exploration. How could anyone not want you, I certainly did.

The shame in the morning, that refused to come, as we giggled our way through the day, it had taken us two years to take the first step to intimacy, while others are receiving love letters from boys, we were content to receive from each other, if anyone noticed us, they wrote us off as two seniors that got on well. In that date and era we knew if we remain discreet no harm will befall us.

My character split into two, I glowed when at school, happy content repeating my name Ethel Odi in my heart, thus passed our snr years, you never visited me and I was never invited to yours, we understood the rules of different worlds.

Our first Separation:
In keeping with family tradition, I am to attend University abroad, I choose Canterbury Uni in Kent, unless you can secure a scholarship as you did for your secondary school education then education for you remains local. Age seventeen we finally exchanged home addresses.

Our last night was spent frantically hugging, touching like two people with news of imminent blindness trying to imprint all in memory. We celebrate a love that is refreshing, satisfying and complete without the burden of sex and pregnancy. Funny enough I doubt we would have known what to do if we had ventured down below. The long kisses and tingling of the breast met our needs, we had both become expert masseurs without training.

I had never come across the word depression, all I know is that England was covered in dark clouds when I arrived in late July. While all complained of the heat, I shivered with loss and a need that couldn't be met.

If I felt London was hard, Kent with all the mad women who hated men refused to wear bras and were constantly in your face with their weirdness, multi-coloured hair, screaming and protesting about something or the other happening on the other side of the world with a focus on natural smells which translates as bad body odour, breathe, there was a period when they didn't wash their hair in protest of goodness knows what. I came to know the word Lesbian, that certainly is not us, we are not lesbians we don't hate men, we eat meat and don't have a problem with the world and most certainly don't dress like men.

Rose, your fatty bum-bum shrank, the weight fell off as the months passed. I was not sick; I was pinning for you.

Ha, here we are Rose, your first air letter card to me, it was snowing that day but the earth lit up for me, the cloud that had enveloped me and stopped me from breathing lifted, I knew that letter by heart before the day was out, I wish I was at your

University only because you are there, I wanted to be there with you.

Dear Ethel,
You wouldn't like it here, too much chaos, you name it it's happening, drugs, alcohol, sleeping with lecturers for marks, sugar daddy sponsors, pimping of self and others, then the cults: you never know who you are talking to and what they want to get you into.

I am blinkered to everyone and everything around me but lectures, I must make it, as the first in my family to go to University I have to bring the grades home. The family is waiting for me to qualify, get a job and begin to educate my younger siblings.

How are you Ethel ?

I miss having my best friend with me. I have a neighbour who said I can receive calls on their phone, this is their number. If you can call, make it a Sunday late afternoon but before 7pm.

For now when I need to hear your voice I listen to the cassette tape of us singing Brown girl in the rain, I hope you still have your copy.

Do you know if you are coming home this year? I remain your faithful best friend.

Love like a river

Rose Odi

Babe, can I call you that? We've always stuck to our names to ensure no slip-ups in company, but babe you are, my babe. We are not too old to flirt.

Your letter saved me, I was one touch away from antidepressant, this simple thin piece of folded blue paper was the right prescription. I came alive like a desert that suddenly had rain, parched until wetted, soaked.

I held it to my chest, slept with it in my bra, Rose touched it. Rose is touching me. I was first in the queue at the post office the following morning. I bought a dozen and wrote four in easy succession before I cautioned myself about your limited budget.

Oh, Rose the joy of getting a letter from you each month, that is what is responsible for the success of my degree then Masters. Five years Rose, five years of not being in the same room as you not breathing the same air, no hug, no tongue exploration, no gentle cupping of the breast none of the things that made me feel complete, instead the unwanted attention of my parents friends children eagerly encouraged by parents who want to keep money in the family, not who you want but another prosperous family so that the money pot is bigger and they become a force to recon with, what a way to treat your children.

Forced holidays to various destinations, all the same crowd, while people eventually began to pair up in friendship some of which lead to marriage I remain devoted to you, a love that couldn't be acknowledged, not spoken about, not shown, a love that burns hot like the very fire described in hell, molten red boiling yet kept in a locked crypt, smiles, polite and socially amenable I bumble along.

I need you Rose; I need my woman across the water, I need my missing jigsaw piece that lies across the Atlantic, but horror awaits me. The two families have decided. I am expected to marry the son of my dad's best friend and business associate, Architect marries Architect. My pledges to come home to sort out my traditional clothing fell on deaf ears; the designer was instead flown to London.

Just short of my twenty-third birthday it is clear my life is not my own, I was born to do as I am told. I am distressed, distraught, life ending thoughts spill forward, I don't want this, I want the gentle peaceful life I have with you. Your letters during that difficult period often brought me back from the brink.

Dear Ethel

I hope this letter meets you well. Congratulations to us, twenty-three with Masters.

You know your best friend is a traditionalist, we do as our parents wish, it is our job to make them happy and by doing what they want we give back some of the happiness they gave us and the sacrifices they made.

Try and make the best of where you find yourself, survive all to give me the happiness of seeing my best friend again. For your

best health, cook a pot full of ginger and lime, boil and simmer for a few hours cool and do a fast the seventy-two hours before your period is due, it will help you in terms of painful periods.
Your friend
Rose

Dearest rose
It took me a while to work that one out but once I understood I never missed those three days leading up to my period. I married a monster, well maybe he wasn't a monster and felt stuck with me the way I clearly was with him. I had hoped to negotiate time before intimacy, but he was having none of it. He had been dating an American he was in love with and hated the sight of me.

Forced is the word he used; force is what I experienced on the wedding night. No gentle touch just brutality that I quickly became used to, sex on demand am and pm, the constant violation with childbearing intent. A pregnancy that never occurred due to my three-day liquid diet. Thankfully the nightmare ended after five years. I refuse to say his name.
I am now my own woman, I throw myself into work, get my own place and begin to plan my way back to you. How was I to know my father himself was a monster who was determined I will marry and remain married. His encouragement of me visiting my homeland for an extended holiday should have alerted me. While I dreamt of time with you my father was lining up husbands.

Dearest Ethel
How are you my lioness, my strong best friend who will pick me up when down, who will bounce back when thrown. When will I set eyes on you, happy to come to England but even better if you come to the homeland. Let me know your plans. On standby to pick you up from the airport if possible. Miss you, my bestie.
All is well at this end, I continue to be surrounded by heaps of money as the financial lead of the Bank but little of it is mine…in all I am content, I have put my younger ones through

school, so able to breathe somewhat myself. Both my parents have stopped discussing marriage as they know the first thing the man will say is stop working, for that understanding on their part I am grateful.

> Let me know when you are arriving so I can clear my dairy.
> Love from your Valie
> Ps: We old @ twenty-nine 😊

That first look Rose, that hug, your touch, your breath, the feel of you, your lightness against the darkness of my skin, I caught a glimpse as we tumbled into bed, we undulated in our movement, no longer the school girls the loving is furious, making up for longing so deep so fierce the first coming together is almost violent in it's act, for the first time I reach a climax, I have heard about this but know not the pleasure, I have orgasm after orgasm and then this feeling that starts like an electric current, pleasurable and painful overwhelming sweeping finally an explosion in my head, I experience my first post coitus migraine, you knew what it was and gently cradled me, keeping the room dark and hydrating me through that first night, then refusing to touch me in the morning in case we triggered another headache.

Oh, the joy of spending that weekend with you. For me you got rid of your home helps, we wandered around the house in flimsy covers and sometimes nothing at all, drinking in the richness of the female body, the sheer joy of togetherness of an attraction that began age 13 against our culture, against our religion a sure sign we will go to hell according to some and to prison in some countries, yet this felt good, actually this felt so damn good, two pieces coming together, a feeling of completeness, yet just outside your gate laid ugliness and it didn't waste time rearing its head.

When my father said dinner guests, I felt uneasy, I asked if I could invite a friend and got a no. I am dinner, I am the menu, what is wrong with this man, has he no other interest in life other than to get me married. I look to my mother for help that has never been there, he totally bullies and controls her, the most you'll get out of her is 'you know your father' This time he is a young widower, his wife died of cancer four years ago, nil children so no complications. He runs his own shipping company and is in and out of the homeland regularly. I certainly perk up when he says the main base will be between homeland and the UK.

Using the fact, I am an only child, I press on the fact that I would like to be in the homeland for both sets of parents who are not getting any younger. The deal is sealed, I come to tell you Rose of the next chapter of bullshit in my life. Roll with it your advice, bonus is we are on the same side of the water, that night you made love to me, it was different, tender, every touch a word, I cried like a child as you gently held me in your arms. This is love, nothing can compare to this feeling we share.

My second marriage is a toned-down affair, we observed a decent period of courtship, I tolerated Alex well. On his part he was an absolute gentleman, didn't try to sleep with me or make any sexual overtures. The register was brought to the house, we were married in front of a limited number and promptly moved to a magnificent mansion two streets from you Rose, yes, the one thing I insisted on was a new residence not where he lived with his late wife.

Alex seemed easy going; we had discussed endlessly on what we wanted. I had put emphasis on friendship which he echoed, how was I to know he had secrets of his own. I'm thirty-one and know bad sex, good sex and out of this world sex called Rose. I know I can tolerate sex with a man to protect Rose and I.

Come wedding night and Alex spent so much time in the shower I fell asleep. Determined to set the pace in the marriage I wake in the early hours and reach out for him, I feel two massive balls but can't seem to find a dick…this strapping 6'3 guy has an undeveloped penis, even without having children I expect that size on a child under the age of seven, it literally is the size of my little finger. I encourage him knowing there will be no penetration, he slams himself repeatedly against me and it's all over. We both clean up and retreat to our side of the bed to continue the sleep.

Our marriage lasted until he got a girlfriend pregnant 7 years later, pregnancy was the perfect excuse. I kicked up a fuss and decamped to Rose's house. Finally, at age thirty-eight I can start my life, my father has passed and my mother is totally spineless, has no say in what I do, the old regime is over.

PARADISO

Dear Ethel
Welcome home, my love, my better half.
Finally, we can exhale, life has felt like I have been waiting for permission to breathe.
Thank you for loving me, thank you for staying strong, thank you for nourishing and keeping our love alive and safe. Sorry you had to go through so much for us to be together.
Thank you for not shutting me out, it has been my journey too. I remain committed to you. I would like to formally ask you to be my life partner, you have been my first, my last my all. You are my strength, support and deep sense of wellbeing, you to me are everything, every moment, everyday.
Love always
Rose Odi

Hellooo! My thoughts and reading moment rudely interrupted 'could you step out please we need to clean and refresh Rose as well as do her observations.
 What is wrong with these nurses are they bred to be rude, asking if I could help, I am again reminded of my identify, no, it would be okay if you are family but as you are a friend and Rose can't give consent we have to ensure we maintain her dignity until she can guide us !!! we'll let you know when you can come back. Out away from the bedside I am kicked.
I step outside the ward and watch as people come and go, feeling lonely and defeated. I wonder how many are masquerading like me, LGBTIQQ as we are now categorised pretending to be friends, white, black, brown afraid of the horror and backlash that will follow. Sympathy for a thief but none for Dykes.
I reflect on the nine nieces and nephews Rose has. I am Aunty Ethel. I wonder if I would be so loved if they know Rose and I are lovers, not just two older spinsters supporting each other rather than living alone.
I begin to shake, lack of nourishment, fatigue, fear, fear that Rose is sick, very sick grips me. I rush out of the side room they

stuck me in, fuck this, fuck the nurses, fuck the system, fuck everyone, I have reached my melting point, as I open my mouth to speak I hear my name spoken lovingly and with warmth, I turn to see Roses' two siblings and crumble, they both envelop me in a massive hug, the first act of kindness towards me in twenty-four hours. I belong again, even if it's aunty status I belong in Rose's family.

I move my biscuit tin out of the way as we gather round Rose, I am no longer alone and the bleep of the machine fades as we talk to Rose, if I wasn't so preoccupied I might have picked up on the language being used, 'we release you from this pain' in my head translated as wish you pain free... the urgent bleeping of the machine jolts me back as the nurses and Doctors come flying out from all areas shouting for a crash team, crash trolley, crash machine.

Throwing all three of us out of the bed area we are left outside the curtain and told to wait in the side room for relatives. Finally I lose it the years of separation, unnecessary suffering, living a lie, denying myself, ourselves, loving in secret, only feeling safe abroad, the missing years, bullying of society into fear of prison sentence

I hear my own primaeval scream as one would the roar of a lion, words tumble out of my mouth as Rose's sister and brother shocked into silence gap at me, open mouth eyes wide like one would on seeing a newly mad woman in the town square.

I can't do this I thunder, don't leave me Rose, I won't survive, don't leave me, I have no one, E is before R, I should die first, don't leave me escaped my mouth again as I felt the shearing pain in my chest, tearing and exploding as the room lite up and I crumbled to the ground, I watch as the light dims only to be replaced by another light coming closer in the distance, in that moment I understood Rose was going before me, a love so strong she went ahead to light the way, her outline in the distance allowed me to close my eyes and yield in totality to 44 years of loving, in the nanosecond left I think of our love, it will remain untold unless someone has the courage to read Rose's letters and tell you who we are. I am a woman who loved another, that's who I am, right on cue merciful darkness envelops me.

LETTERS

Thank you Dr Fahad, this debrief is important, I have never seen anything like the level of distress I witnessed, I was coming on to the shift when I heard that blood curdling distress and to lose two patients within minutes is much, then we had to deal with the siblings of the deceased who were sad, angry and distressed and in denial of the relationship between the Ethel and their sister at the same time, safe to say the ward was unsettled. I am an open minded person and feel incredibly sad for Rose and now we know Ethel, her lifelong partner, we certainly were not thinking of family as we should have. Well, that's me, I'll let someone else speak.

Dr Fahad, I am a compassionate nurse but as a fellow Muslim you know this is haram, the prophet Mohammed SAW in the holy Quran covered what is permitted and what isn't, to me if both women lived, I would hope they realised this is not the path to follow, I hope their sins are forgiven and they make heaven.

I knew the room would erupt and it did instantly, the LGBTIQQ nurses and those who accept others screamed the room down. I waited for the noise to die down, all the time thinking of the dancing boys of my youth, of how much sadder my life is compared to Rose and Ethel, at least they got to spend some time together. I made all the right noises said the right neutral things and ended the meeting before I personally strolled over to strangle Amal who ironically means Hopes but is yet to give one single person hope, a typically frustrated dried up old prune of a middle aged woman she looks twice her 46 years, dampens any environment she is in with her negative cloud, huffing puffing and generally complaining about something while constantly sniffing and adjusting a hijab that refuses to sit right on her.

As we empty out Bisii the CBT therapist catches up with me, Dr Fahad just to let you know patients' property is closed and not sure where to put the tin of letter I have left in your office, someone will pop it down to patients' property on Monday. Dr

Fahad the letters are gut-wrenching, imagine loving for so long and not being able to express it because of all the cultural taboos.

That's alright. I responded before opening the door to my office.

In the privacy of my room I breathe slowly, it's Friday evening, today is the day, I will not be here tomorrow not to talk of Monday, I look around my office, Chief Medical Officer for the past fifteen years, lots of hard work and yet not one solid moment of happiness, the toe curling, deep throat curling happiness I hear and read about never experienced, oh well I get off the bus called life tonight, I have put all my affairs in order, at sixty-two I am a widower of twenty-one years, nil off-springs, just the thought of procreation revolts me, my cousin wife had died a virgin the same way she came to me.

I get up and pace round the room, the debrief session had gone on for ninety minutes, longer than I thought, my back niggled me from sitting down too long, not aware of my surrounding I knock a tin over, there shouldn't have been a tin on my desk, paper floats everywhere apart from a bunch tied with what looked like a faded handkerchief. I recognise it as the one left by Bisii.

The entire hospital staff are aware of the new greatest love story more intense than Romeo and Juliet. Packing up the letters I stand holding the pack, I am curious about Rose and Ethel, two women who were visible but not seen for the loving couple they were. Written on the top envelope are the words For Rose, not sent sharing is Coping. I wonder what that means. Sitting down I untie the ribbon and pull the bunch out thinking of their bodies lying on a cold slab two floors beneath me. I read.

Dear Rose

I send love from my heart and my head to you, the two permanent places of residence for how I feel about you. My dearest, these are the things I cannot bear to burden you with but need to put down.

I am sitting in the middle of a circus, the wedding preparation is in full swing, I am robotic, I am scared, I am helpless. I think of all the things I can do such as run away but you don't know my father! he is a man that must be obeyed, he is such a tyrant I cannot imagine him wooing my mother and having the softness to sleep with her, my brother fares better because of his sickle cell thalassemia status, he is treated with kid-gloves as his next crisis is awaited. You want to see a pale black man come and see my brother. He just looks unhealthy all the time.

He is sitting on the settee watching the show going on around me, his eyes are soft, somewhat sad, as if he can read me. I burst into tears and all activities stop, I sob like the end had come feeling completely empty, all non family are shooed out of the room, I point at my brother and say how sad I feel about his pain, he knows and I know it is nothing of the sort, last night my brother said to me I don't know what you want but I know you don't even like this guy, if you are in love with another guy try and tell Dad, you never know he might reconsider as you and this guy have zero rapport.

At the time I didn't respond as I realised, he didn't consider I might be in love with a female partner he just assumed another man, if he had kept it neutral and remained at someone else, I might have shared how attracted to women I was with him but cry I did instead. My brother is the only one that can comfort me, all others are perpetrators. I cry for me, for you for the unmet need, the longing to end my longing, the silent cry of my flesh for you, the need to hold your hand, look into your eyes, swim in your warmth, come together as one.

Rose my love, my thoughts are all dark and dangerous, how to get rid of reigns in my thoughts, shame and a prison sentence does not allow me to perfect what I will do, who do you know that is about to get married and is filled with thoughts of how to get rid of the groom.

It's the Sunday before my wedding, it's 6:30 pm. I will live, my heart will beat, my flesh will warm, my body will glow with each thought of you is what sustains me.

Talk soon my Valie.

Dearest Rose

It was not a wedding but a carnival, if anyone had paid attention to us and not to their guts for what they could stuff their way through they would have noticed a robotic couple, the love of his life was there. How did I know her? the American twang, while encased with his friends from Uni days where they all met. For a moment I felt sad for him, if he was saying I do to her, what an amazing day it would have been for him, instead I sit next to him, say the right things feed the cake and offer wine all the while hoping for a miracle in which he choked and died with no effort to bring him back. Do you think I am evil? Is love making me evil? Who cares anymore, my life is over Rose.

I can't come to you, my tier of society is all about the name, status, social standing, the etiquette of high-ranking families, old money as it's referred to. My shackles I call it, huge invisible rings of heavy metal on each shoulder and ankles actual weight rests in my heart.

I look around the wedding reception, his mother has asked me several times if I am okay, I tell her I am nervous and share I have never been with a man, do you know what the old hag did, she went straight to her son and told him to be gentle with me, I could see she was also telling her friends and family, a celebration I gather when the bride comes to her marital bed clean and untouched, I wonder what the mental illness term is for this manner of behaviour.

We decamp to The Landmark Hotel in central London Marylebone a short drive from the reception, our wedding gift from both parents is a three bedroom flat in Lancaster Gate the lovely Marble Arch end of it, became a shitty present when I realised both sets of parents had flats in the same building, while not living there they called it investments and used that excuse to drop by regularly.

Rose, I know you won't like this kind of talk but if it is remotely possible to hate one's destiny it will be mine of being born to my father, I don't think I have love for him…he who must be obeyed, he is the roaring flame that begot a lesbian child, him and his manliness blames my mother for only having two children, I wanted six he stated one day, my mother had nearly died with her pregnancies producing two children from seven pregnancies. The entire day he struts with a fat cigar in one hand and glass of Remy Martin in the other, not drunk but slightly happy, planning my life, in his speech talking about the wonderful grandchildren to come, I look at him and wonder how I could be related to a man who has nil emotional intelligence, for a moment I wonder if my father is Autistic.

In the honeymoon suite at a whopping five hundred and fifty pounds a night I get ready for the inevitable: tonight I will be raped, what else to call it, this mean, disgruntled, spineless man who is unable to equally stand up to his father to express his wish is going to take it out on me, I steel myself for what is to come, thanking God for the layer of fat to at least provide me with some insultation, you can't go through what is to come Rose with your slim petite frame, you will break, thank God it's me not you.

My daft as a toothbrush of a mother insisted on a bridal trousseau, ridiculous flimsy material for everything I might as well be wearing net curtains in various colours and patterns, this is not me, simply adds to my feeling unsafe. I am scared, Rose, I am not naive but truly scared of what is to come. I hope it takes place in the dark.

It's five am Rose I've cleaned up the cloggy red brown oozing from me and quietly made a cup of tea, I am on the balcony watching the first rays of the day in the distance, my head hurts because he kept grabbing my head in his hands, my neck hurts where his hand roughly reaches behind to hold me face steady, my eyes hurt from unshed tears, my nose assaulted with the smell of his aftershave that penetrated to my brain, my lips are swollen with a small tear in my bottom lip, my mouth feels like it will never be clean again.

My breast Rose they hurt so bad, this man squeezes them without regard for me, the soreness is so bad It pains me when I brush against myself, my entire chest hurts from baring his weight, something I am not used to, feels like I am being crushed by a bus, below my waist is a mess Rose, my viagina lips are swollen and rub as I try to walk, this man as I will always think of him hurt me, he hurt me Rose, all he could think of was his own pleasure, even when he realised I was a virgin all he say was ' you are tight'

I feel like I did when I arrived here, age seventeen, alone, lost, desperate for you, your face, your touch, my completeness. How am I going to survive this Rose? day one and I am filled with thoughts of desperation, thank God I have not chosen the honeymoon location, he said he will leave that to me. I am not going away with him, to hell with my honeymoon. I am going back to work next week. I am not staying at home to be a fuck buddy to this awful human being, he is a monster, a pathetic example of a man, in love with one settling for other, just for inheritance's sake, I wouldn't care less if father left me nothing just to be able to live my life and life with you.

You see all those lesbians I wrote about and their weirdness at Uni. I now envy that weirdness, I envy them because they kept it real, they could be themselves, love, protest, burn bras, hate or love men, they had freedom and that's what I failed to understand. Their weirdness to me was because they are shackle free. I turn and look through the curtain at the lump in the bed, we are a victim of circumstances, if he was kind and friendly I would endure what lies ahead better.

Oh shit ! while I was lost in thoughts of you I didn't notice him wake up look for me see me on the terrace and come up behind me, the first thing I felt is the erect manhood poking me in the bottom, turning around I burst into tears, in a still voice he states, 'you'll get used to it and steers me back into the room and unto the bed, his entry and violation of me shearing hot pain and dominant, he is marking his territory, I am his land. As he labours away on top of me having the cheek to ask me to romance him pulling my hands and directing where to touch, my one thought is 'I can kill somebody'

Dearest Rose

A week has passed, a week of silent tug of war, of boundary marking without words. I accepted the master bedroom but commandeered the middle bedroom as mine, ensuring all my stuff is stored there and his in the master bedroom. I will lay with him but will not live with him. We have a cook for evenings and the weekend, we also have a home help twice a week, money does come in handy. I concentrate on making myself look as unattractive as possible, if he realizes it's deliberate he keeps his peace but come rain or shine sex takes place twice a day Monday to Friday at the weekend I am lost for count, but endure I do, my body has settled to the assault, his compliment to me ' you are always nice and tight, I like that' I am not turned on you fool, you do not excite me, there is nothing about you that calls my body awake. Ignorant little sod !

We had our first argument today Rose, I thought I would test the water and informed him when he reached for me in the morning, my period had started, he got off the bed, got a towel shoved it under my ass and climbed me, twisting and turning to throw him off so I started the verbal assault, nil effect he did not even miss a stroke, when he finished and wiped himself and saw no blood he went ballistic, telling me if I ever pulled that stunt again there well be hell fire in our house, I married you against my will, so don't wind me up' and to prove his point he proceeded to fuck me again, I just laid there like a lump of wood and detached myself from the act going on, over time dissociation embedded itself in my everyday life with him.

My three-day ginger and lime liquid diet is the bomb, it's six months, no pregnancy to God and the Universe be the Glory. Funny enough it is really getting to him with talks of Harley Street Doctor blah blah blah. All blood screens and scans show normal working equipment for both of us and for a moment I realised if this man had been kind to me for my want, I might have allowed myself to get pregnant secure that the child would remain with me come the inevitable separation. Who on the other hand wants to have a child with this buffoon, tactless so and so who has no clue of the needs of others.

I breathe a sigh of relief when a year into the marriage it appears he is unable to maintain his mad regime of sex-sex-sex, I took a tally once as I wondered if my private part will not disintegrate from all the pounding, Monday to Friday instead of ten it was eleven, a lesson for implying my period had started and at the weekend seven times. The one ray of light it all lasts less that 10 minutes, to occupy my mind I would count his strokes, not once in the years we were together did he make a spark in my mind or body or touch my soul, what he called tight was years of dry-fucking a woman.

Dearest Rose

The one bright spark in my gloom of an existence. I want to share what I cannot share; I know the effect on you will make you throw caution to the wind, and you'll be banging my door down. I don't understand how I got to this place. At work I am the trusted, respected dependable target achieving Architect E as I am fondly referred to by colleagues. Rose, what is mental wellbeing? I don't think I have it. I feel such pain that digging my fingers in my palm doesn't relieve, I feel like a car whose brakes have failed careering out of control. I have no control over my body Rose, it's killing me, my body is not mine, I share with a monster, I do not share willing, I don't want to share, not sure why I am using that word the awful power of a piece of paper you jointly sign, a marriage certificate gives this man such power over me.

I feel so small, so pathetic, so irrelevant once the door to the outside world closes. I start controlling what I have a say in, my food intake, Oh Rose this was a terrible time, restricting my diet. The first day I accidentally scratched myself with my nail, I was trying to pull on a swimsuit as I pulled the edge out of my crotch. My nail caught me on the inner thigh, the small sharp pain felt so good, it was a release of something too big for me to understand. I pinched myself, it gave the same pleasurable pain, I pinched harder and again the same draining of tension. Within a week I had moved to using my inner thighs, pinch scratch and eventually using a safety pin to draw across, the first time it bled I realised the sight of blood was irrelevant. It is the pain that soothes me.

Please don't worry if you ever get to read this, the period of restricting diet, inducing vomit and self harming by scratching lasted for a year and seven months, why did I stop ? I lost three teeth. It was my dentist that gently broached the subject of sudden teeth decay via acid reflux and encouraged me to consider therapy rather than inflict punishment on myself. Interesting her conversation woke me from my semi-comatose state and predictably I turned that anger towards him.

I went from being submissive to being absent, boy did that indifference hit him hard, holy bastard! It hit me like a ton of bricks. This man enjoyed every moment of discomfort he put me through. I have somehow managed to put this period behind me, slowly my weight returned to normal, and the thin lines of the pin lines blended into the surrounding melatonin, I didn't have therapy, putting my pain in writing to you healed me, my Rose my wellness tonic, love, love, love you.

Dearest Rose
I am more okay than I thought I would be, his parents particularly his Mum pops in, with guests we have settled into the charade we are comfortable with, both playing the role expected with nil issues, the moment we say bye to visitors we go back to our different corners: nil use for each other. With his mum I do the occasional lunch and in her I see some of me. I am sure she had once been in love but that departed a long time ago leaving a woman who knows what side her bread is buttered, living in luxury and enduring or living in poverty and suffering. Lunch or tea would be at The Ritz, she always had a gift for me, I think she hoped I would be her confidante and she mine.

By the end of the second year, she gave up. When she gave up my father started, are you two doing the needful to give me grandchildren he will bellow with what counts as a smile for him. It's in God's hands my mother would soothe to placate everyone. Neither of us could blame each other. The tests came back all clear, so God and the Universe share the blame.

London can be the most amazing or loneliest place on the planet. I go through the motions, thinking of you constantly, six hours flight away but you might as well be on Mars, how do you cope?

I made some new friends at work. Rose, they are nothing like me, more like the crowd that scared me at university. I can't make sense of their sexuality, and I don't try to, many different preferences, I stick to seeing people and thinking about people. It's the Christmas period and spirits are high because for once they did not have to pressure me to come along on the outings, I looked at the various ones and chose two. The first is in Soho, Madame Jojo's, you need to come there, sorry I am getting ahead of myself.

The walk-through Soho itself is an eye opener, all manners of sexual promise and pleasure displayed in a manner that makes it clear you are entering a zone dedicated to orgasms.

With the kind of confidence I do not have we pour into a shop, you name it it's there, drops, oils, edible underwear, whips, dress-up outfits and wall to wall penis, double edged ones for females who want to pleasure each other simultaneously, I have never seen anything like it, and no shame whatsoever people made purchases, me I kept a smile on my face acknowledging to myself I know nothing about sensuality. Madame Jojo's is dinner and Cabaret, the food was good, the Cabaret mind blowing. I sang alone, laughed, and roared with the crowd as the performers dragged us into their show, after the show we moved on to a nightclub called Heaven.

Rose we have not lived, here there were several areas to hang out but it is the crowd, gay straight, crossdressers you name it we were all on level ground. Noone watched me or was overly interested in me as I drank in my surrounding, poured onto the dance floor we did and danced to songs I had no idea of but my body moved with the music, I got plenty of attention from women on the dance floor, I love us, when I made it clear I wasn't looking for a liaison nothing changed we danced and hugged and parted with air kisses.

I like Heaven, under the Arches as it's sometimes referred to, pouring out at four am, I have never felt so alive, I didn't want morning to come nor the night to end, half our group had disappeared but as I hailed a black cab for my short ride I feel bitter, bitter that I could be having fun, fun with you, a fun-filled life with the person I want to be with not the shit I have, sorry about my language, actually in less than a week I am using stronger language than that.

Dear Rose

I am feeling drained and ill. Today I came home early from work, guess what I discovered, when I am at work he brings friends home they eat and do whatever it is they get up to. When I arrived early I was surprised to hear music and several voices, walking in I politely said hello and headed to my room. I went back to the sitting room and sat in one of the far corner chairs waiting for the lemon tea I asked for. I am in the same room but far enough to give them space, it's my home and I'll be damned if I must sit in a room while he and his rat pack have the sitting room. While waiting, a lady I hadn't seen appeared from the guest toilet, unsure if she thought I was one of their group, still yacking away on her phone she came up to me and asked me to move, I am in her seat! I looked at her in astonishment, those on the other side of the L-shaped lounge couldn't see or hear us.

I erupted out of my chair like Mt Vesuvius 'bitch I shouted, I will rearrange your face if you don't get out of mine, you come to my house and tell me I am sitting in your chair, if you want to walk out of here the way you walked in you better get the fuck out of my face' my tone despite the music conveyed itself clearly as whatever alcohol influence she was under vanished, I have never seen clarity descend so fast, 'sorry, sorry, my mistake, I'm sorry she repeated before sculling round the corner to where her cronies awaited her.

It reminded me of a throw away statement by a neighbour 'the traffic in this building during the day is interesting' me and my mind your business attitude I just bid the her a pleasant day not realising the old goat was trying to alert me, well here I am alerted. What an insult Rose what won't my eyes see with this madness called marriage.

If I had known all I needed to do was come home early and catch him at his game I would have done that a long time ago, the wonderful fallout of that incident is that he took himself off and would disappear for days, if he goes out on a Friday he might return on the Monday after work, did I look for him or ask him his whereabouts hell no. I accepted the comfort of the empty flat and the peace it brought, slight embarrassment as the staff knew but eventually that was neither here nor there for me.

Thus began a phase when I didn't experience so much distress but also started a different level of distress from feeling like I am invisible away from work. Would you believe I can use people, my love I did stooped to that level and started to hang out with the friends from work, if anyone looked closely, they would realise I gyrated towards the LGBTQ crowd, one guy did comment on why I wasn't hanging out with them I chucked back nil office affair gossip with those I hung out with.

So started a period when I went to all the London iconic gay hangouts, The Golden Ball, Julius Caesar, Taylor's Molly House, Royal Oak Molly House, King's Arms, Compton's of Soho, Halfway to Heaven, Zodiac Bar & Club, Eagle London, Two Brewers to name a few, never have I felt so safe, these friends ensured I got home safely, they welcomed me into their mist, nil push on examination of sexuality they just let me be a pal and hang out with them.

How I wish you could be here, the freedom to connect, love, express, I witnessed it all in the clubs and outings as I long for you, it blew my mind how easily people made friends and relationships grew right in front of my eyes. I miss you and what could be, still I can begin to see the writing on the wall so I began to reduce my association with my new friendship eyeopener group.

Disengagement was simple. I took on a new post, my sendoff party will stay in my mind for a day past forever. We started in a wine bar, then on to a night club followed by the early morning Chinese meal, goodbyes were bittersweet promises to keep in touch made knowing I won't. I got the feeling they know I am gay, tied down by many invisible wires and shackles, that well known prison with no wall's windows or locks. The greatest statement made when I was them was 'we've got you' they certainly did and for that I am enormously grateful for the sanity they brought into my life, thank God for my work gay family.

Dearest Rose

Big mistake, big mistake this new job, sexual harassment, I should have sensed something amiss at the interview but thought the female director Toni on the executive board just valued me. Trouble never comes without spare parts to it. The project I will be working on is led by her, tall for a woman at 5'11 impeccably dressed, not one outward sign of macho man in her, but I came to find out how vicious Toni is. It started gently, inviting me to lunch, quick bite after work. I was grateful for the interest in me and feeling good that in my boss I had found a mentor. Mentor keh…omo this lady na real craze. Working together meant being in proximity most times, sharing rides to sites and generally being within arms reach of each other, again Rose not once did I think Toni was interested in me.

Praise came often and promotion came within nine months of joining the team. What others could see I was blind to, I was being groomed, you would think I had more common sense, but I was totally blind to what was brewing. It started with what seemed to be accidental brushing and squeezing past, hands touching or reaching for the same item at the same time, I just laughed it off as mirroring each other.

Toni is a predator Rose, if anyone tells you there is no female-on-female grooming, they are lying. For eighteen months Toni desensitised me to being around her, spending most days and working hours alongside her. In the female changing room, from mufti to overall and back and hard hats nil interest shown in me, I began to see her as a sista, someone I was comfortable with.

This bitch made her move on a work trip, we were to attend a conference in Vienna, the other participants wanted to make a week of the four-day event so flew out ahead. Toni and I naturally travelled together, sharing her car for the airport drive, enjoying the pleasure of access to the first class lounge and all it had to offer. My undoing is the Southern Comfort and lime, I had two, I was not drunk but lightly merry, the arm under by arm to steady me resting gently against my left breast did not alarm me as we giggled our way towards the forty five minute flight, not used to too much alcohol naturally I feel asleep. By the time we landed all signs of that drink had left my system contrary to the belief the altitude increases the effect of alcohol.

Arriving at the hotel to check in I thought they had made a mistake in the booking but no we are booked into a suite, still no alarm bells, arriving in the suite there is just one bedroom in it a massive Queens bed and still foolish me thinks sista's, we'll be alright. Rose naivety can kill. We have about two hours until the welcome meeting Toni suggests a massage, in no time there are two massage beds set up side by side in the suite. The massage totally relaxed me deeply and was soothing. I feel almost limbless, fifty minutes of sheer bliss. Nil alarm at showers, I went in first and Toni used it next, nil exposure of bodies both of us I thought maintaining the required decorum. As usual she is suited and booted in her high end clothes. I settled for a Lipsy maxi embellished navy blue dress.

If I had stopped to think I would have wondered for a moment if we did not look like a couple, but you know me Rose I can be a total airhead, the admiring glances in the lift and at the reception I put down to Toni's striking presence. Again too much champagne not enough food, we rolled up to our room just after midnight, I slept off immediately, in the early hours I woke to see I had moved over to Toni and we sleep in a cuddled fashion, detangling myself I went to the loo, ensuring when I returned to sleep I kept to my side of the bed.

There was nothing usual in our coexistence in that suite until the last night, again I will put it down to not enough food and luxury drinks of all kinds being pushed, this incident is one of the reason I have not touched alcohol ever again, I know it wasn't just the alcohol but if I hadn't been merry I don't think Toni would dare. Clearly merry we headed upstairs, me thinking what a great sista when she helped me undress for bed, even the way she held me made me think aww she doesn't want me to fall over. I remember sinking into the softness of the pillows and lights out.

I woke confused by pleasurable sensations, I squirmed thinking I am dreaming straining for more of this good feeling that I didn't know exist, as I moved I gradually became more awake, first thing off is that my legs were spread open, my pyjama shorts missing, between my legs in the gloom of dawn I see a head hands either side of my hips my knees bent, still I think I am dreaming. I came awake confused and all instincts to move back were met with resistance as Toni held me firm and gave me head, at some point using one hand to hold me while she pleasured herself.

Surely this is rape what is different from this and my husband, I am involved in a sexual act I am not engaged, I lay frozen I can't pretend I am still asleep I lay there and detach myself, in fairness she has not hurt me and is gentle in all she does to me but violation is violation, I did not invite nor encourage Toni. We are in a strange country. I am away from my support network. She is my boss; what the hell is this? She climaxes noisily, I detangle myself and roll on my stomach, she slide unto my back her entire weight pressing me into the mattress, I thought she is done, lifting herself up to end up knees either side of me she pours oil on my back and begins to massage, she massage every inch of me, parting my legs and massing my private part.

Rose can you imagine, a massage of the viagina ! and still I lie quietly not making a noise used to being brutalised by my husband I accept the fingers gentle inserted in me, would probably have been better if she was rough I might have fought back but what do you do with someone worshipping your body, I also can't hit her it would show in moments, how an earth did I walk into this? Toni gently flips me over and massages my front from my hairline to my toes, she finishes and moves off me. Would you believe that in that early hour of the morning I fell asleep, my brain totally scrambled.

Waking to the smell of toast Toni is washed and dressed we check out in an hour, she smiles good morning and I answer keeping my voice steady, the turmoil in me not showing I washed like you would expect a rape victim to, I may not have experienced the violence associated with rape but rape is rape, rape by another woman leaves me struggling to breathe as I wash and wash trying to get rid of the memory of events of recent hours.

Toni is pleasant, attentive and acts if I am not mistaken coy, she smiles at me a lot, I smile back wanting to rush across the room and knock her head off, I smile back at my boss and vow never to touch another drop of alcohol.

Who do I share this with, what will the advice be, did I enjoy it, no I did not, this is what it is unwanted attention and I am unsure despite my age what the reaction will be if I was to report it back in London, what will happen to me at work, home and publicly, is there such as a thing as female rape. We return to England without mishap, the ride home is heavy. I think Toni is beginning to question my silence, drawing up at our building. She asks if I am okay, when can she see me.

Finally, I speak feeling safe that once I have my say I do not have to remain in her presence. I call a spade a spade and get some satisfaction at the look of alarm from her, reminding her of my marital status and at no time had I encouraged her nor wanted her attention, Toni pales, she finally recognised the level of the incident back in Vienna. I love my job I tell her I love the people

I work with, I do not want a relationship with you, you will continue to be my Boss but never you cross the line with me again, what you did to me in that hotel room is rape, should I, would I report it, it will devastate our lives. I will put this behind me today, you stay in your lane, and I stay in mine. If you ever try that with anyone else and it becomes public, I will testify against you. I detest you for what you did to me, I will never forgive you for taking advantage of the respect and trust I have in you. If I am to choose a partner Toni it will not be you.

From today you must move me to another department, if I get to work on Monday and I am still on your team I will change my mind about reporting. If women can't be safe with each other then we are done for, I will always remember your touch with the horror it brought, you do not turn me on or mean anything to me, and if you try and bully me, I will teach you a lesson you will never forget. Toni, all 5'11 crumbled and began to cry 'I have been in love with you from the moment you joined the firm. I thought culturally you couldn't share how you felt in return freely and publicly. I am sorry I misunderstood you. I am sorry I caused you trauma. I am sorry that because of me you are sad. I hear you and apologise for my behaviour' she stammers.

I listen and I am not fooled for a moment. Taking out my phone I switched off the recording. If Toni was going to collapse, that was the moment, my passport to safety from you Toni, I exit the car and walk into my building without looking back. I felt good. Good that I spoke up even if I couldn't in the homeland arena. Today in my mid twenties I stand my ground to the beginning of abuse, different types but abuse all the same.

Rose, why is my life so colourless, why? I'll tell you why you are not in it. I feel the cloud descending but will fight it. I will heal, I will move on, I am strong, I am brilliant, I am clever, intelligent, I am your Ethel and you are my Rose forever and a day.

No other woman is going to touch me, it is you or nothing. That evening, I attended my first Taekwondo class. The next person that tries it with me I will karate chop them up, my huge backside permitting movement of course, see humour at the thought of you Rose. Your name makes me feel strong.

The cramp and general stiffness in my body brings me back in time, makes me take in my surrounding, it is daylight, I sigh, I have not killed myself as planned, the insulin remains in the fridge, I was and remain totally caught up in Ethel's letters to Rose, it is the feeling of being given privilege to walk in another's shoes. Placing the letters back in the order tied up I make a note of where I am. I pick myself up and go to bed, hoping sleep comes on.

Just tossing and turning from peeping into the life of a stranger where mine is too empty, painful unfulfilled to make it worth sharing. My thoughts adrift.

I am taken back to the first time I will see a man touch another man. We are young and gathered to learn, it is the northern part of the homeland where I was born and raised, watching the most Snr Imam pick a boy up and sit him on his lap I am envious, I want to be the special one that is picked to sit on his lap, as the rest of us sit on the ground facing him and reciting after him, the boy on his lap squirms and he holds him firm moving his own legs side to side, because I am focused on the Imam I watch him rhythmic movement of the boy on his lap, then I see him pull a handkerchief and tuck it under his abaya.

It is the look on the Imam's face that keeps me captured, it is one of rapture as he recites, but he also glistens from sweat that broke out on his face, I watch as he lowers the boy on the ground at his feet and wipes his face with his abaya. I wish I was that boy, what do I have to do to be chosen, I vow to always sit at the front always, sooner or later he will notice me. I like the intense heavy scent of the Tabu perfume they all wear, I can't wait to be old enough to wear it.

I figure I am between seven-eight an age where when the wind changes directions I get an erection, my body seemed to be in a permanent state of arousal, having a bath is my favourite time of the day, the smoothness of soap suds on my little pee-wee, though I don't quite know what to do with it I also know there is something sinful that will earn me a beating if I am discovered touching myself which I do at every opportunity I am alone,, it is hard not to when at night you can hear Baba with one of his wives and he is not quiet thinking we are asleep. As the Chief Imam I wonder if Baba is also bouncing boys on his knee during his lectures.

I am what you would call a handsome child. I heard it so often from Aunties who would press me into their bosom all the while telling my mother what a handsome child she produced, my long eyelashes were always a point of conversation. Where I did not like the bosom crush, I loved being with the women, joining in their singing, clapping along and watching their movement closely. With no one around I would pull one of my mothers hijab and enjoy the silky feel of it against my skin, in private I would go over the dance steps and hip movements of the women until I perfect the sway and undulating hip movements I see. I dance and dance when alone, pretending to have a bosom, squeezing my chest, cupping chest as I see the women do, for now I am allowed to move freely amongst them but I know a time is coming when like my older brothers I will no longer have access to the women when gathered.

Life in general was good, Baba is important in our community, Mama sold provisions and home life was relatively settled, the area of concern is the school where a lot of beating went on, you spoke you were hit, you didn't speak when expected you were hit, it seemed life is about hitting the children into submission, but me I dreamed my way through those encounters, I have minimal interactions with the boys if I can help it, too rough preferring to roll around the dusty ground.

I seek the company of the girls after all I know I am a girl. I am accepted due to my feminine features. If I dared to act macho, I know they would yell at me and kick me out of their gathering. I do all they do, talk shop, talk care, talk about marriage and what we will do when we grow up.

It is a normal Saturday with nothing to signal or hint at the mind-blowing day this was going to be, armed with my tablet for writing I head to the gathering and sit on the floor at the front as usual, our regular Imam is sick, we have a new face, fair skinned with the most beautiful black lips I have ever seen, the kohl around both his eyes accentuate them making me think of drowning in the contrast created, his head tightly wound with the obligatory covering I fantasise about what laid under the covering. Such was my intent that I caught his glance, turning his palm upwards and outwards towards me. He beckons me forward, if I had hoped for a lap I was mistaken, he simply sat me by his foot and proceeded to touch my head neck and shoulder throughout the time of recitals.

I feel like the teacher's pet, with the other boys giving me envious glances and plainly wishing they were in my place. Dismissing others, he kept his hand on me to still me, in greeting him we know he is Imam Nuhu. Looking back, he clearly had no idea who's son I am as if he did I doubt he would have paid me any mind. As if he knew my mind he asked if I wanted bread and tea, how could he have known this is my favourite, that slim loaf of bread that comes with a milky sweet cup of tea from the wandering vendor who bangs the cup against the kettle to call attention to his presence, yes please I respond, he gets up and takes my hand.

I love that little nub of blue band margarine, wishing the vendor will put more, I gratefully accept the bread and tea, squatting down like I see kids do while the elders sit on benches. Imam Nuhu asked me to move in front of him, which I did so we were facing each other. I like how he constantly smiles at me, how was I to know in my loose-fitting clothing my crown jewels are on full display with my squat. I like the attention this man is giving me, while we both enjoy our bread and tea.

He asks me about school and what I would like to do when I grow up, I tell him about my wish to become a Medical Doctor, I share it's because several of my siblings had died because of lack of a Doctor, he tells me it is an honourable thing and encourages me to study hard, he is the first person to plant the thought of the outside world in my horizon, stating whatever Country you are in Doctors are always needed, he shared his experience of studying in Cairo, the richness of the culture and the modern approach to problem solving.

I drink it all while basking in the attention of an adult male and wondering if he will make me a good husband. Walking me to the end of our room he informs me he will see me next week as the Snr Imam had an operation in the big city and will be away for a while he will be covering our classes, without thinking too much I hugged his legs tightly, smile up at him and tell him 'I like him, small child he says I like you too'

Not much needed to know who arrived first the next Saturday, his back towards me while arranging books I ran up and hugged him from behind, Fahad he said without needing to turn, coming round I touched his feet the proper way and bid him the traditional greeting. We stand smiling at each other, me drowning in his beautiful eyes and at that tender age experiencing wanting to be with someone always, I am enslaved.

Again, he kept me close, tender touches and strokes that to the onlooker looked to be comforting a child but in that touch were messages that at a tender age I was able to decipher, I want to be special and he makes me feel special, thus continues the next few years, nil to alarm me in his manners and behaviour towards me, in time I am called Imam Nuhu's son as I grew into his shadow.

I spent more time at his little dwelling given to up and coming Imam's like him, pottering around, eating, sleeping or simply basking in the warmth he extended towards me. Our contact was dominated by education, ensuring I achieved my optimum. As the years progressed my increasing beauty did not go unnoticed by both sexes, compliments came from both sides, the girls wishing to have my grace and the boys wanting my slim tall frame.

The shift to being myself in Imam Nuhu's presence came one night at his place, there was no electricity, while waiting for it to be restored he brought out his windup radio, as music filled the air one of my favourite artist came on without thinking I jumped up and began to dance as I would if alone and safe at home to do so, I moved my body my arms my eyes and swayed my hips like the best of them, Imam Nuhu sat quietly watching me, I smiled and smiled at him my performance mirroring the dancing of women that I had studied like an exam. Sweating and a bit lightheaded, the song finished.

I stood in the middle of the room panting as Imam Nuhu broke into a prolonged clapping session, getting up he pulled me into his arms and then sat back down and nestled in his arms hot sweaty and pulsating like a vein.

I am thirteen years old, developed with the promise of more to come. Taking my head he leads me to the bathroom, there is not much water he says so we share this bucket. We take our clothes off and wash individually. He is drinking me in while I have to be more discreet in case I get into trouble, instead I get smiles and nods from the Imam. Getting dressed we sit outside for a while to help with the heat.

It takes a moment for me to realise Imam Nuhu is speaking to me, are you able to remain perfectly quiet he asks, yes I say nodding to ensure he knew he could trust me to say silent, my thoughts one way, hoping and longing for a melt into his arms, nothing of that sort, he tells me to follow him as he set off towards a small settlement not far away called Tuantuwad. We reach there in less than 10 minutes, avoiding the main area as this is known as the place for drinking prohibited alcohol and general misbehaving with the women there.

Staying on the outsketch we arrive near the edge of a compound, I can hear music and multitude voices, Imam Nuhu indicates to me to move slowly and be as quiet as possible, we both come to stand a short distance from a gathering of many, all men dressed in their causal traditional wear of loose trousers and long shirt top, they are mainly standing with the much older men sitting on chairs placed in a circular manner, well lite even from our distance I can make out who is who from our community, the drumming and singing quietens.

All heads turn in the same direction, I gawk as about a dozen teenage boys dressed in tight fitting clothing come into the circle and start dancing, the same seductive dance steps I have done in private for over seven years, here ends the similarity, these boys moved freely through the crown touching the men, flirting with them, thrusting their body at them, sitting briefly on their lap to tease them, the excitement in the gathering is palpable, there is something in the air, this is a scene I expect to have the loose women I have heard about dancing instead we have boys, the audience is generous with their money.

It is where they place the paper notes that is interesting, tucking it in the chest or groin area, the boys gyrate from one end of the gathering to the others, I also notice some tension. Any boy spends too much time with anyone else, another spectator will use money to turn that attention to themselves. These guys can dance the best of women under the table with the moves of their skilfully applied make-up that made them look even more alluring and that ass, they must have practiced forever to shake their booty the way they can.

The last person I expected to see is sitting there, spending money and touching like everyone else, if he hadn't pinched a boy's chest causing the boy to play slap his hand, I wouldn't have taken much notice, but he turned to laugh with the man behind him and I saw it was my father. Fear gripped me, sensing the change in me Imam Nuhu reached a hand across to me.

I held his hand, providing me with a sense of reality. I had a lot of questions, we sat where we were in the shade of darkness, the entertainment was over within the hour, I then noticed as people walked away the dancers followed various individuals, my father included. I have a lot of questions. We remained sitting long after the departure of others. I understood Imam Nuhu wanted people to disperse without us bumping into anyone, motioning for us to make a move, I stood up with my legs weak without reason. As we walk Imam Nuhu explains what I have just witnessed.

Dancing boys they are called. They identify as women when needed and provide sexual favours for men who are thus inclined. Despite myself I asked why Imam Nuhu gently guides my thoughts, for men with needs how many women are available ? you get married or nil access to sex, religion forbids masturbation, yet the body is screaming for release. I listen quietly, unable to digest my father with several wives is still finding release with a teenage boy, I ask for clarity around this. The bottom line is this was the practice before marriage and remains a pastime that is kept under wraps. Are they having sex I ask outright like a man and women, some do I am told for the majority it is for the act of mutual masturbation.

I want to do all I have seen with Imam Nuhu and wonder if he attends these gatherings himself and how many teenagers he has taken to his bed. Of course I can't ask this, instead we say the usual required prayers against asetan (devil) and prepare for sleep, for the first time Imam Nuhu rests his hand on me, I move closer to him and thus ends that night. In giving me privilege to what goes on under cover of the night he desensitises me further to my need of a same sex partner of course I am the woman so not looking for a feline partner like myself.

I go through secondary school living across two households, I continue to be referred to as the Imam's shadow, going home only to see my siblings, returning to the sanctuary of Imam Nuhu, who when he does touch me it is tender, understanding and patience with the promise of things to come. I am not yet a lover, still a pet.

Predators are incredibly patient people; they remind me of farmers who are prepared to put the work in and wait for the harvest that will surely come if they tend their land well. Imam Nuhu did just that, he nurtured me, feed me, impacted knowledge, validated me, encouraged me, drove me to achieve in my education and to some extent protected me, speaking up when I turned fifteen and my father spoke of marriage, I am betrothed to my cousin Amina, the cultural norm is her first period is at her parents house by the following month all rituals would be observed and she moves to live with my family, her education stops based on our decision if we do not support her studies.

I think of my cousin, who is the cross-eyed same age as me, a girl most people make fun of but who leads at school in all her subjects, no time for people who have no time for her she uses education excellence as her weapon of choice against those who accord her no value. With the support of Imam Nuhu, we speak to my father and appeal to him to allow her to continue her studies while I do the same. Emotional blackmail is the number of my siblings lost due to lack of medical care and the prestige it would be for my father to have an MD son.

Apart from Arabic and knowing the holy book off the top of his head my father has limited education.

Imam Nuhu tells my father of the new government initiative to bring the education standard of the north up to that of the south who are producing Doctors Lawyers and playing on the world field. Valuing Imam Nuhu my father gives his consent, we ask if she can continue her education so she is not a burden for me in the future but an asset to the community, my father likes that, I see the way his eyes twinkle when he speaks to Imam Nuhu, like one would if you share a secret, I feel irritation towards my father, later translates as jealous knowing my father partakes in activities I am preached to will send me straight to burning fire.

I feel some liberation, still plenty of questions but for now nil issues, I feel better than the boys I know worry the farmers sheep at night, another act the community turns a blind eye to, if you ask why sheep was bleating during the night you are told probably spooked by wild animals, yes man the night animal !

Thus, my pathway to studying abroad is laid. I breeze through my exams and in due course gain the much-coveted scholarship. Life with Imam Nuhu continues, every moment spent in the most incredible sexual tension known to man. This buildup is killing me but I recognize one wrong move from me and he will send me packing to my parents. Not once did I realise my protective factor is my age, the age of consent is 21 according to the government.

We have proceeded to touch, touch in the sense of massage as an excuse, my leg hurts, my back hurts, my shoulders feel stiff, let me do the same for you, give the permission to touch making it legit should anyone stumble on us. We are used to each other's nakedness by now, I am doing everything expected of a partner, I am a badass cook, laundry is done and clothes ironed and neatly pressed, the dwelling is kept immaculate. I am allowed to groom Imam Nuhu, oiling his hair and combing his beard before patting it into shape all the while drinking in the heaviness of the scent of Tabu.

With 6th form completed and plans to move to England in August my Nikkah is conducted. The exchange and consent to the wedding is not an issue, once completed the bride retires to my mother's room, I go in to her and two educated youth have a much-needed conversation. I tell her I will not touch her as getting her pregnant means she will not realise her ambition for further education, I tell her I can wait if she can, knowing she has very little choice she agreed to all barely looking at me. Here is the thing, she is my cousin so no chance in hell of ever divorcing her we are stuck with each other it is the custom.

Under cover of dark I return to my main abode with Imam Nuhu, the process of the wedding and watching me give consent must have struck a chord with him, I walked in into his outstretched arms, we hold each other for a long time no words needed just the pressing together of two bodies wanting and desperately trying to melt into each other.

In my fantasy I have always seen myself as the bottom but reality is deliciously different, guiding me to the bed, he leaves me there for a moment to ensure all access to the flat is secure, all windows closed, curtains drawn, I lay on the bed, shivering with excitement and apprehension, I am a few months short of my eighteenth birthday. He takes my clothes off then his, sliding next to me he takes me in his arms, finally after nearly ten years I am treated as I had wished for all along.

The feel of his flesh against mine is beyond what I had fantasies about, though well built and masculine he feels soft in the right places with rock-hard muscles where you expect it. His hands feel like they have never done a day's work, soft like a baby's as they glide over me exploring and familiarizing and marking his territory. Producing a tub of what I later learn is coconut oil he shows me there are nerve endings around the anus I did not know existed. Touching massaging probing then withdrawing makes me arch for more touch. When he finally makes love to me it is gentle, slow, expressive, he knows pain would have made this not as magical as it was, as I lay spent he continues to caress me, years of longing meant he didn't have to do much.

When he turned and offered me himself, I was confused, I have always thought of myself as the bottom, not sure I can do this apart from it all being new. I should have trusted him, when I sank into him I thought my head was going to explore with the pleasure, wherever I got the idea I could only be one or the other flew out of the window, this man that I have adored worshiped walked beside for over ten years is finally rewarding me, I sense the urgency in him the need to love me, owe me, dominate me, submit to me all in the short space of time left.

We cried exhausted with the emotions of the day, slept in each other's arms to be woken by the cock crowing its head off somewhere as dawn approached, thus started another round of frenzied lovemaking, needed like two lost in an ocean clinging to one raft… Nuhu was a raft and I noticed the calling of my name. He asked me to say his name over and over like it needed to be ingrained in his being. He told me he loved me so many times I would have given him anything he asked for in that seventy-two-hour figure. It wasn't until I was on the train on the first leg of my journey to the international airport that I realised if I had stayed in the homeland, he still wouldn't have made love to me for several years, waiting for adulthood the only protection he has should we be discovered. I left my entire heart with that man and begged him to keep it safe.

Crying unashamed the entire clan and well-wisher thought it was my connection to them, I cried for my lover, my Imam Nuhu, my man, my anchor in a world where I cannot be myself but elders can under cover of the dark, I think of the dancing boys and what a rotten life it must be, passed around by a bunch of married men who will not acknowledge them or the acts that goes on under cover of dark if they come across them in broad daylight. I wonder why we are like this, looking down on anything western but carrying on the same way under cover of darkness, holding back women from self actualising when in the West women are proving they are equal partners in innovation and groundbreaking work in all areas of development.

The average age girls from my homeland start having babies for the top tier of society is age 15 once they've completed the equivalent of GCSE for those with understanding husbands otherwise it is whenever the period kicks in. Thus, we have several generations in full view with a new baby mum aged fifteen grandma thirty, great grandma forty-seven, two greats sixty and seventeen-seven, with the ninety-three too many greats bringing up the rear, I'm sure you get the gist.

School of Medicine University of Cambridge no less. We are deserving and qualified to attend this prestigious setting, we have higher grades than our various western counterparts but because it's not western passes we are treated like the visitors we are.

At 6'3 I turn heads, but the wrong heads are the forward ones constantly inviting me out and wanting to get close. The dedication to getting laid is something to see, children from top tiers of society looser than those who are paid for hook-ups. Our starved loin foreign students dive in shagging their way through the first year coming to their senses as exams and submission dates approach. In fairness that place is so cold you need human flesh to truly warm up. Despite travelling down together it was clear we wanted to avoid each other and be able to live however it is we imagined.

Our allowance is generous as we are the first set sponsored to study abroad. All sorts of pastimes opened to us, from legit sports to those who wanted to try every hallucinogen available, making the dealers rich as money seemed to flow unending from wealthy parents who gave money to quill their conscience.

Despite the strict religious upbringing most of us drifted the way we wanted, on the odd occasions I went to the social club on site I was greeted with the sight of my fellow homeland folks drinking and enjoying the women, totally haram, isn't it or is it depending on where you are and what you believe is the right things to do. I have seen too much back home to dare criticise anyone, because of this we remained cordial whenever we were forced to sit down together. After the first year successfully completed, I found myself searching for a Nuhu.

English Nuhu came in the form of a lecturer, initially all seemed normal, the checking in to ensure all is going well with my studies as a foreign student which is part of the welfare role he has, there is nothing to suggest he is inclined towards me. Gradually the subtle signs and communication begins when we are chanced. I began to accept his study invitations until invited into town for food.

The pleasure of Indian cuisine is the nearest thing to my halal palate, and I gratefully accept. Munching our way through a feast he asks me the usual questions about my background, I am older and wiser thus permitting him to set up the scene. At this point I am still teetotal so very much in control when he sheepishly asks if I want to come back to his place. I agree, hoping for some good sex. What an experience, we get back to his place and he asks me if I like pain, no, okay I do he shares, if I don't mind spanking him, this excites him, not an issue, I take the paddle from him, note that way he slides his pants down and lays across my lap.

I smile at him and start slowly allowing him to guide me, pain pleasure I am unsure as he makes all noises, he even cries, guiding me to hit harder or begging me for mercy I roll with it. His ass is red and hot on fire when he finally climaxes straight onto his rug. This has been an experience but not done anything for me, I allow him to unzip me and suck hungrily as he brings me to my own relief. I close my eyes so as not to see him but imagine it is Nuhu.

Once the much longed for relief came, I wanted to distance myself, yet I knew I had found my own slave, someone who felt for me the way I had felt for Nuhu. It did not take long for the presents to start arriving, outwardly a lecturer looking out for a student. In the safety of his flat I beat him with the paddle as needed, he in turn took care of my needs. Thinking this will be it, I relaxed, nothing indicating he was just warming up.

The pattern is the same, study, ensure grades remain on par for a first class, dinner Friday or Saturday in town then back to the flat, in no time my body became accustomed to the routine. Today is different. He hands me a box, three black silk handkerchiefs and a smooth shiny ball. He talks me through slowly and I understand today we move on to sadomasochism. I follow his instructions, legs tied together, repeat with the arms, ball in mouth and silk tying it in. It keeps the ball in his mouth ensuring nil other than the ability to grunt. I have permission to beat him within an inch of his life, I start slowly, watching his eyes for pain, turning him regularly and watching his hand for the safe signal. I crisscrossed that man's body like one would expect on a plantation.

When I slowed his eyes begged me to carry on, there is only so much you can do before your muscles begin to ache, summoning the last of my strength in a situation that I find crazy unique I land several blows with the paddle moving out of the way in time as he convulsed his way through ecstasy, would he let me untie him, no wanted to stay that way for another 30 mins, eyes closed I can only imagine what may or may not be going on in his head.

Finally, he signals for me to untie him, I do so but don't want any sexual relief myself. It is the first time I will taste alcohol; I ask him for a glass of wine, what I have just done has scrambled my brain slightly. Mixing the wine with coke I drank long and hard and yes it went straight to my head totally relaxed I see him in a more attractive light, pulling him onto his knees I take my frustration out on his, no gentle love making for the man who just wants to be paddled, I see the panic in his eyes and carry on, who are we both going to complain to. He is submissive to all I do, when I finish, he asks if he can get up, I nod yes, disturbed but unsure why. I later realised it is the move from I am not inclined towards being the submissive to taking the lead, I balance things in my mind, I am not butch, I just happen to be with a submissive, it will do better than soap in the shower.

This is the way six years passed at university, despite the discreet way we went about our so called lives I lived in fear, the kind that keeps you awake and makes you shiver when with your fellow country people knowing they will turn in an instant if they sense I am not inclined towards the ladies, in my few interactions I mentioned the wife back home so this seems to have secured me a pass from closer scrutiny. I am a newly qualified medical doctor, aged twenty six. I have stayed in England without once going home unlike the others as the government provides a ticket once a year in terms of money, I apply for the same and send the money home instead. I finally realise I am scared to return home. Imam Nuhu and his wife plus mine must surely await me. I know which one I thirst for.

England is offering all sorts of job opportunities to retain us. I took a post at UCL and moved to South London, amidst lots of false promises from me to the Professor, how was I to know somewhere along the line the delightful spank me please professor had become unhinged. I settle in well not once did I consider there was someone in the background pulling the strings, I just thought in all areas of allocation work pattern and early opportunities I was simply lucky, London's gay crowd do not take prisoners they are loud confident sure of themselves very visible and give no apology, they overrun the parastatals holding the most powerful positions and looking out for each other.

Jobs are discussed and recommendations of the best suitable person are put forward and agreed over a drink or squash match, the rest is just formality, the lovers get the choice of jobs be you male or female as long as you have a same sex partner you are well taken care of.

I am cautious and do my best to live quietly. There are too many Homeland people in London both at work and in my locality. The nurses flirt endlessly with me, I give back as good as I get, if they suspect I am not attracted to them they keep it to themselves. I work and work so I don't stop to think, it's like I have turned off the sensations and zombified myself, outwardly doing all that is expected and dying slowly inside with fear, dread, loneliness, there is no I to me because I can't say who I am.

I am Bisii he said in an interview, black nail polish with a fair haired husband who clearly adored him, Anthony, even the name as it rolls offs off Bisii's tongue sounds seductive, I change what I am watching, again wonder when will me here be able to say I, this is who I am! I am who again? I am the conditioned son of a Chief Imam who likes the dancing boys but will not hesitate to have me stoned to death if he knew I liked and slept with men. Well you know the saying the status quo must change and mine didn't just change it thundered.

I have done all I can to avoid the topic of the wife back home, I can't bear to think of her as a person, Amina my cousin, just a wife. I get notification that a passport has been obtained and she has applied for a spousal visa. I prayed the British Embassy would refuse but you know the British when they should say no they say yes. Overnight I develop gastric issues, the stress of her imminent arrival freaks me out, we are two strangers, the Nikkah feels like it took place on another planet, I have lived in denial but now I am about to face my wife, even the word sounds offensive.

I can't eat or sleep because the stinging in my belly keeps me awake, a punishment of the past and things to come, that stomach ulcer stayed with me the rest of my life, just like that stress induced. I think of my environment, nothing in my lifestyle or presentation to give the impression I am anything but a fine looking man. In public there is no sign of the feminine me, not the dancing boy nor the paddle whacker. I am just the trusted Doctor who when I walk on to the ward works tirelessly and is loved and liked by all, also fancied by many.

I have no choice but to prepare for the arrival of my spouse. Curious to know what will be landing on my doorstep I enquire about her and her achievements, would you believe it she has been allowed to continue her education probably more as compensation for a disappearing husband who refuses to return to pick her up. She has a doctorate as an Archivist, this is new to me, I wonder what she will do when she gets here only to be told she has a job offer from the British Library in London. Oh well, she is educated and appears to have some independence, I can understand her going for a quiet job like that of a Librarian yet clever enough to push for higher recognition for self.

Arrival is in six weeks, work commences eight weeks from arrival, it should give her time to find her way round and get used to the hustle and bustle of inner city commuting. It's spring and yet I feel chilled to the bone, I don't want a wife, I want to be the wife.

The truth is I have forgotten what she looks like and paid little attention to the periodic family photos sent over the years with her standing meekly. I pull these pictures out and scan them, I need to have a faint idea of the person I am meeting at the airport. I remember cross eyed!

I got my cleaners in to give the flat an extra good clean and set out to the airport that fateful day like one attending my own execution. That train journey into Heathrow was torture, I felt sick to my stomach not to talk of feeling lightheaded. Father has sent word I am to take her to the registry to ensure she is recognised as my wife in the west. Instead of the woman I am meeting I wonder and hope she might have news of Imam Nuhu, either way I know I will prob gently to extract any information about him however minute and insignificant it may seem.

The years have treated her well, nil fat dumping that sometimes rolls up to horrified men who have become westernised and recognise the importance of maintaining a decent body mass index. I while away the time watching the horror and look of despair on the faces of spouse who are now used to women who look like they stepped off the magazine cover, now welcoming a lump of lard that has been told the thicker you are the more your man will love you, maybe before their men got on a plane and left the country but not after exposure to the West.

If I wasn't so busy distracting myself I would have noticed her immediately, she calls my name softly in greetings, blow me, not sure what I expected everything but this slim rather attractive quietly spoken woman, I return her greeting and so detached from her I smile and welcome her like you would a visitor, taking her suitcase I lead her to the train for the ride back into Victoria. What happened to the cross eyed cousin ?

I am grateful she is educated, she carries herself well and doesn't gawk nor freakout at the escalators. I am also relieved she didn't pack the entire homeland in her suitcase as people have arrived with what seems like a mountain of luggage, a large case I handle leaving her with the smaller case, we take our place on the train, she sits next to me leaving a decent space between us. I look at her and feel how I would if my younger sibling was sitting next to me without the excitement of their presence.

I keep quiet while she drinks in the scene, I let her know we get off at the last stop so nil hurry. She is wearing a trouser suit with a high neck shirt, her hair is covered by a lovely turban, low cut shoes and a smart black handbag, she is actually passable but not what I want. I think of my ulcer and name it wifey. I wonder how strong she is for what lies ahead, I hope she is a strong woman who has the resilience she will need once the picture becomes clearer.

Arriving at my building as we get out of the black cab used for the short ride, I see someone standing by the main entrance, I see but my brain refuses to acknowledge the man standing there, my brain is scrambled, why today what is he doing here, why has he turned up, of all the days he could come looking for me he chooses today. I smiled politely and introduced my wife, if she was more in tune she would have noted the hostility which she took to be western reservation.

Taking her into our flat I pop back down to see my old Professor, old is an understatement he has not aged well, what is it with fair skin when it wrinkles, it is vile. My skin crawls to think of the years of sexual encounter with him, I don't like what I see but keep my mask on, he is in London for a conference and thought would surprise me, I politely explain the situation and ask where he will be staying, was planning to stay with you he replies, how come I have never noticed how narrow nasty his eyes are and his lips so thin they do not exist. Still I smile a sixth sense warning me things can go either way, he is so tense I can see the muscles in his face twitching, explaining my family had sent the wife I leave it hanging in the air.

Gathering himself he moves down the few steps I follow him down as we walk to the corner I know the situation is explosive if I don't handle it well, I have not seen this man for several years and yet here he is, my placements on acute admission mental health units kick in, this man is in a high state of some form of mental distress, get rid of her he says to me, I gawk at him, get rid of her I repeat, you don't know my culture sir, she is not going anywhere, she was sent to join me as I didn't go and get here, she is here and there is little I can do about it, ensuring my voice comes over as one helpless in the equation.

I want to see you. He states a complete change of direction, his voice soft, seductive even but with nil effect on me, I look at the liver spots on the back of his hands and arms and see my safety flash away in front of me.

I am to be blackmailed I think fast but have nothing on him to put him in his place, is this the fate of remaining in the closet. Let me know where you are staying and I will catch up with you, he reaches for my hand, I keep my expression neutral but inside I feel rage that is if we were somewhere isolated I would have strangled him there and then, I'll be in touch he says it sounds more of a threat than a friend saying see you soon, hailing a black cab I say bye and watch the cab drive away he doesn't look back, I take it as a bad sign.

Returning to the flat the wife is waiting patiently, not sure of her expectation, I ask if she has located where everything is while she is waiting for me . Please just go and pock around and make yourself at home but home for me is no longer this place. With paddleman arriving without invitation I need to make plans to protect myself, while listening to her dribble and taking nothing in. I am thinking of what next, when it comes to me, a simple but effective solution to the wife and paddleman. Not a bad cook, we ate in a relatively cordial atmosphere, not unlike a brother and sister.

With wisdom she begins what must be the most painful conversation of her life, avoiding english she speaks arabic ' we are both in the same boat, I will understand if you have made a life for yourself here and I clearly don't feature in it, please bare with me, tolerate me like you would a sister, we are both in an impossible situation of the old school, promising children at birth no thought for a modern world in which there is a choice. I want to thank you for insisting I can continue my studies, it gave me some freedom as I got to work in several places away from home over the years.

I won't call myself modern but I also know I will not be an embarrassment to you. I am a peaceful person who is easily content. I am scared of the life that awaits me here as many years were spent in the shame of a husband not coming back to get me nor was I free to move on. Please consider me a sister so that we can at least cohabit without too much stress. I start work upper week I will do my best to fit into your schedule if I make a mistake please correct me, I only make a mistake once, by this point she is in tears'

I say the first thing that comes into my head, 'do you care about someone back home ? she nods and looks at me wide eyed. Taking the advantage presented, I tell her I understand and will endeavour to ensure our living arrangement does not cause either of us distress, I tell her to stop crying and reassure her we will be fine despite the start of the nil choice we had. This seems to reassure her as she goes about clearing the utensil, she tells me to sit down, I obey this is new to me. Once the chores are done, I tell her we are equal partners in this house so not to feel she has to pick up after me.

Her response is hilarious to me ' I didn't betray you she say, just that we liked each other nothing happened between us, I smile at her thinking she's finished, I come to you a virgin she says, oh no, too much information, I don't need it nothing about her turns me on, in my head wife is a sister just as she asked to be treated. I tell her to use the bedroom. I have an early start so I will take the sofa. She doesn't challenge and disappears mercifully to the bedroom.

By now I have a raging migraine, that feeling of a sinkhole erupting, pulling the bed settee out. I settled down for the night, playing events of the day back in my mind.

I am on edge the next few days as I try to focus at work and the activities of orienting wife to the transport system and her work location plus the borough we live in. I didn't have long to wait for the paddleman, finishing an early shift I breezed out the doors and who was waiting but the paddleman with his stained teeth and smile that looked like a sneer. Youth truly is a time of foolishness nil attention to detail just a drive for the moment to enjoy the thrill the flesh the comfort the wildness of adventures no one stops to think is this person sane. Reaching for my hand he pulls me aside his knuckles bony and nobbly, gripping my hand he says 'I'm sick' my blood runs cold, sick what sick, what type of sick, cancer he says I have prostate cancer, I continue to stare at him in shock, he has not say anything more serious that would affect me, I try not to show my relief.

I have been given till december he says, it's september, what does he want from me. I still don't know where this is going so I suggest the hospital cafeteria, taking our seats. He looks at me with what I suppose is the nearest thing to love in his eyes. You truly have no idea how special you are to me, you mean so much to me, you let me be myself, you didn't make fun of me nor ridicule what I wanted. I do not regret the time spent with you but feel hard done by the way you walked away and never looked back. He puts his hand on my lap. The panic of someone seeing him nearly has me jumping out of my seat. I think fast twelve weeks to live, surely if he was my patient I would be showing him compassion, picking his hand from my lap. I hold it above the table and ask him how I can help, what can I do to support you I ask.

Paddleman fills me in…well seeing I can't stay with you I have made arrangements to stay in a rented apartment until I need hospice care. I would appreciate it if you can spend some time with me to make the passing easier. I have no family, no ties to the north and having taken medical retirement I could only think of reaching out to you, suddenly he begins to cry, what is it with the past week, I move closer to him and comfort him, a few people look at the black guy comforting a white man and assume he is a patient or patients relative they smile at me in gratitude of sorts.

I feel myself softening, I have shared endless hours of passion with this man beside me, my initial reaction was fear of exposure and having not heard from him for several years I was not too pleased to see him just pitch up on my doorstep, it takes me a moment to realise I did not give him my address, I'll ask about that another time. Shall we go to your place? I find myself asking. Nothing prepared me for how close he had found a place to me, try five houses away, he has rented the ground floor of the house for three months, this is a man who is not trying to fight his illness, with his illness on my mind I mellow considerably towards him.

I am the one left crying shamelessly when I realise all along he has been pulling strings behind the scene following my career advocating for me with his fellow gay controllers, making sure I am well looked after. I cry for myself, I cry for the woman stuck in my house, I cry for paddleman, I cry for a life I want but can't have, I cry because I fell in love with one of the pharmacist who is sending me mixed messages, he joins me for lunch everyday is friendly enough but walks away without a backward glance. I cry because I can cry in the private space of this man that I no longer even want to remember but our exploits brought up. I cry with the relief that he does not have any illness he could have passed on to me. I cry because it is not easy being gay.

I am in a self made prison, me, my own jailer, the horror of coming out and losing all I've worked hard for too much to contemplate. I am spent and it is the one dying that hands me a cup of tea, as I sip it the bell goes, he leaves to open the door and in walks two care staff, he has truly got everything arranged to meet his needs. He asks if he can leave my contact details with them, I write my name, address and phone contact for the nursing staff, palliative colleagues from an agency I know, costs will be astronomical.

Thus begins twelve weeks of half living at home and five doors away. The wife says not to worry and to help a man who helped me in the past in his final days, she asks if there is anything she can do to help, he doesn't want her anywhere near us as he puts it. I watched a human being shrink before my eyes, yet he fixed his eyes on me like looking at me would restore him. Sometimes I am uncomfortable sensing he is hoping for a different kind of affection but he holds his peace knowing I have a choice and can leave and not return. He did not die in December but made it to the second of January before passing away peacefully from all the morphine given to keep pain at bay. Paddleman's passing is the end of an era, a release for me of fear of exposure, a drawing of my breath so I can continue to remain safely in the closet.

I will never understand white people for as long as I live. In March I received an official looking letter, it is a copy of the last will and testimony of paddleman, it is from a solicitors firm asking me to make contact to formally hand over what I have been bequeathed by paddleman. I attended the appointment not taking in much of my surroundings and walked out of that firm owner of a property, shares with various companies like Boots and Marks and Spencer, staple British companies as well as a foreign swiss pharmaceutical, in total paddleman has left me assets close to one million nine hundred thousand pounds. He was not lying when he said he has no family, somehow he had cared about me enough to want to leave me a gift, I say a gift as more money than I got went to various charities.

I keep this news to myself, disposing of the property in Cambridge I bank the money in an account that just rolls it over and makes me a decent interest with one instruction no letters were to be sent to my address if I want to know my total I will pop in the bank. It is February the wife's arrival coming up to six months has made no difference in my response to the female sex, I wonder what she will do if she knows I wear her clothes when she is out of the house, I particularly love the feel of her underwear that's in satin material the smoothness of the material on my body is sensual taking me back to my youth and the love of my life.

For her end she has not come near me nor tried to initiate any form of intimacy, we truly are like siblings and have moved our interaction to being able to spend time together over cards, ludo or scrabble games. I live in a strange era, I believe her when she says she is a virgin, well virgin she will stay. Having waited two years and with more than adequate funds in the bank we bought a house in Battersea, an up and coming area because of the proximity to Chelsea. Three bedroom house affords us all the space we need, no friends or relatives to visit, we settle into a routine, she has the two smaller bedrooms. I use the large bedroom, we have not slept in the same room or bed to date both agreeing to peace without verbal communication.

If she suspects why I don't want her she doesn't say but I give allowance for female intuition.

I remember vividly when I asked about Imam Nuhu, it's the first time she comes near me close enough to touch, she looks at me and says she is sorry, I wonder what she is sorry about, she she is speaking but I don't want to hear what she has to say, he died in a car crash on his way back from his wedding, I am told he was driving himself and his bride in a convoy of cars , it was raining and his car skidded off the road. I do not believe that for a moment , my Nuhu has died because he couldn't live the life mapped out for him.

My only love, my heart,my awakening, my pleasure, the very man to take me to heights I heard about but didn't think possible, I think of my dancing days, the pleasure in his eyes, his waiting until I was an age where he would not be accused of molesting me should we be discovered, I remember his beautiful amber skin, the curl of hair around his genitalia, the smell of him, his cleanliness and attention to self care, nails always kept short and clean, the attention to clean sharp crisp clothing at all times, those twice a day minimum shower and the smell of tabu occasionally old spice.

I can smile at my memories now, till date I have a bottle of old spice in my cabinet to me it's not old spice but Imam Nuhu. How can he be dead, such a beautiful person? If only we had both been born on the right side of the ocean, we would have loved, lived freely and now that things have progressed, married, taken each other's name and taken our place in society.

The pain in my guts reminds me of yesterday's prescribed medication not taken, engrossed in Rose and Elthel's letters I have read through the night not bothering with my normal routine, I move away from the window and fix some cereal to enable me to take my cocktail of tablets. I need sleep but I am a man on borrowed time, Rose and Elthel are making me relive my life. Imam Nuhu and paddleman are my life but what about the disasters when I have dared. I shiver with the same fright I did in the past when what I thought was a relationship began to demand I take care of him or he will out me.

Not all is plain sailing in the gay world, not just money but the demand for sex making me hate myself and what had once been a beautiful and fulfilling coming together of two individuals. I am a victim of domestic violence on many occasions, men who become monsters behind closed doors soon cured me of the hope of meeting a loving man, perhaps it is just hard for an older man to find love. I lay on the bed for a while but sleep will not come, I get up and retrive the tin of letters , making myself comfortable. I begin to read from where I left off.

Dearest Rose

I started work in the new section, it is quiet and boring, just what I need. Home is a mess,but he leaves me alone. The sexual demand has lessened to the rare occasion, he realises no child is coming forth from our alliance so he is not wasting his energy on me, to my relief he is barely at home, he has a new focus and I couldn't wish for anything more. I concentrate on work but Toni for her foolishness is not done with me. We meet at the main company meetings, she looks at me like one lost, totally pathetic like a lost dog, I glare at her and swear on one occasion she went to the toilet to cry. Her behaviour is so far from her statue, she fancies herself in love with me. God help me, I can't be with my love and there is another woman crying over me and saying she loves me.

Her memory is selective. I remember her for forcing her attention on me. She clearly thinks there was some sort of connection, I tell her quietly to stay away from me, I am not moved by her tears and confession of love. Rose did not be alarmed but Toni started to sit in her car across the road from the flat. On some occasions weather permitting she would stand next to the Hyde park railing looking towards the building. Not once did I go over to talk to her. I parked most days aware of her sitting in her car but never acknowledged her presence. I have heard and read so much on social media about same sex fatal incidents, I religiously went to my self defence classes. Sometimes I will peek at her from the safety of my flat even from the distance you could see she was either crying or just sitting there looking across at the building, this is usually in the evening after work until quite late.

Once I realised she left once the lights were out I started to ensure the flat was in darkness by nine o'clock more to help her than me needing to go to bed, on the days he came home that silly cow would be there till early hours of the morning. During the months she did this I kept one of the kitchen knives in my side cabinet, despite knowing she would never get into the building and if somehow she achieved that getting into my flat would be near impossible.

Rose I do not realise there are so many mentally disturbed people around me. I eventually hear through the vine Toni has had to have some time off to deal with personal issues, that translates as her taking an overdose. Do I feel guilty, no, nothing to do with me, I am not going to get drawn into her rubbish, there are enough women in the world for her to find someone else, the irony of me having no compassion for her when I am in love with you and can't be with you. What a crock!

I realised same sex relationships are more intense than heterosexual relationships, I wonder why that is and what the remedy will be, this all or nothing approach can't be healthy.

Rose my darling, the years are beginning to blend into each other, I am waiting for something but don't know what, your letters keep me sane. I long for your touch, the sound of your voice on a continuum not just on the phone, I wish to see you, hold you, make love to you, drown in your eyes, breathe in your perfume but more than that I want the smell of your sex in my nostrils. I want to blend into you that where you stop I continue and we become one, am I asking too much ? One thing I am sure of is that we will be together, how, when and where I have no idea but I know it will happen so I wait patiently in our thirties. It's good to hear of your progress and your dedication to family.

How I wish we are in a position to fulfil our union. Do you know that if we lived in the West we could have children? gay men are donating to same sex women who wish to have children. I drown in the sorrow of what we could have and can't. I have diagnosed myself with Roseitis. It is a condition where there is a deficiency of Rose. You are the tonic I need. Something is afoot with my husband. He is restless. I pray it is another woman and he has reached the end of his road with me, it has to be that as my parents would not hear of the word divorce. Please let it be what I think is another love interest that will make him lose total interest in this dead end marriage.

Rose I am so stressed I am missing meals again, I caught sight of myself in the mirror and realised if I am not careful I will be back in square one, so I have brought in a nutritionist,, the cost is okay, I simply eat what is put in the fridge for me over the week for balanced meal. I must invest in my body, it is easy when I think of it as for you Rose, I must look after this body until I can present it to you.

This is one of the greatest days of my life, I have a full house in the presence of both sets of parents. I wonder who has died, but nothing is said about death, my excitement begins to mount. I sense whatever takes place I am going to come out of it well. Bingo, it is out! all the waffling and going round the houses, He has gotten someone pregnant. Rose I should be given an oscar, I get up and coldly say ' as you are able to get someone else pregnant it means we are not comparable, I also wish to have the joy of motherhood, it is not going to happen with you so please let's go our separate ways, how was I to realise that statement about right to have a child would set my father off on a hunt for a replacement husband.

The separation was swift, she is four months pregnant. Ours is the fastest, most quiet divorce finalised three weeks before the baby's due date. I hear my ex remarries, I am finally free Rose. I am free my darling. Please wait a bit more for me, we are nearly there.

Too much celebrating too soon, I am hit with excruciating stomach pains the following month, my period feels like I am bleeding out, a trip to A&E and diagnosis of multiple fibroids. Rose my darling I opt for the operation, it's keyhole surgery, I told them to take everything out, only you and I will know, I will tell you when I see you. What a relief, the healing is painful and takes a while to feel back to my normal self. I am given a hormone patch for those that are now missing with the removal of various female organs within me. Oh Rose what a life, I no longer need my ginger and lemon drink, but also the realisation there will not be opportunity to fulfill the role of motherhood.

Just as well my parents are unaware or maybe it might have helped to stop my runaway car of a Dad had he realised I no longer had the internal works needed to birth. His subtle suggestion of a visit to the homeland fills me with such excitement. I reflect on my invisible prison walls, as a grown up woman no one can stop me from visiting the homeland to see you but I know the consequences of coming to meet you, I will not return to England then all will be lost we will be outed and excommunicated by all around us, is it even possible to survive such an event. The plans to visit are underway, I am recovered and keen to step on terra-firma. I don't have long to wait, it is of course the usual exodus of my parents and I.

I mourn my brother, why did he have to die, his death has made me a cellotape for my parents they stick on and cling on to me for a life, I am their life yet I feel no closeness to either, I'm not even sure I like them, their style of parenting is do as you are told, even at my age talking to Dad can be fraught with difficulties can you imagine being shushed at my age. I try not to be too bitter and take comfort from knowing they know nothing about me that I don't want them to know. My father was so angry once he threatened to write me out of his will, probably the only time I stood up to him, I peeled with laughter and managed to walk out of the room my throw away at him, ' how can I miss what you have not given me, if you give and take back them maybe' mother as usual is her placid self, that of peacemaker role. They just seem so mismatched I still don't get them.

Rose, there is another incident I need to share, remember Pete the fine boy of our teen times well I bumped into the fool as a birthday party, a rare attendance for me but one Mum and Dad insisted on the old crowd, anyway off we went, not a bad setup the cocktails and finger food followed by dinner aspect was fine, there was a break where soft music was played and people mingled while we waited for the celebrant to make another appearance. How an earth Pete found me is beyond me but found me he did, he shares he is married with three kids, and proceeds to tell me about other aspects of his life that is of no interest to me, I listen politely, shall we exchange numbers, we do that still no issues as he walks away to join his friends, you know these guys seemed to have missed the maturity boat.

Anyway as the evening wraps up coats retrieved goodbyes are being said with the usual promise of see you soon, thinking Pete is coming to say bye as he detaches himself from his little group I catch sight of the others looking and smirking, Pete comes up to me and within their hearing shot states ' right Ethel your place or mine' You know I am not a violent person but I was not under my own will, I landed him a slap so quick even I was shocked and made a point of walking past his friends with a large asshole statement.

If I thought that was the end of it I was mistaken, guess who is waiting downstairs the next day with a bunch of flowers, he had spoken to my dad and convinced him we had a misunderstanding if my father had any common sense surely he would have checked with me what the misunderstanding was about and if okay to give my location details out. I declined the flowers and tell him to leave, I remember the rumours from years back of him forcing himself on girls and how everyone said it casually, he has that reputation they say, noone thinking or saying it's not okay, it is assumed you know so if you entertain him you are saying yes to sex.

You need to go I say, foolishly letting myself into my building, he follows me in, I remain downstairs and reiterate he needs to leave, I am telling this fool to leave and he in turn is standing close to me blocking me from moving away from him talking rubbish about how he has always been attracted to me. The arrival of the lift and a neighbour I had never seen who worked out the situation and immediately addressed me as 'darling I was getting worried and tired of waiting upstairs for my baby, come to daddy he grins.

I moved past Pete as the stranger put his arm around my waist and drew me close leaving no room for doubt we are together. Pete is a third of this man's body mass and isn't hanging around sputtering something about I read the situation wrong he turns on his heels and that was that. Here is the hilarious bit: the stranger and I watch him cross the road and drive off.

The instant the car pulled away the stranger jumped away from me arms flapping and the tone changed to the most feminine I have heard in a bit. Alright he tweets, I'm off, are you okay, I thank him/her no name given and head upstairs. Letting myself in the tears flow not because of Pete's behaviour but there is a man in my building you couldn't get it more butch in appearance but totally feminine and living life on his terms. I cry for me because I still don't have my I, until the time I can say I am…I remain incomplete. Life is so empty, I want to live and not just exist.

Dearest Rose

All is in place for the departure to homeland tomorrow, additional luggage allowance needed for your gifts, a suitcase that when Mum asked if I had space I said no and refused to open it, that woman. The countdown has begun, in less than twenty four hours I will be in the same physical environment as you my dear heart. Love lives on. It has flourished even without contact, what to expect when I see you. Random thoughts intrude my mind, thoughts so sexual I feel I might lose my mind, my body tingles, over-sensitive to the drought that is about to end, it will not rain, it will be an avalanche. I love you, I need you, I want you. See you soon my sweet Valentine.

HOMELAND

Nothing much has changed, the same intense smells once you leave the safety of the aircraft assaults my nostrils. Men in charge, women busy in the background, seen not heard, disposable in some instances. Nothing much has changed it's still the same dirty crusted crowds of people that I left behind that still exist at the airport they push they pull and they smell, the sweat that has dried over and over again on unwashed bodies who barely have time to go home to take care of the personal needs under the pressure of earning a living yet they cheerful they're welcoming and they make me feel connected, it's a good feeling I just have to make sure I don't breathe too deeply.

The plus side is I am home. I am on the same side of the Continent as the love of my life. Rose is a breath away, Rose is a short drive away, Rose is flesh that's waiting for me. It's great to be home. I feel like someone who's been released from a prison sentence that had no end date at point of sentencing a nightmare that simply would not end that has gone on and on and on perpetrated by my parents who think they know me and know what I want or what I need but who has made the last few years of my life a misery, well I'm home and the new chapter is beginning I can't wait to see you Rose.

This is all about Rose, my one and only, picking up from the last time we met, yes I know we're now in our 30s but what is age ? what are those numbers in the face of love, love that now puts a tilt in my walk that squares my shoulders up that's making me look everyone in the face and feeling totally invincible. I am drawing lots of attention from the men, which seem to please father no end. Well, if the old codger knew what was making me burst with joy, I would be finished at the airport. I can't wait to see my missing part, the bit that completes me.

Luggage collected we signal to the porter to proceed, I'm not surprised when we're led to the executive car park, this is money talking we literally walk out the airport turn right and the car is there we're loaded up in no time and pull away from the airport it's a short ride. I know we are home when I see the red and white Montana, home is less than 10 minutes drive from where I am. I am in love with terra firma. When I got out of the car I touched the ground with my palm and I pressed that palm to my heart. Mother notices me and smiles and she says 'how traditional for someone who's been in England for a long time it's good to see you're connected to your homeland' if Mother could hear heart beats mine is about to explode with joy, with expectation that's just sweeping through me for my woman.

My childhood house seems a lot smaller now that I'm grown up I walk through the house memories of my late brother, of us growing up seen and not heard, fear for father's behavior and reactions when mother tells him that we haven't done as we've been told when he's been away, this house holds no good memories for me and coming back to it I wonder why my age I didn't opt for an airbnb even wonder why I'm traveling with my parents but it's conditioning, I've been conditioned as the only child they've got left I have to let them hang on to me like barnacles.

What should I do? How do I get away from them? When all I have on my mind is Rose, my father's voice cuts through my thoughts. Let's all have a shower and then meet back downstairs. I think food should be ready in about half an hour, shower! food! the only person I want to see and I want to eat is Rose and the only shower I want is with her but like the well behaved child to well behaved adult that I have been molded to be and expected to be I head to my room and do duly pop into the shower, feeling refreshed I dress in a loose gown and head downstairs despite the fact that it's late in the evening we're eating out on the balcony in that direction lies my Rose's house I just need to get through tonight and maybe some parts of tomorrow,

I'm going see her that's all that counts I send the home help out across the road to get me data so that I can use my homeland phone, I've got to have a local number to be able to call and speak to Rose nothing closes down in this city, if you wanted to buy a SIM card and data I'm sure you can find somewhere that's open at 3:00 a.m. in the morning it doesn't take long the help is back or maybe I should be polite and say the maid is back and she hands me both the phone that now has a SIM in it and also data I watch my parents like a hawk, how fast can I eat pledge tiredness, escape upstairs to talk to Rose in peace. Finally we say our goodnights, what a relief.

That call, the pick-up, your hello and I burst into tears, I am in the now, here, that moment of knowing we are both local, I want to race out of the house to your place, I spent many times looking at your address thanks to google earth, I know that house and street like the back of my hand, a stone throw yet still as far as England.Your greeting, your voice, I practically creamed myself, your voice caressed me, my being, my soul, my entirety, all I could do was repeat your name over and over, our conversation well, that conversation lasted through the night, ask me what we talked about and I couldn't tell you…but we talk nonstop.

You started with welcome home, my Rose's voice reassuring, embracing, settling, connecting and finally anchoring, the steadiness of your voice and the manner in which you welcomed me over and over I knew I'd made the right decision all my life and for the rest of my life I will continue to do so Rose, that right decision is you, what did we talk about, we spoke about things from school, the joy of meeting, the strength of being there for each other, the mountains we had to climb, the valleys we have to crawl through and the hills that we had to walk around, we spoke of the rivers we waded through, we spoke of life and it's demands we spoke of the unfairness of the culture we were born into, we spoke of the struggles but we also spoke of the triumphs, the win-wins, the little wins, we giggled over the fact that we managed to stay under the radar, nothing has changed.

Rose still does it for me, always has, always will, we spoke about jobs, we talked of family expectations, disappointments, lack of understanding, tunnel vision culture, we spoke of the fact that our life is planned and we are expected to toe the line, we spoke of parents and relatives who didn't stop to ask us what we want, what is of interest to us, what did we like, where did we want to go, what did we want to do, who would we want to do it with, where do we want to do those things, the assumption is that the child is stupid despite you getting a degree then your Masters you're not invited to step up the rug to become an adult alongside your parents they know best apparently and I shudder to think of how many young people like me around the world are living in the closet, cannot be themselves wouldn't dare to be the themselves, and then the end results.

The depressive moods, the anxiety, the withdrawal from social contact ,the breakdowns, the unexplained mood swings, the lack of joy in any setting but most important of all the overwhelming feeling of lack of fulfillment as people live their life day in day out ticking the boxes but not their own expectations, of society ticked, expectation of parents expectation of friends, expectation of siblings and extended family ticked but not yours. Within the question you're almost irrelevant, who cares what you want as long as you are that son or daughter that they can point to with pride and say she's one of us or he's one of us not a thought for what pathway you want to take.

Then we have the results, anti-social behavior reaction, misuse of drugs, alcohol, sexual disinhibition, sexual dysfunctions, sexual deviance. Just you name it, it has a link back to the one item if I cannot be me and if you cannot be you then who are you, who are we. I look back on that first night and I don't know how but I knew you will wait, Likewise I waited for you and now that I'm back on the same side of the ocean nothing is going to take me away from your side when I go back to England it's to tidy the living and nonliving up and head permanently, there is no way after tonight that I'm going to live away from you, because that's not living that's just existing and I no longer want to just exist I want to live, I want to love, I want to laugh and I want to do it with you.

It's Saturday tomorrow and I'm coming for brunch. I told my parents I'm catching up with you and other childhood friends, they delighted with that... oh I can't wait, I can't wait to see you, I can't wait to feel you, I can't wait to touch you, I can't wait to taste you, can't wait to melt into you, can't wait to hold you in my arms, I can't wait to run my hand through your hair, I can't wait to hold your head in my arms and have your face in front of me ,I can't wait to see the darkness of your pupils the way it darkens when the light catches it. I love the white of your teeth and the succulent pink of your lips, I love the way your tongue darts in and out when you're excited about what you're talking about. I love the way you wave your arms around to emphasize a point. I love the way you carry yourself, the way you walk.

I wonder if that has changed ever slim Rose. I love your figure, the lack of hips for a very strong solid body. I love the contour of your bottom. I love your ankles, you have sexy feet, can't wait to see all this. A shower probably will be the best place to rediscover but then as long as we're together bring it on. Finally I love the way you say 'you get the point'

The Cock crowing at dawn in conjunction with the call to prayer of the local mosque forces us to say good morning and good night. In a few hours time I'll be knocking on your door, we said so much, so, so much water under the bridge. We're just starting our chapter. I worry about our happiness being so fragile, so delicate in its infancy. Still all these years it hasn't been allowed to grow, like a disabled child who has been written off this is all they can manage yet here we are. My rosebud is about to blossom and fill the room, filling our lives with the most amazing scent that nobody can control just us.

I pray life treats us well, treats us kindly. I pray life allows us the joy and pleasure that we both deserve. I pray we are able to continue moving around in high society, right there in front of all but invisible because to date that is what has protected us. Same sex relationship is Taboo, fake as this our society because we do know it goes on especially in the upper tier with the upper class where money and threats control. We know It goes on but they treat it like a fun pastime and crack down if you dare try to tell.

What is it anyway, it's about one-on-one, it's about falling in love, it's about wanting to be with someone, it's about who you're with, who you want to wake up next to, who you want to share your hopes, your dreams ,your disappointments, your fears, your aspirations, it's who you reach for at night for that cuddle, it's who you want to make love to, it's who gets you and completes you so what if they're the same sex and long to walk side by side.

Rose I ask all these questions and I don't even have an answer myself, it just goes round and round in my head, the freedom to live in a country where you can be who you want to be as two consenting adults, coming to the homeland is like stepping back in time, don't do this, don't do that, this is how we do it, don't, do that ask about it, I'll tell you how I feel I feel like grabbing you and getting the hell out of the homeland and living abroad where if not acceptance there is at least tolerance no one's going to come and protest outside the house, no one is going to threaten to burn the house down.

No one is going to come in attack us or when we're walking down the street no one is going to invade our privacy abroad in the West but in the homeland we're not safe, not even for a moment no one must suspect us, no one must see our joy, my love no one must have any course to think we are in a relationship, remember we discussed it, you are aunty Rose and I'm aunty Ethel to all, not lovers, not partners, not each other's joy in front of others just aunties, if that is what we will be that's fine, if that's what it takes, but for me... I see my love.

My arrival Rose, I take you in and we just stand there drinking each other from head to toe. I love your hair, I like the way it's been bunched up like two nice two handlebars. I love your face because it's clean and free of makeup. I love what you are wearing that loose white linen top and trousers standing there with one hand in the pocket just smiling at me, even your shoes say class, me in my jeans and t-shirt smiling at you like a million dollars ,you just smile back not touching even though we're arm's length we just stand there.

This is what it's about when you find the right person communication goes on without you saying a word it's the look, it's the body language, eyes, the slight tilt of the mouth, angle of the head everything says something and I hear you Rose, I hear you loud and clear while I wait patiently because I can tell not yet.

You call the gateman and the maid and you release them for the weekend leaving where I am you follow them both out and lock the gate from the inside I watch you as you stride back towards the house I've never really thought who's male or female in our relationship just equal partners but I noticed it now I don't know if it's your job the way you hold yourself upright rigid striding taking long steps I know that's to reach me quickly and then you come into that sitting room and I'm still standing in the same spot, you open your arms I have never moved so quickly my life, the moment my body touched yours something exploded in me that I thought I would drown in that moment of completeness.

How many minutes pasted, we just stood there in that embrace I don't even think we kissed immediately we just held each other and gave each other warm courage contact as we hugged over and over again changing our arm me with my arm around you and then you with your arm around me the neck the upper body the waist touch touch… my entire body felt like a system of nerve endings, if nothing else everywhere you touched jumped and responded to you, every sense, every fiber, every nerve, every muscle, my flesh quivers as you hold me and gently stroke me, after all these years that first kiss I cannot begin to describe.

The exploration, initially gently then building in its urgency wanting more then more I can't remember when the clothes came off where we in your room did we make it that far I just remember sliding into your bed and you sliding in next to me, again lots and lots of holding touching, exploring, discovering, reconnecting this is mind blowing. This is how it should be this is what sex should be for everyone exciting breathless you think you're going to go out of your mind as you try and blend, literally blend, melt into your partner's body if you cannot get this feeling when intimate with someone you're with the wrong person be it the opposite sex or a same sex partner.

What Rose and I have I have no words to describe. I have never felt this way except with Rose this is it I am home, I am where I belong, I have been through some awful awful times, it's been Rose who's been my anchor, it's been Roses giving the reassurance and even when I've been lying under a man tolerating sex my thoughts have been Rose get me through this. Rose helps me, Rose strengthens me, every conversation with Rose has done that, each conversation my darling has given me exactly what I needed to survive and survive I did to make it safely back onto this shore that is you.

At some point Rose you get up to get me a drink and then we had something to eat we've been together now a couple of hours and it still the touching the kissing the marvelling and the laughter either cracking each other up still going down memory lanes avoiding the difficult conversations that I know we'll eventually discuss but today is not that day today is about us healing and moving forward and planning and ensuring that we're still radar safe, locked in the closet for our own safety.

We laid there for quite a while and this time when you took me in your arms, it was always going to be different than first love making as adults, oh boy, I wish for everyone to find a partner that takes you to heights that you never began to even imagine exist. A partner that touches you in zones that makes you cry out for more and more and more and you begin to plead and yet you you're not quite sure what your pleading about, that sensory overload, oh yes and please as they touch you here there everywhere it feels all at once and you don't know whether you're coming or going and you hang on to them for dear life because something is building.

It's starts in your toes and it creeps up and it starts with your hair on end and as it cascades down from your neck it builds up from your toes and explodes inside you and you make this noise from deep within you as you jerk and convulse, your entire body feels like electricity, it crackles and crackles and crackles and finally this almighty release like a firework and then the gentleness of your partner holding you, caressing you, allowing you to have that high and experience that awesome orgasm and climax and still gently reassuring you, allowing you to come off that high slowly while still making sure that every moment counts, unlike a man the husband who turns around and goes to sleep, why am I even comparing, been there done it not for me.

I lay there pouring with sweat as if I had showered, sliding on the satin sheets when I try to snuggle up to you again that's when the laughter started because we were both sliding all over the place and then I remembered your needs you anticipate what I'm about to say and put a finger to my lip I'm fine you say and with that I threw my leg over you shovel the other leg underneath you pulling you to me and this time it's me that attends to your needs I follow your lead I listen to responses and keep doing the right thing with the right encouragement Rose you are even noisier than I am when you climax it's a crescendo not unlike an orchestra going off a mixture of english and native language none of which I understood but understood fully the language of love, then you laid spent, panting heavily as you struggled to catch your breath I am blown away by us. I'm absolutely blown away by our level of passion.

If we keep this up you say you're going to kill me we're gonna die if we carry on like this, we laugh and love and it's okay at this moment in time everything's aligned the stars are in the right place the moon is in the right place the universe itself is saying it's okay I'm doing my best to ignore the headache but it gets worse and worse and worse until I asked Rose to turn the light off you can feel the pulse on the side of my head pulsating away, I apologize that I think I'm having a migraine never had one before and not quite sure why now of all days, not a migraine but post coitus headache.

Rose you explained it more and water followed throughout the night, in the morning when I reached for you, you gently detangle telling me to rest we've got the weekend and I don't want to trigger another headache … trigger it, trigger it, I say I'm happy for you to trigger it, you get up to make me a cuppa, from that morning on Rose you made us tea every single day we were together, that was day one in our adult life. My precious Rose, I write this while back in England to tidy my affairs and move back to the homeland. I write with a heavy heart because I am married again, if my father is not a curse I don't know what is.

Again it is the sharp pain that brings me back into the presence. I am so lost in Rose and Ethel for a nanosecond I completely forget who I am, where I am, how I feel, what I feel, the pain, the emptiness, the loss, that feeling of realization the light at the end of the tunnel is officially switched off, my plans upside down, I shouldn't be here anymore, I should be dead at least 24 hours yet here I am. I'm living my life through somebody else's letters, I can see that it is possible and should have been possible for me to love, to live, to be loved, to belong and yet here I am a carcass of a man riddled with illness waiting to die, wanting to die but a tin of love letters has stopped me my tracks!

What now, what next? Do I finish reading and still take the insulin overdose ? There is something waking up inside me. I may be old and tired but there's a jigsaw that's beginning to fall into place. It's beginning to form a hazy shape. I feel something shifting inside me, dare I call it hope, dare I name it, just a deemed dim light, so dim, like a dim candle in the distance, the pain reminds me I need to nurture myself if I'm not going to die today, I need to water myself.

I need nourishment. I need my regular medication and I need to look after myself. Getting up and stretching I realized most of the day has gone by, switching on the lights I head to the kitchen I've barely got any food I wasn't expecting to be around. I use my phone and order takeaway, the usual stuff. There's a million and one restaurants serving all sorts of ethnic foods. You just need to ring them up or order online. The country has certainly changed from when I first arrived.

I am lonely, I am hungry for affection, for love, for companionship, for friendship. I am lonely except when I'm in the hospital while I'm at work but the moment I say goodbye the loneliness overwhelms me. I am on my own and I have no one. I am that one person surrounded by people yet is the loneliest on the planet. Most of my colleagues go home to someone, the few friends I have go home to something, dog, cat whatever. Since I started reading Ethel and Roses letters from what Ethel has written I only need to hear one side of the story to know that everything I hope and I dared to dream about they managed to achieve while I've spent my life hiding in a closet, a closet so big so deep so cluttered with hoardings I can't find my way out from the fear zone, in short I stayed firmly in the closet.

Where do I start ? Is it the culture, is it society's expectation of me, is it family expectation, the expectation of friends, Homeland government ? Why can't I be me ? I wonder the shock and surprise that would be on people's face if I put my hand out and I say hello my name is Fahad, I'm gay, I wouldn't dare, I haven't dared, what's the point anyway my body is giving up, it's ravaged, it's just a matter of time but I'm not prepared to wait for those years when I become incapacitated I'm gonna go while I still have the capacity to make the decision of whether I stay or I go.

    I have been in love for such a long time, his name is Paul, my Rose is called Paul he's a pharmacist, he's lovely, he's gorgeous. I invite him out and he always accepts, we do lunch, we do dinner but never any sign that he's attracted to me, clearly he respects me a lot, maybe too much and looks up to me. We have discussions where I can't remember what we talked about because I just drown when I'm in his company I want to touch his face, I want to kiss his lips, I want to smell more than he's aftershave, I want to taste his skin, I want to touch his skin, I want him so badly to want to touch me and feel me, hug me and give me a sign that he's also attracted to me, is it foolishness? Is it madness ? How can I wait for over 25 years ! over 25 years of carrying this affection for Paul.

    Nothing has changed from the first moment I set eyes on him, to my darkness, his lightness, the milky white of European flesh, blonde hair like Adonis, or a Viking. Shy and reserved, it took a long time to draw him out into friendship. After all, I'm over 20 years older than him and he probably sees me as some sort of older brother but he is nothing of the sort to me. He haunts my thoughts, he haunts my feelings, he haunts my very existence, he's on my mind the moment I opened my eyes and he's the last thing I think about before I go to sleep yet all it reminds me of is how deep is my closet, the ding dong of my doorbell brings me out to my thoughts.

    I thank the young Asian delivery guy and give him a generous tip. Will I be ordering next week? Will it be an obituary next week? who knows if Ethel and Rose once loved why not me. I've had choices but dating sites can be a meat market, the downside of gayness has never appealed to me, the casual sex, the meeting at the pub, what I've wanted is a relationship to build a home to build a life, someone to talk to, someone to share, someone to walk with, someone to spend time with, to sit in silence or to engage in conversation, someone to echo what you've said, someone to correct, someone to learn from, someone to make mistakes with, someone to argue with but someone just someone and for me it's Paul.

Paul is my Rose and I've watched my Rose flourish grow from being just a Pharmacist to now the Chief Pharmacist, he is just down two corridors from me, every day I walk past when I have no business to just to catch a glimpse of him and in fairness to him he seems to sense when I'm around and he'll look up and wave, followed by that quick step back to my office to ask if he'd like to do lunch or dinner and in all those years he's never said no but he"s also never invited me home. I've never been to his house. I've never met his family. The friendship has remained in the corridors of the hospital. Having lunch together in my head is a date to him. It's lunch, grabbing a bite to eat after a late shift.

For 25 years I've lived for those moments I think of my late wife quietly living like a mouse in my life co-existing alongside each other, never seen each other's nakedness, living like brother and sister whether she was happy or sad I cannot say but I never mistreated her and yet I never loved her not even when we had visitors could we pretend any physical attraction, it simply wasn't there we both accepted it and despite me being a medic when she got sick with cervical cancer I just thought it was ironic all these women sleeping around from an early age infection after infection jumping from man to man and yet a woman who had never had sex is diagnosed with cervical cancer, the irony of life indeed I wonder what Miriam would have written if she wrote letters about her life, I wonder what it would say about her about me about the wretchedness of being stuck together.

Living in a goldfish bowl moving around each other without actually touching yet aware of the existence of each other. I think of the quiet way she greets me and retreats to her room. I think of how her life could have been if our parents didn't make the choice for us. I think of what could be for me if I was indeed the captain of my ship. I remember I once loved and that comforts me but then with the comfort comes pain. My late wife was a good woman. If we reflect on life she accepted her lot and never caused me to raise my voice, not even once, she played the part of a woman well despite her high qualifications. On the few occasions that we had to step out together she walked just that extra half a step behind me. She waited quietly beside me until introduced and she never spoke unless she was directly addressed.

We never had a holiday, where were we going to go, there's no point going on holiday, holidays are for people who are into each other, who at the very least are friends, we were housemates, we were polite and cordial but you couldn't even call it a friendship. I feel sorry for her, I feel sorry for me, I feel sorry that we lived in a status quo that probably slowly killed both of us, killed the lightness, kills the fire of life, killed our drive and just turned us into two people that year in year out went through the motions ticking the boxes doing what's expected of us, working paying bills.

The people around us assumed we didn't have children because we had some difficulties and gradually the question about do you want kids? Do you have kids? How many kids have you dried up?

I'm done, pushing the rest away my appetites no longer great, the food I could consume in one sitting now takes me at least three attempts to finish, it's not a bad thing it's worked well for my weight while people my age waddle around with a six month pregnancy belly I'm relatively slim not bad to look at, the hint of part Arab blood, that slight hint in my hair continues to make me quite attractive someone once said it reminded them of Omar Sharif, they've kept me amused they've been my friends they've been my siblings they've been the companionship that I needed but then even in the midst of them I have been alone. So what now I asked myself? What should I do next? I'm no longer thinking of suicide but then if I don't die now death awaits in the future at most a couple of years, unlucky a couple of months, noone knows the order of exit in life only arrivals and that's because we can see the belly of a woman swollen with child, the order of exit makes no sense and only God has control over that.

What should I do? What should I do? I don't even have anyone to talk to who I go to with my problems. Who can I say can you help me to. I am in my 60s, gay and I'm desperate to have a partner again. I can get a partner tonight if that's what it's about but the meat market has never been for me. I like it clean, I like commitments, I like to know I'm the only one, I like to receive what I give and mutual dedication, the gay scene is much too fast for me, it scares me, still does so what do you do when you're male and attracted to other men? you build up character and barriers and you become everybody's best friend, best uncle, best brother, you become a funny man you have little anecdotes to share, little jokes, little peep talks, all just so that nobody focuses on you and asks you those meaningful questions.

What do I have to lose why am I so scared, what's the worst thing that can happen, actually disclosing how I feel to Paul could be the worst thing, should his response be, no I'm not that way inclined, how do I come back from that, the relationship is gone, that's it no lunch, no dinner meet-ups no Paul that's what's kept me a prisoner. The fear of losing Paul of losing the only contact that Paul and I have Monday to Friday. At least every couple of days I got to sit down with him for an hour it's better than nothing yet here I am prowling around my own flat like a locked up tiger what do I do, what do I do, will I die if I confess and share how I feel with Paul what's the worst thing? he can react badly to me that will surely send me running for the insulin oh God! what a life. I've achieved plenty, recognition, status, money, I have money I can't take the money with me it's certainly hasn't brought me happiness, it's made me very comfortable it's made me never have to worry about bills if I see something I like I can go out buy it and then what ? the items don't meet my needs, they just serve a purpose.

What is this recklessness I feel, what is this new bravado, why am I suddenly considering telling Paul how I feel, the horror of him reacting wrongly and badly will tip me over the edge and I've been standing on the edge of this cliff forever and a day wanting to jump, waiting to jump but opting for the wind to sweep me off yet that wind never whipped up enough to knock me over the edge of the cliff. Rose and Ethel do you know what fire you've started? Dutch courage, because for the first time in my life I want to take the bull by the horn. I want to call Paul and ask if he's free to meet, I want to tell him how I feel but I want to walk away without losing his friendship. If he says no he doesn't feel the same way, I still need contact with him. So how does that work? The motion in the mirror distracts me, I look at myself in the mirror and I see an old man, a silver fox not bad looking, good figure, nice physique but old will someone that much younger than me want much to do with me.

I know how I feel about intimacy with Paul but would Paul see me as someone to love, to romance, to touch and be intimate with.

These thoughts are now killing me slowly, the why, why, why, can I not be me all these years of empty living, of suppressing my needs, too scared of everyone and everything, actually the moment I take that white coat off I feel like there's a target on my back, put my coat on and I'm the guy in charge. Why is life so cruel? Why are people so mean? Why is society so hard? Why can't I be me? surely it's okay as long as it's consenting adults you can be what you want to be but let me be me. I want to be comfortable in my skin. I hear sobbing from a distance, it took me a moment to realize it is me, totally broken, overwhelmed, empty, lonely, struggling. All the predisposition for male suicide or should I say adult male suicide article I tick all the boxes.

What am I living for? my prostrated slowly killing me, I'm in pain you can't imagine. I'm either struggling to wee or struggling not to, don't even want to think about it. They say regular sex for a man is good for the prostate. No wonder I've got prostate cancer if the research is right. I could cry forever and a day but what does it change? nothing, so what do I need to change?

How do I recognize the change I need to make? how do I not make a fool of myself as they say, can I take the risk ? Will it be worth it? Finally if I don't try I will die. One drink for courage,I pick up the phone and dial Paul's number.

He picks up on the second ring. Can you imagine the second ring he answers, his voice, oh my god his voice, oh ye Universe, he's voice, 'hello stranger he says' I smile catch myself in the mirror and I smile again, my face, my mouth, my body, my entire posture just evolves into this amazing person I don't even recognize. The person standing in front of the mirror, 'how are you doing?' I ask, 'I hope you don't mind me calling you at the weekend' 'I was wondering if you're free for lunch tomorrow, I know it's Sunday, short notice but would you like to meet for something to eat. We meet at Charing Cross station, stroll into Chinatown, eat seafood or steak. Is it doable for you? "Give me a moment,' Paul responds. I can hear chatter in the background. Then he's back and confirms tomorrow is fine. Let's make it two, 'I say good, great stuff, I'll see you then.

I'm not going kill myself today because tomorrow I'm having lunch with Paul until then Rose & Ethel are going to keep me company, sharing the life they lead. I wonder what the trauma is that kept Rose writing after they were together, she says she was in London packing up to move permanently back to the Homeland and is married again! That's a surprise, so yeah I guess it's reflective, at least she has something to reflect on. My reflection is the emptiness behind the emptiness now and the emptiness that possibly lies ahead if things go wrong tomorrow.

I need more painkillers I realise as I fix the hot water bottle it's one of the few things that helps, just gently propped underneath my legs the heat acts as a distraction from the pain not unlike a TENS machine standing by the window looking out across the Thames I pick up the next letter Ethel to her Rose, I envy them because they had courage, having found each other they had the courage to find each other again and that's what I'm going to do tomorrow. I'm going to have the courage to tell a married man that I have been in love with him from the first moment I laid eyes on him and there's only going to be one of two outcomes he also cares for me or he doesn't, so there, I've said it, I accept it, yes I'm not going to die today.

Dearest Rose

There's no bastard like an ex-husband, money grabbing, irritated by the fact that you rejected them or simply pissed off that you manage to get away from them, yep! There's no bad man like a man rejected, if I tell you that he tried it on when he came to the flat to discuss the percentage of how we were going to share the profit from the sale of the flat. I'm not even sure the words to use my dear, he addresses me as my dear! Has this man completely lost his sanity?

Does he have an onset of dementia? this man that terrorized me that made my life so miserable, calls me my dear, straight away my antennas going off, inside warning me to be careful and to scrutinize everything before I sign it. That Instinct is what made me tread very carefully with him. I don't worship money, I use money, I spend money and all my life money has been my friend. I've always had money, never any greed about money. I'm a fair person and as far as I was concerned it would be 50/50, but not this man, oh my dear you don't need money like I need, you know I have young children, they go to private school, yeah, like what's that got to do with me, get out my face man, he makes a comment about how amazing I look, how I'm glowing!

I came close to saying to him my partner is making me glow but I knew he would think it's the new husband and I'm not going to let anybody take the grace of what you've done, so I hold my peace… wow Rose it's not easy emptying a house, it's not easy shipping things, I know they just sentimental stuff but you know they were things that I'd collected over the years, things that meant something to me. Furniture, crockery and all sorts but I got it done. I got the paperwork done, I moved out on time and got 50% of the money we made after settling the mortgage.

Miss you my darling. I miss you every single moment I'm away from you, despite this new marriage business you know you are the only one for me. This new chapter in our life we're going to get through. I say this with full confidence because I am not the kid who doesn't know her mind. I'm a grown ass woman with needs, with her own unique quirky taste who found everything she's looking for in you, you're the one that I want full stop, the fact that I have the baggage of a new husband is neither here nor there. He's going to get your leftovers if ever there's any sort of intimacy.

This time though, you're so close I can smell you, I can feel you, I can taste you, I can love you and that's exactly what I'm going to do every day. I can't wait to be back in your arms. I've also made a decision not to stop writing. I think it'll be really strange if this avenue that has kept me sane year after year is locked down. I'll keep writing to you but obviously you're not going to get these letters, love you my sweetpea, see you soon.

I get up and pace, if I am honest my mind is no longer fully on Ethel and Rose. My inner restlessness grows as feelings long dead are resurfacing, coming back in waves, the feelings that I had for Imam Nuhu. the excitement that starts inside that then creeps and slowly spreads out to all areas of the body. I thought these feelings were long dead? it's rearing its head, feels tingly all over, excited, apprehensive at the same time yet just longing, longing to be loved, longing to be held, longing to be touched, longing to belong, longing to be validated, longing for someone, someone with the name Paul to say 'yes, it's okay, here I am for you, I see you, I feel you, I hear you. This is either going to be one hell of a triumph or it's going to be a miserable gut wrenching experience that will tip me over that edge.

The edge that Ethel and Roses letters pulled me back from, but is it right? is it fair? that I put the responsibility of my well-being on someone else either way it's called desperation, will he accept me an old man but a man, old man with feelings, old man like a volcano that's been forced to not erupt, it stayed bubbling, rumbling, year after year, after year and now it wants to explode the explosion is either going to be one where everyone's been evacuated ahead of time or everyone in its path gets buried.

Paul has been on my mind, in my heart, in my waking thoughts, in my sleep fantasies, 20 years! It shows what a coward I am. I've watched this guy grow and stayed silent, he's got engaged, I stayed silent, he's got married yet all the time there's been this parallel line of friendship. His friendship with me, my friendship with him, on my side under the guise of professionalism, on his side? well I'll find out soon. I haven't had an erection in years with the prostate nonsense going on and here I am with a hard-on! it beggars belief doesn't it just! the name and the thought of Paul. Prostate cancer has to take a back seat, yeah! There are some things that science can't explain. If Paul and I had become partners, my prostate would be in a healthier shape.

Who knows but here we are it's what it is and I'm rolling with it ,at least I live in a country where it's not a 14-year jail term if I'm discovered to be the homosexual I am, man loving man, it's how I'm made, it's who I am, it's what I am, it's what I need, it's just me. I am a man who's only attracted to other men, yet I'm a man with no confidence when it comes to love matters. I'm too scared of name calling, of image, of society, of shame, even today to venture out and say 'I am ga that's where I'm stuck. It's the cowardice that means I have lived a pretty lonely life since I stepped on the soil of England, what's different? What's changed? I'm still lonely, the only fulfillment that I've ever had in my life has been with Imam Nuhu, the professor was neither here nor there, he just filled in a stop gap and as kind as he turned out to be to me, as amazing as his legacy has been making stupendously comfortable financially, there was and there is an element of him that revolts me yet part of that lies with me, the inability to say no, to walk away from him.

The pleasure that I got from mutual masturbation, the pleasure from penetrative sex, when it did happen, the pleasure that I got from having this delicious secret that nobody knew about. The pleasure I got was just feeling superior that I, a boy from a dusty village in the middle of nowhere had pulled this super intelligent man with so many alphabets after his name. Still I've never felt affection for the professor. I don't look for him, I don't think about him nor feel physically attracted to him, he had a need, I had a need, we simply met halfway. Once I graduated and moved away I just wanted to distance myself as much as possible from him, still here I am today I'm super comfortable because of his kindness, in terms of sexual satisfaction or sexual needs encounter my last time was with him and so the years continued to roll by, unlike Ethel and Rose who had hope I don't have anybody that I wrote letters to, I don't have anybody who wrote to me.

I basically don't have anybody. I've distanced myself from my people for fear that they will discover the real me. Why is it that my sexual identity goes against me in their eyes? Why do people change when they hear a sexual preference not in keeping with their ideology? Pacing around I've managed to work up an appetite, back into the kitchen I get my second helping and still this semi-erection sits in my lap, I thought with all my prostate problems that was going to be an impossibility but Paul's voice, thoughts of Paul, ideas about Paul, juicy thoughts running wildly in my head and my body responds, I wonder again what the doctors will say. Resurrection is the term, I feel good and at the same time I feel bad and I feel like I'm developing a fever it's the fever that you get when you're anxious and you're excited at the same time and you're apprehensive, there's just so much going on and yet I have many hours to wait out.

I need to be patience, anything could go wrong I dread the phone ringing and it's Paul to say sorry I have to cancel, really is that happens it's straight to the fridge I'm going for that overdose because that just means that's not only has the light at the end of the tunnel gone out the tunnel has now been bricked up.

I wish I could make someone walk in my shoes, you need to walk in my shoes to understand me you need to walk in my shoes to be able to relate to what I'm saying health without money is a nightmare money without health is a greater nightmare but worse than those two things is life without love, physical, psychological the entire love triangle without that fulfillment in life is a nightmare, walk in my shoes, I get up alone, I eat alone, I drink alone, I am alone for at least 72 hours straight in a week in my property, nobody ,no pet, no hobby, just on my own, me myself and the missing I. My public persona when I step out the door. I'm a respected physician. I walk into the hospital and I am acknowledged. I connect, I speak to people, people speak back to me but then they go back to their lives and I crawl back into the home that's my house there is no warmth, a workman commented once that there was a lack of family pictures in the house, then my wife was alive.

Poor Miriam, we didn't stop long enough to take pictures much less think about framing them and putting them on a wall, that house is a house not a home, that house is my prison, my mind is my prison, my body is my prison, my thoughts are my prison bars, I have been serving a sentence for so long.

My thoughts turned to Imam. I remember the lazy days with this amazing man when I could be me.The touch of his skin, smooth, velvety and warm to touch, his beard, beautiful thick rich black hair, shiny with the care that he gives it. I love the way he turban's his beautiful pristine white muslin material, wrapped around his head expertly then thrown over his shoulder. I love the billowing white robes. The way he carries himself, the smell of Tabu perfume that lingers long after he's gone. I love the shape of his hands, the cleanliness of his nails, always cut short. I love the way he looks after himself. I love this man and he doesn't exist anymore, if asked about soulmates Imam Nuhu the late is my soulmate.

I haven't found anything to remotely measure close to this man, I miss him every day, I miss his wisdom, I miss how safe I feel when I'm with him. I missed love making, be it gentle or hurried, be it kinda close to violent in nature, a bit erotic I just miss him. I missed the smell of his sex, fresh, nothing about him irritates me. I totally surrendered to him and him to me.

I take a moment to think of how difficult it must have been for him to get married because he's a man that loves man. I wonder if he was able to consummate his wedding night. I struggled to remember how he died, it was a car crash but I don't remember what Miriam said. Did she say he died before his wedding or on his way back from the wedding or after his wedding my memories are not as great as it used to be but this is what I wonder about? Was he able to force himself to make love to a woman? When all he wants is me, who makes the rules, why do we have to toe the line? I know for a fact that those who make the rules most of them have a boy on the side, they have a man on the side, they also have the same urge, this same need for total and complete fulfillment with same sex partners.

Many are sugar-daddies, they sponsor the young boys who are in University, they keep them, they pay their bills in return for sex, in return for companionship, yet they sit there in the light of day making the laws, passing judgment, wearing their strange white wigs, saying you have been found guilty of homosexual behavior and so we're sending you to rehabilitation, you're also going to serve prison time where we are going make sure that we change, we will change you, we have methods.

Who are you going to change! you can't change a human being, you can't change how they're made that's not possible, you can force them to consider alternatives but trust me their redial the reset button will always go back to what is them, what defines them as a person, oh dear, I've become all philosophical, it's not going to achieve anything.

I actually feel envy, some irritation towards Ethel and Rose for how things worked out for them, somehow they managed to navigate but that's the difference between a lesbian and a homosexual man, the lesbians are there in plain sight yet nobody sees them because they diversify themselves, live how society wants them to live, while living their true self how they want behind closed doors and that's what we're not good at, as a man I have not been able to pretend to be what I'm not in public or even behind closed doors I have just turned myself into something that is asexual, can you imagine asexual, you wouldn't know where to put me if you had to place me somewhere.

If I was to share with you who I am, hell will break loose, there will be the usual shock, disgust third person might sympathize and say oh how sad and that's all that will be attributed to me, no doubt the achievements, the multiple alphabets after my name will be forgotten, my people, my tribe, my culture will now mention my name and say it with disgust, with a twisted mouth with horror on their face with disdain in their voice, that's what's kept me a prisoner. I don't want people hating me, can you imagine, people who don't know me hating me. So here I am, until tomorrow it's me.

For it to be myself and Paul I can only wish myself luck with tomorrow. Ethel and Rose have kept me alive longer than I thought. Let's hope Paul throws me the line that I need for the short period left. I need to get some sleep. I know I won't sleep without some sleep aid. A bunch of letters have literally kept me hooked, given me hope, scared me at the same time. I look forward to tomorrow. It's a do or die type day. I hope Paul is favorable towards me.

Ethel and Rose, if you can hear me where you are and if it's remotely possible for the dead to intervene and bring about something delicious, something amazing, a blessing, that feeling, something that would mean that I also have the flesh of my flesh in Paul I hope you can interfere as good women do. I hope the universe intervenes and Paul says yes to me, yes to companionship, yes to be loved, yes to be with me, me as a person, a man who wants to love him. Now finally I know who I will leave all my assets to if he says yes, I will change my current will.

I slip into sleep easily, as I drift off my thoughts are filled with a jumble of Ethel, Rose, Paul Miriam, Imam, the laws, homeland, England, the now, yesterday, University, the professor, my work, life, my ethics as a person, as you can imagine sleep was not restful. I had nightmares about Demons, vivid dreams about being caught in compromising positions. I had nightmares so intense despite the diazepam I woke up shivering, scared only to fall back into more troubled sleep, people accusing me, taunting me, calling me names, telling me what a bad person I am, 'old man you should know better' on and on it continued,

I wake up in the early hours covered in sweat, cold and frightened, is this normal? What can I do? Who can I talk to ? nobody, this is my prison, this is how it's been, this is how it always will be unless Paul changes things. Change will come with Paul saying yes to me, Paul saying he cares about me, Paul saying he's happy to have a relationship with me, Paul saying he's okay with sharing.

That's what I want to share, that's the word, where he doesn't disrupt his life or his lifestyle, nor his routine but shares and knows that he's a part of my life while I'm a part of his. I'm not a demanding person. I will fit into his life, I am totally sure of that. I will fit into his plans at the end of the day. The most I have is six weeks to three months so what the hell I just want one last tangle before I say bye.

I go back to sleep more nightmares, being chased, being called names strangers pointing at me while I'm walking down the street, faggot, gay, disgusting, what a shame, a fraud that's what you are, to think we like you, we trusted you, we invited you into our homes, hope you haven't been trying it on with our sons, we can't trust you ? Can we ? you're gay so you'll always try and pick up the men, what's wrong with you ? it's a disease, you need deliverance, you need help, it's a mental illness, you are possessed you don't realize that! the abuse carries on and on,

I wake up time and time again drenched in sweat, I'm anxious, I know I'm anxious it's my anxiety coming out in my nightmares, the fear of being outed, then rejection, the fear of being made to feel small, not wanted, doesn't count, I feel invisible already, if things go badly with Paul that's it really, I simply longer exists, just a name, just a functioning surgeon. What is the point of it all at 4 a.m. I can't sleep much in spite of the Diazepam. I get up and go over to my workstation, I pull out the pen and paper, I write.

Dear Paul

It's so early in the morning and I'm looking forward to seeing you this afternoon but I'm scared. I'm scared because I've been lonely for a long time and I'm not sure I know how not to be scared. As a man in my 60s, petrified of receiving love, of getting loved, of experiencing love yet even more petrified of being rejected, of being discovered, of being outed after all these years in the closet. A lifetime built on commanding the respect of others delivering the goods as an expert, a respectable member of the immediate community and I'm putting all this on the line to be loved by you Paul.

You've been my friend for a long time, I've always felt more than friendship for you. I'd hoped that at some point I would have the courage to tell you how I felt but that courage never came instead it was replaced with fear, fear that is dare I tell you, you would stop meeting with me, you would stop being a part of my life, you would stop counting me as a friend. I want to be more than a friend, I want to be your lover, I want to share secrets with you, I want to share my fantasies with you, I want fulfillment with you, I will fulfill you in return. I want to be a part of your life that's not too hidden. I want to be able to walk down the road with you and if somebody says to you who is this I want you to be able to say my friend, yes I want you to be able to say the Silver Fox walking beside me is my very good friend, that will do me if you can't say partner.

I'm not a bad looking guy I know that, at six foot three I cut quite a figure I've looked after myself, my hope is that when I share how I feel about you tomorrow you'll find me attractive enough to say yes let's move forward, let's share this, let's love, the other side of the coin is if your reaction is negative I don't know what I'll do.

You see my dilemma over 20 years of friendship will either deepen tomorrow and be taken to another level or be completely crushed like an egg shell, discarded without a backward glance, well there's no two way about it, it's either nay or yea, if you say yes, I'm probably going to take you back to the Chelsea apartment, that beautiful place overlooking the Harbour. I don't have any tenants there at the moment, if we're going to be intimate that's the first place that I want it to take place. I'm going to be super generous. I can't take my assets with me, so I'm going to spoil your wife because she is the one who's going to have to share you. I'm going to look after the two of you now and when I'm passed. I'm going to make sure my presence in your life leaves positive footprints.

I hope you find me attractive physically, I hope you allow me to get physical with you but most important of all I hope you value what I have felt, carried, nurtured and protected for over 20 years for you, more importantly I pray that you treat it with the respect I deserve even if the answer is a no.

I'm feeling very Rose for her Ethel at the moment, the tin of letters has been a catalyst for me, it's allowed me to look into someone else's life, their longing, their love, their coping mechanisms, their patience with time, the hills they had to climb, the roads they have to navigate but always finding each other. I hope that I get my happiness ever after with Paul because at the back of my mind sits heavily the early exit if it's a no. What's the point of hanging around, I fail to see the point so Rose & Ethel wherever you are fingers crossed for me that I find my happiness ever after.

I dress with care, a nice casual brown linen suit to accentuate my skin tone, I drape a scarf around the my neck I think smart casual not overdressed and yet not jeans as I'm taking you to Yi Qi Pan Asian, it's supposed to be the best in ChinaTown. I just want everything to be memorable about today when you look back. I don't want you to look back at any part of it and feel what a waste of your time, what waste of your afternoon, what a waste of a Sunday. It's not that far from me and the distraction would help. I look forward to seeing you. YSL Jazz is my choice of aftershave, heavy intimate, I use just enough amount for whoever is near me to sniff the air hopefully in appreciation, I used this because I once heard you say years ago that you absolutely love Jazz and so I kept a bottle at home, never used it to work so it shows you how many years I have been hoping, dreaming wishing that today will come, when I can wear Jazz for you. I head to Chelsea first.

I give the flat a quick go over there is red wine, white wine, champagne, on the table is whiskey, brandy whatever your choice of drink it's there for you. I even ask the flat to wish me luck that when I come back later today I'm not on my own. My first with you Paul has to be somewhere neutral. I don't want it to be in the house where Miriam lived unhappily, where I've stayed a hostage in my own created prison, money has never been an object, in that, life in the West has been kind to me, I close the door and make my way out it's time to face my Demon or Angel.

I'm a few minutes early, you're already larger than life, smiling at me warmly, we shake hands then go in for the man hug that men give when they are pleased to see each other, patting each other on the back followed by 'are you okay' ? have you been waiting long ? the usual chit chat but I also observe the admiring glances we're getting from men, from other men rather than women wondering if we are a couple? I lead the way out, we take a leisurely stroll cutting across Trafalgar Square we head into Chinatown, the place has such amazing reviews I'm sure it won't disappoint having booked ahead, we arrived a few moments early, we're offered a glass of aperitif of some sort or the choice of tea while we wait we both go for the rice wine, it's warm, we cup it in our hands and look around the restaurant appreciating fine dining, in no time at all we are shown to our table.

The conversation flows easily, you are a friendly person Paul, quite easy going, of course the conversation initially focuses on work, we have a laugh about this person, that person, this policy that policy, this usual shake up, you know nothing's changed, it's just that the chest pieces get moved around but the game is the same in the NHS so having had our fill of that I ask you about family life, married to a dental assistant I know your salary is the major one for the household, you talk about her for a bit, marriage is good, marriage is okay, it's got it ups and downs, good days, bad days, times when you just feel like you need to give each other space etc etc.

All stuff I know is normal in relationships. We start with seafood. I can't fault the food, we talk, we appreciate the food, we keep it on the superficial level for now. As we get through the third course thinking of dessert I pluck up the courage to ask you what would you have been doing this afternoon if I hadn't asked you to meet me ? Not a lot you reply just watch the game, grab a couple of beers with friends and potter around the flat, not much. My wife tends to spend every other weekend with her elderly parents in Bean, Kent so I'm very much left to my own devices, no children so no Daddy duties.

I take a deep breath and find courage, there's something I need to share with you Paul, I hope I do not offend you or destroy the friendship we've had for over 20 years, to my shock and surprise Paul you lean across and you put your hand on my lap and you look me in the eye intently, you say to me 'I know you don't need to to say anything, I know how you feel about me, I've just been waiting for you to say something'

What kind of wait is that, what did he just say !!! He said he's been waiting for me to say something. I could cry but I'm in a restaurant full of people of our class, it's not the place to ball your eyes out. Paul has been waiting for me to say something, I feel like slapping him around the head, I feel like kissing him, I feel like hugging him, I don't know what I feel for a moment. I'm just bombarded with feelings, he knew all along, well hang on, slow down. What does he know and that's what I ask him.

What do you know ? he responds I know you like me as a man, I know romantically you want a man, I'd hoped over the years you would have said something or reached out to me, it's the reason I've accepted every single lunch or let's grab something after work, but not once did you express how you felt so in a way that meant that I wasn't sure if it was okay for me to say how I'm possibly feeling about you, I had hoped that the way we interact, the way which I always make time for you would help to get the message across.

It's eerie you only have to walk past the pharmacy and I can sense that you're there I'd hoped you would have the courage that

I didn't have as a young person to tell me how you feel, can we drink up and leave because I really want to talk to you, that is if it's okay. 'Let's finish, to hell with desert' I stammer, I'm not sure this is what I had imagined, but yeah Ethel & Rose must have done their job in heaven, for 20 years I've nurtured and held a love for Paul, here he is sitting in front of me telling me that I've wasted 20 years by not being courageous, whoa! this is hard,sad, this is a difficult pill to swallow. I watched him every time we were together, I watched him like a hawk, I watched him with the hope that there might be a sign however little I would have picked it up and run with it but no nil sign to say you can take things further.

My assessment is that he's always treated me like an elder, that elderly uncle, that older brother to look up to, to emulate, his role model. I mean how do you cross that line from being someone's role model to say to them 'I want to sleep with you, I want to love you, I want you to come into my bed, I want to take care of you, I want to spoil you, I want you to call me your partner in private, I want to be your better half, I want to be your second half, I want to be that missing jigsaw puzzle that completes you. How do you go from being looked up to as a role model to saying to somebody come to me, to my bed, let's be intimate.

If you know the prostrate you know it's an absolute wicked, wicked instrument to a man. I need to pee, I need to pee now, I am either struggling to pee or I'm peeing all the time, paying up for lunch I tell Paul I need to step to the toilet. I'll wait for you by the door he says and off I go to the toilet it takes a while for me to get the body to obey, probably because I'm a bit stressed by what I just heard, some excitement too, yes, what next? What's going to happen today, is it this evening or tonight? What's it going to be like making love to Paul for the very first time? I guess I take a bit longer in the toilet than most people do but having finished I walk towards Paul, he's got his back to me and he's on the phone to someone. As I get to the door and put my hand to push the door forward I hear the following and it turns my blood into iced water, just chills me to the bone. I guess he's speaking to his wife.

Babe, I know he's dying, Paul is talking about me and he's making fun of me he's referring to me as the old goat, the idiot, filthy bastard, no idea how I feel about homosexuals, talking shit to me well he hasn't got anybody else so I'm going be friendly, and make sure that the fool leaves me everything he's got. I know he's got nobody else, he's certainly got no family I have heard of, his wife died, he's got no kids, he's never spoken about his folks back home so baby this is our opportunity to reap big by sowing a little, else the fool might leave his money to Battersea dogs home.

He continues to talk to his wife unaware that I'm one step behind and I can hear him. Paul is angry, he seems to be full of rage, he's not the guy who sat opposite me who put his hand on my lap and told me he's always felt the same about me, he likes me, he knows I like him he was just waiting for me, this is some nasty angry bastard of a man, this is a man that I don't want to meet on a dark night, this is not the Paul I know and it's scares me.
Stepping back momentarily in case he turns around I feel my body changing, I feel anger, I feel real rage, absolute rage towards this man that for 20 years I kept quiet, kept my peace, never overstepped the boundary ensuring that I never did anything to hurt him, scare him, put him off me, this fool who just ate £360 worth of food is on the other side of the door talking about me, making fun of me, calling me names, I can't even say it, he called me a waste of space, he called me homo, disgusted he said and yet he smiled at me, he touched me, he had me believing that there can be something between us. Okay this guy has not seen or experienced me as a madman, he's about to because I'm the mad man who's only got a few weeks to live, a few months at the most but who's got all the money the greedy Paul wants. I'm going to treat this guy like my bitch.
Paul is gonna be my whore, in an instant, there's no longer any thought of loving, there's no feeling, there's no connection for me anymore, I'm going to use this guy, the scales having fallen from my eyes. I can tell right now he's a worse human being than me because he's further in the closet than I have ever been, hating gays but more gay then the gayest man, deny self, he thinks that by being nice to me I'm foolish enough to hand over everything to him, well Paul you are in for a surprise, actually I think we're

made for each other and thank goodness I heard what you said otherwise I'll be walking around with roses in my eyes, bells ringing in my ears, fooling myself that the love of my life loves me.

I start to cough so that Paul will be aware that I'm approaching as I push the door to swing it open he tells me to hold on he's waffles on and says the wife says hi, I said to send my love and engaged in a she said giving a response back each time that Paul relayed. To her thank you for taking Paul out, thank you for being there for him, we really appreciate you, I respond, that's okay I'm always here for the two of you thank you for letting him join me for lunch I look forward to seeing you at some point, take care, Paul ends the call.

Flagging a black cab we head back to Chelsea. I am going to deal with this man, he is about to receive all the frustration I have experienced since Imam Nuhu. Paul is going to bear the brunt of years of unfilled needs, this nasty conceited man. He's going to be at the receiving end of my shaft, if you don't know what a shaft is, go and ask anybody from the homeland they will tell you. I am scared of what I'm capable of and I know I'm capable of a lot. What makes it worse is that same line of thought: what do I have to lose ? very little.

It's interesting to watch someone closely without them realizing their game is up, that's what I do. I watched Paul's expression as we went into the flat. He loved the fact that he could see the harbour , the yachts and small boats in Chelsea harbour. I love this place, he says over and over I love the high ceiling, I love the rooms, I love the way you decorated, I love the location. Yes, I love it too, I love the rental income even more I joke. White wine, Red wine, Champagne, Brandy, Whiskey, what's your choice I ask, Paul settles for Remy Martin's, this man has taste maybe not the money but he certainly has the taste I open a special preserve bottle of Remy Martin's.

I don't drink, can't, too scared of blotting something out when you're drunk, I give him a generous glass as he steps out on the balcony, I watch him, I can see the clock in his head going click click tick tick tick, yeep would love this place if the old boy that's me decides to leave it to him. I'm not sure what sort of fuck you think you're going to give me to be entitled to a two bedroom property in prime location, worth well over a million pounds.

The problem is when you think you have a fool but the fool has you as their fool I don't even want to touch Paul there is something revolting about him, I'm amused when he puts one hand out to me and beacons me over I walk over to him and he slips his hand around my waist and pulls me close, this is comical! my dream, my hope, my fantasy.

All these years is happening yet all I want to do is beat this guy into tomorrow for the horrible things he said about me, for his true feelings that he's hiding right now and for a moment I'm apprehensive because actually nobody knows I'm here with this guy so he could hurt me and leave me here but he won't because he's greedy and he already has a plan with his wife, let's milk him and let's be there for him and let's ensure he leaves everything he's got to us, very simple plan if it works. The manner Paul is caressing my hand puzzles me, is he not new to man on man contact?

Taking Paul's outstretched arm I step backwards so he has to follow me back into the flat brandy in one hand my hand in another I ask him if it's okay I kiss him ? he nods, taking the leading I kiss probing teasing sucking tasting, holding him in an embrace enough for him to move but tight enough to not pull away, when I pull back I catch just for a brief second the shock on his face his response is instantaneous, I can already feel his erection, so like the other thousands and millions of men throughout the world you're also homosexual and your covering it up by getting married doing what society wants you to do, what family wants you to do, what's expected of you, you're also hiding deep in a closet, how many sexually encounters have you had on the side, but then also from the tone of your voice and the way you ridiculed me I wonder how many gay men you've also bashed, well I'm your nemesis, I'm your karma and karma has arrived.

Shall we, I say leading him towards the bedroom he tries small talk, I find you so attractive, oh gosh I did know it was going to be like this, if I did I would have said something to you all these years, I smile at him holding his gaze I begin to undress him he makes all the right noises he's enjoying this, I'm miles away in my anger. I know your're gay so all this is to line your nest, yet all those abusive words, you are such a waste of time, I've clocked you Paul, you are poor, I know exactly who you are and what you are, you are a faggot just like me, well let's see how you like this, bending him over I keep my clothes on, I touch him, stroke and play with him, then love him up before he had a chance to even think do I want to be bottom or top?

I begin to take possession of him but there's something about him that disturbs me, I cannot unhear what I heard and I feel myself begin to go soft he asks what's wrong and I tell him it's the excitement I waited so long and overwhelmed I say, I close my eyes and think of Imam Nuhu, instantly hard as a rock totally solid in seconds and then I begin to ride Paul, I didn't make love to him and if there was a feeling in what I was doing you could call it irritation you could call it disgust you could call it anger and you could call it 'flog the bitch'

I listen to the noises he makes and I look at his back as he arches his back up and pushes himself backwards to receive me there's nothing gentle about me I take him hard and fast he cries he mumbles he talks I don't really listen to what he saying I'm too far gone I'm too cross making sure he doesn't cum on my bed I stand up when I come and I finish him off with my hand tissue at the ready he tries for a cuddle, I tell Paul to get dressed we need to go he's puzzled he looks at me, is something wrong he says, I repeat the same crap no it's not you it's me.

I just feel completely overwhelmed. I'm happy but what next? I need to go and think and just understand how this is going to work for us, it's going to work just fine. Paul reassures me, we're going to be fine, he says we're going to work it out. I'm going to spend time with you. I'm gonna be with you as long as you need me in your life. I'm going to love you, I'm going to be your love, I'm going to be the one you reach for.

While Paul gets ready I ask him for his bank details. It's interesting how he doesn't even hesitate just reels it off, his bank sort code and account number. I transfer five thousand pounds into his account and say to him buy your wife something nice, he doesn't see the amount he doesn't know the amount but I have no doubt that the moment we part company he'll be checking his bank balance he earns a decent wage but nothing on the level that I'm on. I lead him out of the flat very quickly you know we've been in there less than an hour I feel like I need to have the place aired, fumigated it just feels like this place that I'd romanticized our first meeting, our first intimacy just feels contaminated, maybe I should have taken Paul back to my house but what is done is done we make our way back to Charing Cross where a polite bye and handshake of all things with a talk soon I watch him head off to jump on the train.

    I stroll out the door of the train station, so lost in thought not really bothered which direction I'm going but knowing I don't want to go home yet I find myself in front of Trafalgar Square again they've got the usual pop-up market there selling burgers for 15 pounds to idiotic tourists who believe it's homemade, handmade and the usual no additives no chemicals as natural as possible, ignored earlier in the excitement of being with Paul I wander around looking at the tourist hundreds just shifting like sand not looking where I'm going I I end up saying I'm sorry I'm sorry several times having walked into or bumped into people

    I smelt him before I saw him as I reached out to steady him, steady myself at the same time saying I'm really sorry he turns around to say it's okay and I stare into beautiful eyes in a tiny little perfect portable body, his either Chinese or Cantonese or Korean he could be from anywhere, he tells me in his gentle voice it's okay sir it's quite crowded here, saying sorry again I reach out my arm and introduce myself it just felt right there was something about this that felt okay taking my hand he pumped up and down and introduced himself as Yong, as with his small delicate size his hand is small, we stand there holding hands just smiling at each other communicating volumes without saying a word.

    I speak first. Would you join me for a drink ? That would be very nice. He says we move away from the crowd looking for a wine bar, I'm looking for something. I look at him as we walk. He's well dressed, his suit screams money, his leather shoes though casual. I know good qualities when I see it, Casadei my guess.I wonder about this little man I've just made friends with as we find a quiet corner. He chooses red wine. I asked for orange juice. We mainly smile taking in the environment and the crowd around us when he speaks again he is softly spoken choosing his words carefully.

He's here on business, he's in the UK every Thursday he flies in to pay his staff he says he owns businesses based in China his main export is to London, he likes to be a hands on owner ensuring that the middleman management is not mistreating his staff who are the backbone of his business he talks about his business but he doesn't say what it is and I don't ask I'm a little bit taking a back when he asked if I'd like to join him at his hotel in Docklands I tell him I'm not familiar with Docklands. He insists let's get to know me he says, I fly out tomorrow, why not I think no risk no gain it's been quite a day. I accept graciously he suggests we have a walk around which we do, we stroll around like a couple of tourists looking at this, looking at that, marveling at a world of junk, junk that we keep manufacturing, collecting, hoarding and leaving behind when we pop our clogs.

With the sun's going down and we moved towards the train station we converse easily about everything, the world, politics, the ozone layer, the melting ice, finances, England, China, families the gen-z generation, he's into classical music apart, from the Kora I have no interest in classical music but we talk easily, there's something about us two very attractive smartly dressed men sitting side by side on the Dockland Express that attracts attention, women look at us and smile men look at us and you can see they're trying to figure out couple or they just business associates.

I don't mix much so I'm not aware of how other people live. I am taken aback by the luxury of the property we walk into throwing his coat on the back of a chair in the opulent dining room, I've never seen anything like it okay I don't know anybody at the Docklands but when you walk into a flat and you're on I think it's the fifth floor and there's a pool on the same floor for the owner you begin to get the idea of where I am, the decoration is exquisite black and white minimalistic, amazing lighting, the place just smells amazingly clean, you can tell there's an army of people working tirelessly behind the scene to create and maintain this magazine page living room, by that I mean the lighting, the chandelier is something to behold I watch in amazement as he picks up a bell and he twinkles it an older Malaysian woman appears from nowhere they speak rapidly and she gestures for us to follow, she slides the door, I'm treated to a 16 seat dining table I didn't even know there was this much space in Docklands much less these kind of properties.

I've been in some exclusive places but this is on a different level the doorbell goes and he goes ah my neighbor! I think we might be joined by one more guest. How do you feel about Arabs? He asked me. I have no idea what I'm doing here and for a moment I wonder if I'm safe. Am I being set up for what I read about countlessly or heard about on TV happening in the gay world. I hold my peace and smile, that will be nice if you're expecting an Arab nothing of the sort walked in.

What walked in is an absolute poster boy for middle east countries, dressed impeccably in western clothes, his hair wavy black and thick, he smile making him look more attractive, I can smell Papillon perfume, he knows I can smell him, he smiles again as he walks towards us Introductions are done we seat at one end of the table Yong at one end at the top end and the Arab whose name is Faisal sits opposite me we talk, we eat, we drink, he drinks alcohol that's fine it's my choice not to there are people of faith who drink alcohol. I don't judge because I don't want to be judged.

The meal was scrumptious, clean tasty and fresh that's all I can use to sum up the food little portions of seven to eight courses by the time we're finished I was pleasantly full, Yong suggests we moved to the terrace, awesome view of the Thames you can see across to Greenwich and beyond, sure get what you pay for it's an amazing view as the sun begins to dip makes it a picture perfect view of the 02 canopy.

I'm not aware exactly when it was that Faisal asked if I was okay and put his hand on the back of my neck starting a massage, 'tell me to stop if you don't want me to touch you' he says I turned around and I looked at him, all my life for fear of my religion, my culture, my people, I have hidden in the closet now here I am, known you guys less than two hours, you're touching me, you feel comfortable to touch me and I feel comfortable super comfortable to receive your touch. I wonder was it a coincidence that I met Yong? Was he looking for someone like me? Yong just stands back leaning on the railing looking at us.

I look at him and wonder what he's thinking and wonder how many times this scene has been played. Tonight I am on the menu, I don't mind. Faisal's hand is no longer on my neck, he's moved to my shoulders, it's down at my waist it's doing things to my body and Yong just stands there watching I can see the effect it's having on him, I've never experienced anything like this in my life.

Professor and Imam Nuhu were one on one, this is different, shall we go in sounds like it's coming from a long distance, yeah shall we go in just in case there is someone watching remotely let's go in, I sit down long legs spread out in front of me Faisal sits on one side of me Yong takes the other side I'm older than this two so I'm gonna ask them exactly what they want ? we want to make love to you they say, we want to worship you, we want you to know that we're here for whatever it is you wish to do or you wish us to do to you, you just have to tell us, we're both clean, we get tested regularly so if you're concerned about diseases and safety not here, we both clean and we keep it safe using condoms.

I pull Faisal in for a kiss while I let my hand rest on Yong's crotch, I've gone from being lonely to living the dream. I've already had sex once this afternoon and now I'm in a flat in Docklands being ministered to by two foreigners. I've stopped thinking about race and culture and religion if I think about it I'll lose my erection so for now I'm just going to live in the moment, if it's Ethel and Rose up there that are making things happen for me they need to slow down because from nought to ten is a little bit too much, yet in no time at all arms and legs are everywhere mouths are kissing cupping sucking touching feeling, the place echoes with groans and moans, hungering for more, a guidance of the hands, the body, the legs.

I look around the bedroom for a moment, massive it's got too many mirrors, including the ceiling the mirrors placed strategically where you look up and you see what you're doing for some reason excites me more ever, I've never had a threesome and here I am in my 60s looking death in the eye and I am in bed with two really hot guys, what more can a man want, now grateful I didn't take my planned insulin overdose, thank goodness somebody left letters in my office, thank goodness I knocked it over, thank goodness I had the nosiness to start reading, that's what's kept me alive that's what gave me hope, that's what gave me the courage to speak to Paul, though Paul turns out to be a closet asshole, like me a fag who got married, he talks negatively about homosexuals yet one himself.

I am not sure where my strength is coming from but I'm going to deal with Paul. If this is what is meant by hatred, it is dangerous because it's as intense as love so when you love someone and you no longer love them the intensity of that dislike is the same.

Right here right now is blowing my mind, never in a million years did I dream I would find myself where I am right now, two gorgeous men who are worshiping me, in between we take it in turns to make each other feel good. I've lost count of the orgasms. I've lost count of the climax. I've lost count of the amount of pleasure from me as a person much less the other two people I'm with but eventually we're sated and tired and sweaty the room absolutely stinks of sex, now there's something in me that wants to get away, I get up first and I head into the shower, I wash and get dressed, they're both still lying in bed looking at me, you can tell they do this a lot, I'm grateful for the experience but this isn't for me I need more than this, whatever this is, damn! I'm glad I enjoyed it. I got the chance to experience this.

Where do you need to go, Yong asks ? Chelsea, I said Chelsea Harbour, uber in five minutes I'm told, would you like a drink while you're waiting ? no thank you, this something I'm no longer enjoying the sight of these two naked guys after our sex marathon. I want to leave and I want to leave soon. It's the woman's voice that cuts through my thoughts to say the uber is here.

I give them the best of my smiles and I thank them for an awesome time, they understand they won't be seeing me again without us even communicating it verbally they've made my day, actually they've made my life because this is not something I'm going to experience again but boy or boy in 24 hours I've gone from being a lonely 60 something year old to having sex one-on-one and then a threesome and I don't even know how many times I came I just know that right now I must get to bed or I will drop where I'm standing.

It is an old man with a smile on his face that entered that uber.

Dear Ethel & Rose

I'm not sure what's happened today but clearly based on my spiritual beliefs you heard me and you intervened, Paul is not who I think he is or rather Paul's character is not what I thought it was would you believe Paul turns out to be homosexual like me, if not it all has been too easy with him. I know greed has played a part, he's befriending me because he knows I'm dying I didn't even know he knew that I have prostate cancer and that I have a short time to live so again that brings up the issue of has he breached confidentiality somehow to know about my information but you know what, that's neither here nor there the thing is to hear him discuss me in such vile terms has been difficult.

It's not easy when you carried a torch for someone for so many years only to find out that person you've been longing for, falling in love with, maintaining that love under the guise of friendship is a complete moron, I'm hurt but who do I tell, I'm hurt and angry because he thinks it's okay to mess with an old man like me, an old dying man for that matter, to get hands on my assets, well the next few weeks are going to be fun.

I plan to enjoy myself, all these years of lack of sex I'm fulfilled, as I walk to my grave and Paul is going to be my bitch. I am going to use him the same way he wanted to use me, nothing is going to be changing in my will. Battersea dog homes will be second happiest. Paul is not deserving of anything but what I'm going to do is I'm going to keep the bait going this is going to cost me around 50,000 pounds I've decided once a week I'm gonna give him a check or transfer money to him 5,000 pounds will keep him hooked and then I'll do whatever I want with him.

I plan to live all my fantasies Paul is going to put up with, he has his eye on a different picture. I have my eye on him and that's the way it's going to go, for the first time in months, in years I sleep without sleep aid, I sleep the sleep of the peaceful, I sleep the sleep of one who is not worried about anything, I sleep the sleep of exhausted flesh, I sleep the sleep of a head that has absolutely nothing going around in it, finally I sleep the sleep of one who just wants to switch off and is finally able to I sleep, I sleep very well.

Ethel and rose when I get up there I'm going to find you and I'm going to give you the biggest hugs you've ever received from a stranger, thank you, thank you for letting me walk with you thank you for stopping me from what I wanted to do, just thank you for your letters.

Dear Rose & Ethel

It's Monday morning and I'm wide-eyed and full of wonder about the last 24 hours, was that really me, me no sex, no affection in years, absolutely none since the professor and all of a sudden I had sex with three men in less than six hours, something's different, something's changed something's right, this is blowing my mind yet I'm grateful, I'm grateful to connect with human flesh again. I'm grateful to be able to express my sexuality even if the latter part of yesterday was a risky situation.

I used condoms so I should be okay, it's the light of day now when I look at myself in the mirror I don't recognize who's looking back at me and I asked myself what next ? is Trafalgar Square the place to stroll to, to hook up, I think that's what it's called, don't care now that I have Paul exactly where I want him.

I no longer desire him, I am so angry it's unbelievable even his name no longer has the same effect, the love that was in my heart and that's what scary one minute you love someone and the next minute you absolutely want to kill them, all that affection vanished the moment I heard what he was saying about me, me an old faggoty fool, you're going to see how clever this old fool is.

I've never felt more insulted in my life and it makes me question was this affection that I've always had for Paul or a way of me just distracting myself and getting on with everyday life that as long as Paul was on my horizon every day he gave me hope, I got up, I got dressed, I went to work just for that bit of lunch with Paul, or grabbing something to eat after work, of seeing his face, of looking at his body, of just breathing the same air in the same space.

This is a man that has stopped my dreams forever, in a moment he froze my thoughts, my hopes, my feelings, my needs, for as long as I can remember from the moment I set eyes on him. Now look how he turned out, an absolute disappointment, the moment I entered him I realized that he was not new to anal sex, there was no resistance, there was no be careful, be cautious, there was none he just spread himself and gave himself to me, somebody's been giving it to him, that's much I know from my encounter with Paul yesterday or maybe several people have been giving it to him, my caution to myself is to always ensure that I wear condoms.

Despite my plan to give him money I'm going to treat him like the whore he is, how dare you Paul, you and your stupid woman, how dare you want to inherit stuff that you've done nothing to deserve, well let's rock and roll, the ball is in my court and I'm gonna control the dribble.

I noticed though that there's a spring in my step as I get ready for work, as I stroll around the building I wonder if anyone noticed that there's something different about me in the way I'm carrying myself, there's this additional confidence that comes from having control.

I've never been in control before, I've always felt controlled by my need as a homosexual man, today I look people in the face and I speak straight at them the shy Fahad who's been hiding away like the moth has become a beautiful butterfly, we talking here of Fahad who got laid several times yesterday, hasn't been laid in years and all of a sudden he's cup runneth over. I go about my job diligently, a post where I haven't told them that I'm dying I don't see the point you can't tell I'm dying to look at me. After all with Prostate cancer all they do is monitor before taking action, slow growing, yeah right !

The morning goes quickly and I make my way to the pharmacy, Paul smiles at me differently this time. After yesterday the silly little shit clearly thinks that he's got me eating out of his hand. Let's go do lunch. He smiles at me, like an idiot not realizing that he's been clocked. I think the smile is supposed to convey a delicious secret only we know. I play with my lunch in the same manner that I want to play with Paul. I'm going to be the naughtiest person possible before I depart from this world. I take the condom in my pocket out and show it to him. He smiles back at me and says let's do it. I nod towards the disabled loo.

It's one of the out of way places where no one's gonna knock on the door, I tell him to go in first I'll join him I watch as he goes into the disabled loo I'm only a few steps behind him I step in and without saying much, bending over pull his trousers down put the protection on and just take him I don't even say anything, he makes all the right noise that he thinks I want to hear but it does nothing for me. I simply put my hand over his mouth. I'm not interested in Paul's pleasure, I'm just interested in my drought that has ended.

Once done I ensure that I see the condom flush away. I'm not interested in the Clinton scenario where my semen is produced. I walk out of the disabled loo and don't even look back. Five thousand pounds means I can just about do anything I want to do, there'll be another five thousand at the weekend. I will pound this guy so much. I just wish after I go there's a way to watch his face when he realizes that nothing has been left to him. I head back to work, not noticing, our ward Occupational therapist Al, short for Ali who saw me emerge from the loo didn't think anything of it until Paul also emerged.

I'm buzzing. Is this how you felt ? Ethel & Rose when you finally got together ? this energy, this electricity that's just cruising through my body, the slight pain from my right scrotum is nothing, that is the prostate reminding me it's not very happy but it's what it is, I get through the afternoon's consultation can I just say to note I purposely have not brought the tin of letters back to work I still have some reading to do but I've also started to add my own writing to it.

 Ethel and Rose's letters must not be the end of it, I want my letters to be added so that at some point in the same manner I got to read their letters and took a look through the window of what their life was like perhaps somebody else might read mine, hopefully I hope they'll have some compassion for me if they don't at the very least my letters say I was here! like Rose & Ethel I mean in Plain Sight yet nobody saw me so I'm also sharing what it's been like and what it's like right now.

In all the years I've worked with Paul he's never sent me an email but I get an email now with emojis. Would you believe the silly sod he thinks he's playing an old man, well, my dear I am playing you and you are going to be so played. I send back a smile emoji and a hand tick emoji, this can't be real, I get a reply Paul, wants to know if we're getting together tonight this guy is a whore he's just confirmed it, getting laid is something he's clearly been doing on the side in a closet somewhere, he's too eager to be with me.

I tell him I'm busy tonight but maybe tomorrow night we can get together. I need to go home and process Sunday some more. I need to reconcile myself with my behavior because this certainly is not the reserved Fahad for some reason I've become a stark raving sex machine.

No, I'm not a menace but something's gone wrong because all I can think about and want to do is get laid but angry sex that's what I'm interested in because I'm not going to get loving sex, expressive sex, validation sex, love language sex. I'm having sex that literally I'm paying 5000 pounds a week for and no I'm not going to take any prisoners. I'll be rough and angry. I'm going to do exactly what I want to do because there's no genuine affection for me from Paul and so Paul's going to receive from me what I can only think of as a bam bam bang bang bang bang no more, no less. Intrusive ruminations are hard. The more I try not to think about Paul the more he creeps into my thoughts.

Ali or Al as he is called knocks and appears with a cup of lemon balm tea for me. A cordial relationship over the years, Al asks how I am and follows with would I like to go for a bite midweek after work, I know very little about him aside from the professional contact so say yes as a form of further distraction for myself, agreeing on Wednesday after work, seven pm Paladar, he gives me the details located between Elephant and Waterloo turns out to be an award winning gay-owned Latin American restaurant.

This is the first time in a long time that I've had an appetite, a proper appetite, a roaring appetite like the old me, not the sick man with prostate cancer, I head to one of my favorite food holes, today I have a little bit of everything I like, no problem on my mind, no loneliness in my mind, no partnership on my mind, nothing on my mind, just good quality food. I look around the crowd and wonder as I eat lamb succulent grilled to perfection, vegetables, couscous with little bits of dates, little bits of almond little bits of everything good.

I wonder like me how many married men with children sitting here live their second life in a closet or secretly alongside the public life, should we all be honest and say who we are and what we prefer, both sexes will become scared, marriages will dwindle, I want to get married, I want to get married, it'll be like now we got to test you out first are you really heterosexual not same sex orientated but can't say so and wants to marry a wo/man to cover up that fact so you can carry on living your double life, now that is a mouthful.

I chuckle quietly to myself as I enjoy my meal, I wash it down with freshly made orange juice just the way I like it and I carry on looking at the crowd playing that game of work out who is who, the men sitting together, are they really who we think? the two men in the corner speaking quietly suited and booted clearly professionals are they just friends or are they both trapped in a world where the only breathing space is this Turkish watering hole? where they can come and sit in a corner and dare to talk the talk they can't talk publicly, dare to talk the talk they can't talk freely, even the chef seems feminine, I wonder what his story is, I wonder if he's got the nerve to stand up and be counted instead he hides in a woman's role flip flopping around the grill grooving to the music doing his own thing, good luck to him as long as he is happy that's what it's about.

 At the end of the day happiness and where we can find it, where we can get fulfillment as a human being, the hierarchy of needs, ability to tick off each tier of those needs. I'm not too bothered anymore. Tomorrow is what matters, I've got two important appointments, with the urologist online, the other face-to-face with my lawyer at 4 p.m. I need to make things more airtight, then there's a phone call I must make when I get home. It's going to be a difficult one.

I'm going to be speaking to my sister in the homeland. She's one person who has remained distressed with my lack of appearance all these years. For my part I have kept an eye on her remotely, the benefit of social media through her children. Zariat has four strapping boys all married and given her grandchildren, spread between USA and Canada, though Zariat continues to reside in the homeland she is a frequent visitor to the children returning to the homeland late November to avoid the cold, heading back abroad in May.

The new Fahad makes his way home, I have things to do just a little bit of extra tidying up and a little bit more of my letter writing. I don't want to go quietly without leaving my own footprints, by that I mean my real footprints not who you think I am or what you think I am but to share who I really am. Where has the pain gone? I haven't needed painkillers today, was the sexual release what I needed, what my body and soul needed to feel this good. I have been foolish for so long, could have been paying or just take a toyboy like all these other older men like me, a younger man who would satisfy my needs and whose needs I would take care of, pay his bills or whatever.

Thoughts of Paul has kept me a prisoner within the walls I created myself, so here death is round the corner, it's not easy to care for someone for so long then hear them say these awful distressing things about me, well it remains what it is, so Rose & Ethel thank you for beginning this journey but as it's not you who is going read my letters let me try this.

Dear whoever,

My name is Fahad. I'm a surgeon, a very successful one, I married Miriam who I was betrothed to as a child. I've lived in England for a long time. Correction: I hid in England for a long time. I am a man who loves men, I am your definition of fraud, who has lived right under your nose but yet you did not see me. I have done everything expected of me hailing from the homeland be it religion, be it my culture, to the outside world I have conformed and been the perfect role model but when it's me, myself and I.

I cannot think of anyone who has led such a miserable empty unfulfilled existence, a lonely existence, an existence with no light in it, no colors, no joy, no fulfillment, no excitement, just existing. wake up go to work do something amazing in someone else's life for their health and well-being and then come home, come to a house, to a sad woman, Miriam who respects herself and keeps to herself, a woman who moves around the property like a shadow keeping out of my way, not wanting to be seen or heard, knowing that it will not be reciprocated.

I am the man who comes home from work and disappears into the other room, only emerging to eat barely able to stand being in the same room knowing I'm responsible for her misery, you know something reader I do have a conscience too but I'm too far down in my hole to be able to make any sense of what I could have done different, the fact that I have a doctorate doesn't mean I have all the answers, it doesn't mean I always get it right, clinically yes, in my private life no.

I wish I'd be more promiscuous, I wish I had found a lover, I wish I had had the courage to get on to the gay scene, I wish I'd had the courage to do all the things that I fantasize about but could never get around to doing, I wish I hadn't been such a rat, so scared hiding in a hole, if I sound angry, I am, I'm angry at myself, I'm angry at my parents, I'm angry at the fact that they tied me to a woman, and angry at Imam Nuhu for dying, I'm angry because once I heard about his death, that became a full stop. I'm angry at the professor because what he offered me was not the way of life I wanted. I thought I was using him, but it turned out he was using me.

I'm angry at the world basically, angry because I have not been able to stand up and say I am ! And that's what's killing me, those three simple words 'I am gay', I'm going to die without saying so verbally, but read this, I am Gay. Despite my accomplishments I have behaved myself, despite living in England. I couldn't live openly as a gay man, living in fear of putting myself in a situation where I'll be discovered, outed. Such an ocean of fear, of desolate feeling, not experiencing the joy that it brings to find somebody who simply loves you back. I used to dream of finding a man and getting married when same sex marriage became legit but I can't even date, I can't get beyond looking at Paul, fantasizing, looking but not touching, I wonder how many opportunities I've missed over the years because of fear.

I couldn't look beyond where I felt safe which was with this man in a pharmacy under the same roof, down the corridor from me, the thought of moving away from the norm that I knew scares me silly, all six foot something of me, all the time nightmares, about me being in a sexual position with a man and somebody kicking the door down, family friends, religious leaders, the police, they've come to arrest me, that is my fear of exposure but let me tell you something I once loved and I was loved.

Imam Nuhu, my love, my heart, my soulmate, my joy, my mentor, my friend, my all. I have loved and I have been loved and I know what that feels like, that feeling of complete peace and satisfaction, connection and being connected, knowing that you matter, that feeling of not just doing things for yourself but considering them. that look. that touch. that communication without even opening your mouth. knowing you're on the same page, same goals, same wants, same wishes, same hopes, same worries, same fears and that nurturing of each other meeting each other's needs, ensuring each other is okay, the public persona, the private persona that you both have.

Then delicious secrets our exploration in the early days within the boundaries, just waiting, waiting for me to be old enough for us to be properly intimate the buildup of that the sexual tension crackling all the time, I tell you, I have loved and I know what it's like to be loved, the scholarship to England felt like a curse, in the end six hours and 20 minutes flight away from the love of my life, that six hours and 20 minutes that felt like Mars, felt far away than Saturn, Jupiter, the galaxy, you name it I was here, stuck here. I couldn't rush back home, the allowance given to go home once a year was directed to help my father, there was no other source of money until the professor came on the scene and even then his money was for taking care of things locally, you know enough but not quite enough for me to get up and go do something like buy a plane ticket but enough to keep me ticking over in exchange for a part of my body but certainly not my mind or my soul, that was already taken.

I am yet to meet anyone as neat and tidy, clean and lovely as Imam Nuhu. He ticked all the boxes and the icing on the cake,he got me and I got him, I miss him every single day every moment. He would never have said any of the horrible rotten things Paul said about me, in all the years I was with Imam Nuhu not once did he make fun of me, if I didn't get something, if I didn't understand something he patiently taught me, he patiently corrected me, he's criticisms were constructive, he explained why before the concept of the white man came about sandwich theory, Imam Nuhu was already using that when it came to constructive criticism.

He would praise me first and pinpoint all the things I had done right, then the middle bit he would explain what hadn't gone right what was wrong what was going to be done about it and then the top layer again he would praise me he would acknowledge my efforts and he will encourage me to say yes you can do it, I never met anybody like him the moment I left the shores of the homeland.

I remember he is face, he's nose in particular, what a handsome man, he's velvety skin, beautiful not a blemish this amber liquid gold I couldn't get enough of and he in turn accommodated me, he accommodated all my peculiarity, my fears, he let me explore, he validated me, he let me know it's okay to feel what I felt, he exposed societies pretenses.

I wasn't the only one who found another man attractive, it was going on in the top tier socially, yet all this was held under cover of dark during the day the men were responsible heads of homes, commanding, teaching, making the rules, ensuring we toe the line but come darkness out came the dancing boys and off would go people to enjoy themselves overnight returning to their houses in the morning the choices always there if they wanted to sleep with a woman, she was at home, if they wanted to have fun with a young man he was out there they just had to go down to the little village that was known for this.

Really, I'm grateful to Imam Nuhu without his input I truly would have believed I was a freak. I remember the first time I told him I like to wear women's underwear. I love the feel of the silky polyester, the smoothness of it, his response, he created a little drawer for me of satin female underwear. I remember the brand Rama, it was mine, I could wear them whenever I wanted and as soon as I got to his place the first thing I used to do was have a wash and then change into those lace edged underwear, that's what I mean by he got me, he let me be who I wanted to be, I thrived under his directives, academically, physically, emotionally, psychologically and personal growth. He invested in me, in return I ensured I made him proud of me.

Everyday matches me towards my death but I no longer live in fear, I have accepted what is to come, I reflect while getting ready for work this Tuesday morning I wonder what else suddenly changed what more has shifted for me. I'm not bringing Paul back to my house I don't want him to contaminate the beautiful ambiance that now exist in my house I will take him back to Chelsea I'll pound his brain out there because that's all he is a pounding object, how can someone be so greedy, how can someone be such a disgusting human being, how could I have been so wrong about Paul. I admit Paul has got to me, he still remains under my skin and that's because of how much I hero worshiped him from afar, desired him, lusted after him, thought about him, dreamt about him day and night and yet here we are Paul doesn't even like me.

Well here we go six weeks to three months. I'm gonna rock and roll my way right through to the grave. I'm going to give my sister a call this afternoon, because of the time difference I emailed her son, her number was forwarded to me immediately I hope it won't be too difficult a conversation because I'm the one who cut myself off from family and the homeland, though I didn't feel I had a choice.

Dear whoever

Today is a big day, speaking to my younger sister, someone that I've loved all my life but stayed away from for fear of her being disgusted by me and no longer looking up at me as a youngest sister does with pride, with love, affection. I have missed her so much, I've missed her every single day. I've thought about her all the time, prayed and hoped that her experience of marriage was a happy time. Social media is a fantastic tool and the pictures of her that are there with her children and her grandchildren she looks good, healthy and for that I'm grateful. I hope I haven't caused her too much pain so that I will not be met with bitterness. I hope as blood siblings we will be able to pick up where we left no matter the years and distance that has taken place.

I'm not sure how I'm going to start the conversation when I call her but I will start. I'm sure the moment she hears it's me your brother that will be enough, I never did anything to hurt her when we were young. I've got two procedures this morning once it is done I shall head to my office, no lunch with Paul, I need to get the ball rolling with my sister I have to let her know about my diagnosis I have to let her know that my will has instructions for her, best to keep it simple, she can find out the nitty gritty once I'm gone. I have to get details from her as to where the solicitor contacts her once I pass.

Plenty that's not going to be pleasant to talk about but they have to be said and I need to get my house in order, the fact that I've been told six weeks to three months is neither here nor there I know the medics are not God who can decide he's going to take me sooner or even let me live longer but you know those are the guidelines that I have.

So off I head to work still that spring in my step has not disappeared in fact my entire body feels good, I feel good and for some strange reason I can't explain I'm not experiencing erectile dysfunction as would be expected, perhaps that's because I haven't had enough sex all my life that despite the prostate issues if the stimulation is there and it's right and everything aligns I can definitely perform, chuckling to myself it's too early in the morning to be thinking about sex as I begin to feel myself come aroused, letting myself out of the house as if others can tell there is something different about me the people around me are reacting differently to me perhaps it's me I'm making eye contact, I'm saying hello, I'm saying good morning, I'm nodding to people. This is what I should have learned how to do a long time ago, come out of my shell a bit but anyway it just all feels good.

Dear whoever

My life has been turned upside down let me share with you what happens this afternoon, following the surgical procedures I went to my office and I dialled the number that my nephew had given me, it rang twice before Yasmin my sister picked up the phone and I said exactly what I'd practice, my sister this is your blood, your brother' I was met with heart wrenching sobs she cried and cried and cried and I had to get up and lock my office door because I ended up sobbing like a child. I was no longer 60 something years old. I was once again small, her teenage brother who felt incredibly guilty that he had walked away and not looked back, it took my sister a while to settle herself and all the time she cried I just told her I love you, I love you, I love you over and over, this turned out to be the most difficult 50 minutes of my life because never did I think that I had affected her so badly, so deeply, the only name for it is trauma that's all I can think about that I had traumatized my sister so much.

I accept what it must have been like for my parents, a child who went abroad never came back, he took care of them, sent money home, made sure they were taken care of but they never set eyes on again as he didn't visit nor send for them. I'm sure I would recognize Yasmin if she was to walk past me in the street but would she recognize me these were all the things she said over and over again eventually her language changed to 'brother I love you, I miss you, I want to see you, my eyes hunger for you, my heart wants to hold you, my arms need to touch my older brother in greeting' followed by a fresh round of tears on both sides.

I am a good listener and answer her questions as they rain down, keeping the obvious out I share how life has been for me in a strange Country, when she asked why I didn't return I tell her my mentor the only person who understood me encouraged me pushed me to be the best version of myself died, without Imam Nuhu to guide me I would have felt lost I said, Imam Nuhu dead, when she asked me ? was it recent, did you keep in touch with him in Alexandria, did you visit Egypt. You can guess when a conversation doesn't make sense. Yasmin I said I was told Imam Nuhu died going to or coming back from his wedding. Yes, Imam Nuhu died but that was the lesser Imam under Imam Faved Sultan the chief Imam.

I can't breathe, I feel ill, my chest feels tight, I am light headed, a knock on the door distracts me telling my sister to hold on I open the door fear there might be some complication with the patients, it was Al with his customary cup of herbal goodness, he took one look at my face and practically pushed his way in the room, locking the door behind him, I walk back to the phone and tell my sister I'm back, Al places the drink near me and sits across me, I don't have the strength to tell him this is a private conversation, Imam Nuhu is alive, your shadow and you his as we teased then.

Imam Nuhu was another person who missed your return, he did a lot for our community. Under his guidance, both girls and boys began to get good education, girls were allowed to stay in school past age ten. So many people began to travel as well, to the big cities and outside the homeland, learning trading and bringing back new developments in farming, building water access you name it even roads and other town planning developments, that man became our hero, he could tell the world was changing and if we didn't adjust we would be left behind always inferior.

He got a job lecturing in Alexandria Egypt, he became a well known scholar. He never forgot us as writes twice a year, the two Eid seasons, and his letter is always read at the main mosque. He is alive and well, Fahad, he lives in Egypt and like me his heart will be glad to set eyes on his little protege. With Al in the room I am unable to tell my sister the more serious news of my imminent death. I ask her to get her son to send me all the information I need for the family addresses etc. I promise to call her at the weekend and give her my landline so she can leave as many messages for me as her heart desires. We end our call with prayers for each other.

I end the call and burst into tears forgetting for a moment Al is in the room with me until I feel his arms round me enveloping me, that's all he did, hold me like I am a child, I cried and cried while he gently rocked me. Starved of affection, my role or scope of practice is out the window. I am Fahad, I need compassion, I need someone to say it's okay, I got you. I try to step away from Al and he says no…I remain in his arms, two men holding each other, nothing sexual if anything more powerful than intimacy. He sensed when I was finally calm and gently sat me in the chair handing me the drink. He insisted I drink it despite the lukewarm state. I do as I'm told feeling a bit embarrassed.

Al is talking. It is the mention of Alexsandria that gets my attention. Al is Egyptian and is familiar with the area as that is where he grew up, he knows the mosque my sister mentioned like the back of his hand and thinks he has met Imam Nuhu several times at his lectures. I asked him to describe him and he had it down to a tee, he then blew my mind adding he's got several pictures back home a group of them once took with Imam Nuhu. If he means a lot to you we can go to Alexandria, it's a four hour flight. I was thinking of going home for a few days, if it's okay with you we can go together, I'll be as visible as you need me, once we've found Imam Nuhu I will excuse you. I smile at Al feeling weak and a little dumb for the first time in a long time. Can you help I say, it's been quite an afternoon, first time speaking to my sister in thirty five years I say.

Al logs in on my system, tickets are booked for Saturday morning, Superior City View Room at the Four Seasons Hotel, uber to and from the airports at both ends, I just nod in agreement, then I realised he has done my booking and was setting up to do his I insisted he add his booking to mine and not to worry about the funds. For the first time I thought of drinking alcohol, drowning my sorrow, my pain, my sister just told me the man I had spent my entire life loving missing wanting, has been alive and well all this time. What is wrong with people? Why can't they communicate accurately ? My life has been one long misery because of nil differentiation in the Imam Nuhu that died. I email my admin, I need emergency leave next week, all necessary colleagues copied in. I am not thinking of anyone but me for a change.

A message flashes up from Paul. I delete without reading, bloody nuisance.

Al asks me if I am okay, I assure him I am, nothing to hide he just saw me at my most vulnerable. If you don't mind would you like to bring our meal forward, we eat and if there is time stop by mine I have a good idea where the pictures are, if not okay I'll find them and bring them in tomorrow, no, no I respond your idea is fine, let me know when you're done and we'll make a move. No sooner does Al leave that Paul comes into my office, in all the years we've worked under the same roof he has never come to see me. I look at him through red eyes, for the third time my office door is locked he comes and kneels next to me all concerned, I don't understand nature, I am sad angry and yet I get a hard on, I undo my flies without a word and guide his head to me, a flash of surprise and Paul does what he is good at, but no the erection would not subside, pulling him up and between my legs I bend Paul over while he is between my legs, I move him back unto me, he holds on to the desk and does all the work.

I come a second time and leave the condom in place as Paul gathers himself, wrapping myself in tissue for now I will clean up when I go to the loo. Paul is not sure what to do with himself, I reach for my phone and transfer another five grand to him, I still have plans for you Paul. I tell him I need to step out and he gets the dismissal, as he walks away his phone vibrates in his pocket, the alert, he steps out then steps back in and mouths a big hello, whore I think. I washed for an unnecessarily long time, I didn't smell of Paul but needed to feel clean. I'm tired and trembling from the rollercoaster of events today.

Returning to my office a million questions cross my mind. How has Imam Nuhu been? Has life treated him well, did he marry, how many wives, how many kids, grandkids, more to add to my will. Has he thought about me with love and fondness or am I a dirty secret? I have to know.

I am in my sixties and he is well into late eighties. I need to see him, like Rose and Ethel. I remain incomplete with my soul mate. I am so muddled right now. I just drift and drift, yesterday and today clashing like a tornado.

Al's return brings me out of myself, shall we, gathering myself I follow him, he has a car, sitting next to him as he expertly negotiated the traffic I realise I know nothing about him other than he looks after me with health food stuff which I receive gratefully but don't ask for and don't miss if not forthcoming. I sit back for a moment thinking of how I am in plain sight and not noticed, well I have pretty much done the same for many. When we did get to the restaurant my inner turmoil momentarily stemmed.

We are in a gay joint, I read the reviews of this award winning restaurant, the food bears witness to that. I am now curious about Al I'm trying to see him for the first time, what have I missed about this man and what does he know about me, what does he recognise about me what sign do I give that made him feel comfortable to bring me here to a gay restaurant, it really did distract me from all the jumbled up thoughts in my head.

Al is good company he seems to know when to talk, when to keep quiet, he sits quietly smiling at me and in a way looking quite concerned, the kind of look that I guess I would give somebody that I care about, I need to tread carefully here because I don't know what I'm walking into he's a colleague that brings me drinks, yes he's a colleague that saw me at my most vulnerable today and comforted me, but he's also a colleague who's turned out to be Egyptian who's offered to travel down to Alexandra with me because he's going there anyway, he knows the place he thinks he's met Imam Nuhu he's got pictures at home somewhere so yes right now I don't know what I'm doing I don't have any plans I'm just free falling that's the only way I can describe it free falling so dear whoever is reading I hope that I don't crack when I hit the bottom, I hope when I get to the bottom of this I come up feeling good.

For the second time in days I'm heading to a strangers house I've given up trying to make sense of the past couple of days and the experiences I've had, I'm just going with the flow I don't have any other answer I don't have a plan B, we finished the meal and head to Camberwell we park along ColdHarbor Lane, crossing the road we walked down Love Lane and turn into another Lane all you can see is just walls and doors, we walked through one of the wooden doors I can't believe I'm in Camberwell, you need to see this property to understand what I'm talking about this is an amazing property in the middle of a cosmopolitan area holding its own there's the oasis that you walk into that's called a garden, Egyptian grass taller than me, down the path is this beautiful two bedroom bungalow, really beautiful place it's when we go in that I realized the loft is open plan for the three bedroom.

 What a lovely place to live, what an amazing place to wake up, I compliment Al he smiles back at me politely and offers me a drink I say yes to a nice creamy coffee and while I drink my coffee and look around which he tells me it's okay to do he dives into one of many boxes and eventually I hear the hear the words that I'm waiting for, 'here we are' he shows me pictures of a group of them that all traveled back to Egypt to hear Imam Nuhu's lecture at the end of which they took pictures with him, these picture were taken 12 years ago I look at it and time stands still, my hands tremble then the tears flow I I feel like a child who has been lost for a long time and suddenly a stranger recognizes me and says I think this is who you are and I think this is where you're from, for me it's no longer homeland.

 I need to get to Alexandria, I need to get to Egypt, I need to see Imam Nuhu, I need to speak with him, I need to see if he remembers me. I hope he remembers me I just want to be in his presence, I want to talk to him, I want, I don't know what I want to do but I want to do everything, I want to hold him in my arms, I want to thank him, I want to smell the scent of him, that heady coy Tabu, I want to share what my life has been, I want to hear what he's been doing, I want to hear how he's been.

 I think it's incredible that Al who was worked alongside me for so many years is the one that's producing the pathway to do this, I am so grateful, eventually I get myself together and stopped crying, I realized he's crouched next to me he's even put his arm around my shoulder and he rubs it gently as you would to comfort a child, I didn't even feel Al when he sat next to me and then the most natural thing took place he turned me around slightly and the next thing I knew I was in his arms a fresh set of tears commenced, he allowed me to cry, the second man who allowed me to be me.

Now begins the puzzling question: is Al gay ? does Al know I'm gay? if he knows I'm gay where is this going, this just seems to be yet another angle to a confusing shape shifting period, it's taking on yet another new dimension, I accept Al's embrace, it's not sexual it's comforting and in that comfort is a promise I think of friendship.

Once the tears stopped I pulled back and thank him, he cups my face in both his hands smiles into my face and tells me 'I have longed for this moment, I have dreamt of this moment, I have wished for this moment, lived for this moment, I have spent the last years walking beside you, talking to you, being in the same room as you but never showed up on your radar. I've tried endlessly to find the courage to speak to you so many times, to tell you how I feel about you, that day just never came. Please don't be offended by me touching you if you don't want me to touch you, please tell me, I have loved you from afar for a long long time with this Al burst into tears, it's me who's now pulling him into my arms to comfort him.

There's something wrong, the world is crazy, my remaining time here has turned upside down, things are not making sense anymore I have gone from Sahara desert drought to drowning in sex, wadding in people telling me they care, at least Al seems genuine, he seems like me an easy going man, mature enough to know what he's saying and doing I hug him to me, I hug him so tight when he lifts his face up for a kiss I kiss him gently probing but very very gently there's no hot breathless passion here.

It's a kiss of acknowledgement, it's a kiss of comfort but I also hope that I convey to him that it's a kiss of what's possible and what's to come and that's how we spent the rest of the evening looking at the pictures getting ready to go to Egypt and making small talk but lots of touching and comfortable body language nothing physical, nothing sexual just a comfort in each other's presence a state that I have only ever associated with Imam Nuhu.

When Al drops me home I invite him in, nobody has crossed my threshold in a long time but this feels okay, this feels right, this is Al and it feels good to ask him in, he only stays for about 10 minutes, in that time I know this is going to be something special. I hope fervently it will be the something special that has escaped me over the years, but I'm shattered, too much has happened, I can't think anymore my brain has short circuited, my thoughts are overloaded, mentally I feel like my head's going explode yet psychologically I'm full of hope when we go to Egypt I can once more be in the presence of Imam Nuhu.

Despite the lateness of the hour I checked my email, my nephew has sent the details I requested. Logging into my account I transfer bulk funds into my current account then set up a daily direct debit to ensure the transferred sum is sent over without hassle of money laundering. I know I will get called or emailed by my bank, I only need to confirm and that's that. I am too wired to sleep, I pack for the journey, looking at the booking details I wonder why Al booked business class and not first, I go in and pay the difference to upgrade us. As late as it is I call my sister again, I tell her I love and miss her.

I finally tell her about my Prostate issue, men's problem she says, she will pray on it. I don't tell her I'm dying, that can wait. We catch up properly on homeland gossip. She told me she had a feeling I would call her back tonight, I laughed. She has always been the closest to me and can announce my arrival just by me walking into the compound without her seeing me, she senses I was nearby, she had never got it wrong.

I tell her I am going to Egypt to see the Imam as she calls him, she hopes he remembers me and shared that last they heard from those who saw him his sight was beginning to fail from the many years spent writing using poor lighting. Again my sister ends the conversation with prayers for our meeting in the near future, in a few months she will return to Canada via the UK to spend time with me. I tell her about the money and assure her though it's a large amount, I am wealthy and can afford it. Besides, I wish for her to distribute it to her children in a fair and equal manner. For the second time today I feel good, and it's this thoughts that follows me into my sleep, for the first time in a long time I wake up from my sleep as I ejaculate, the memories of Imam Nuhu colliding with Paul, the threesome and now Al, my body needed the release.

The hours between seeing the pictures and getting on a plane passed in a blaze. Al behaved like a hired personal assistant, sorting out everything from my door to the airport and on the other side, speaking fluent Arabic. We are through customs and on our way to the hotel. Al jokes we waste money flying first class as nil alcohol, he pats my hand discreetly in the back of the car. Check-in was another non event in no time we were in the suite, I have to be honest the lushness and plushness of the environment is lost on me. Al advises me to have a lie down, he is popping out and will be back soon.

I take a shower and lie down, what is it about Egyptian pillows, I soon find out, when I woke up it's four hours later, I can see the soft glow of a light in the distance, getting up Al immediately increases the dimmer, he has sat on the settee watching me sleep, he knows I am broken and needed the rest. Would I like to eat in or downstairs? I opt for downstairs.

This place is beautiful, the weather is warm and not uncomfortable, the breeze is gentle whispers of hidden pasts, the table is set against the backdrop of the infinity pool, the lighting playing its own fandango of glows. I can't tell you what we ate, just that each dish melted in my mouth, Al seems to know just what to ask for. We are having coffee when he clears his throat, Al visited the mosque when he left me. He explained the trip and was given Imam Nuhu's location.

Imam Nuhu lives about a ten minute car ride or half hour gentle stroll. Can we go there tonight? I ask if it's not that late, we were on the 06:00 hrs flight getting to Egypt during daylight hours, it's now only 7:30pm. Al persuades me to wait until the morning, pointing out I/we would be able to spend the day with Imam Nuhu. I am grateful but impatient, I recognise the need to hold my peace else I will appear ungrateful.

We moved to the main entertainment hall. There are several choices, I go for the traditional dancers, the music and atmosphere brings me some pleasure. I am within a hair's breadth of my precious Imam Nuhu, what is a few more hours wait, we will leave after breakfast. Retiring to the suite Al heads one way and I call him back, sleep with me I say, I don't want to be alone, that is exactly what he did, lay next to me and hold my hand, his body just touching mine, is Al my Ethel ? had I mistaken Paul as the answer to my prayer, this little time will tell. It felt good not to sleep alone, Al like me is clean smelling, he is clearly comfortable with me, nil feminine traits to observe in him, just a confident middle aged guy going about his business.

I tense and he senses it, what's wrong he enquires gently, can we lock the door I am worried about someone walking in on us in the morning, no chance of that he responds, he's left a message with front desk no disturbance until he calls down, he had waited while it was entered on the system, I relax and turn to his.

I kiss his forehead and Al hugs me, that's when I feel the wetness of his tears, scoping him into my arms I held him and assured him we will be fine, again nil promises but I won't do anything to hurt him, I find myself thanking him for caring about me and hold him till his tears subside, thus we feel asleep in each others arms, a hope, a dream, a thirst I never thought would be fulfilled. My last thoughts before I drifted off is how smooth Al's skin is, how lovely it is to have a man in my arms and not be angry.

The Egyptian sunrise is harsh, you look from the inside and have the usual foolish idea of a visitor, the view is picturesque, you step out and it's like an oven, how can it be 24 degrees at eight am ? Thanking Al for his sound instruction to pack light linen clothes I can feel myself already sweating. I ask if we can send someone out to buy a bottle of Tabu, I don't want to visit Imam Nuhu without a gift, I also have with me still secure with the paperwork from the Bank the equivalent of twenty thousand pounds in Egyptian pounds. I hope to find Imam Nuhu living well, I hope my little bit will add to that wellness. Armed with the largest bottle of Tabu we are on our way by 10:00 hrs. I can see we are in an affluent area as the streets get narrower, busier and noisier, the cacophony of noise is deafening, the riot of colours unbalancing the eyes, I am grateful for my sunglasses and the barrier it gives between me and the streets of Alexandria.

In no time at all we draw up outside a large white building that stretches into the distance. The place is in contrast to its location, it's a sprawling building with all the usual beautiful green lushy African vegetation that you would expect to see. I'm suddenly nervous. I'm not sure what to expect. We get out of the car and walk to the main entrance. You can hear recitals going on quietly, the prayer recitals I also did growing up. I'm grateful for the fact that we're expected because as soon as we walk to the front desk and Al introduces us the man behind the desk presses a bell and straight away another man appears and ushers us along the corridor.

We walk for what feels like several corridors left right left right left right, this way that way finally we came out onto vegetation again and walk towards a white bungalow just set apart from the main building, I notice several bungalows like that, my hands are sweaty, my legs are shaky, my heart is thumping away, my vision blurs, my throat tightens, I can feel tears welling up.

The man knocks on the door which is quickly opened by a younger man, we step into a cool sitting room with a high ceiling, beautiful but simple interior, we're shown where to sit. I sit down and stand up immediately there's so much going on for me, right now I feel like the little boy who's waiting to see Mum, I remain standing with my hands behind my back a sign of respect in the homeland my head bowed I smell him before I see him and because my head is bowed I do not take in his appearance immediately. I look up to see an elderly man, full head of grey hair like me but dignified in his stance, dignity is written all over him. He holds on to the hand of the guy who let us in and told us to sit down as he's led to a chair.

I remain standing, it's like I have gone deaf momentarily, I cannot think of what to say, this day, this moment that I never thought was possible, I feel hot, I feel cold, I am overwhelmed, I think I'm going to pass out, feeling light headed, I must have swayed because in an instant Al stands up and guides me back to the chair. We exchange greetings and small talk, observing all protocol as we are in the presence of a man so highly respected I am sure the people attending to him would have thrown us out if we stepped out of line.

Small talk while all I want to do is run across and embrace Iman Nuhu, the saddest thing is that it became very clear very quickly his memory is way long gone, Al does the talking because my tongue remains stuck to the roof of my mouth. I looked at the man sitting in the chair before me, all white garments, clean, crisp spread and glowing around him and I long for him still, I physically ache for him the young Imam Nuhu long gone in his place this dignified elderly man within who lies my precious Imam Nuhu.

I get up and I cross the room I kneel down beside him and I hold his hand and I put it on top of my head he leaves it there and says a prayer, I look at his eyes and I can see the cataracts as he prays for me I wait for him to finish. I ask him if he remembers Fahad from the homeland, he apologizes and tells me his memory is not so good, I give him the bottle of taboo, he holds it, squinting he unscrews it and smells it, something must have touched a memory I noted when he came into the room he did not smell of taboo he smelt of Oud, I wondered if he stopped using Tabu because it reminded him of us, our time together, our love, what we shared.

Imam Nuhu held out his hand, I can tell he's far away from this room, he's far far away from us and an idea comes to me I open my mouth and I slowly begin to sing the song from a show that we never missed, Imam Nuhu reaches out with his other hand, I give him mine, despite the Tabu he holds my hands tight, the young man attending offered and took it from him, Imam Nuhu covered my hand in his and as they say with dementia patient the long-term memory can be solid. Imam Nuhu begins softly to sing the song with me, when he ends he begins to sing the savory song that they sing in the village where the dancing boys are and I know even if it's only for a moment or two he remembered me, within his memory I live, within his heart somewhere I know I exist.

When he finishes singing the song I asked him how he is, he answers me, 'I have been fine, everyone around me has been kind to me, I want for nothing' he said yet when he said I want for nothing he squeezed my hand so hard it made me gasp and then I lost him, in the next moment he let go of my hand and was apologizing that he couldn't quite remember events. I tell him it's okay that I'm just pleased to see him. I'm glad to see him. I inquired again about his health. I asked about his family and despite my questions he was unable to answer me, the young man attending filled in the gaps for me.

Iman Nuhu had never married, he had dedicated his life to Faith, he didn't have children, he had lived quietly, when the opportunity came to lecture in Alexandria he made a decision to move here permanently. Suddenly Imam Nuhu reconnects again, I am happy he tells me, I am content, I have lived a good life, I have many many children even though I didn't give birth to them, I have enjoyed family life because each of my children have brought me into their family they've turned me into family member and for that I never experienced loneliness but I'm old my eyes are not as good as they used to be and so I am limited in what I can do. I hope young man that when we met I was kind to you and that I brought value into your life. At any point if I offended you or wronged you, I ask forgiveness. I wish to die peacefully when the day comes.

This is it in its entirety, I have met, I have seen, I have touched, Imam Nuhu, my cycle is complete, I have closure. I do not regret the missing years anymore. You can't turn the clock back so what is the point but I wish that I had made different choices so that I hadn't let the fact that I have same sex feelings or want sex relationship stop me from keeping in touch with the family. I could have lived here quietly and happily with Imam Nuhu, we would have continued to be careful like we were. I would have passed as his assistant and I know my life would have been different but it is what it is. I am grateful for this opportunity to put the full stop to this part of my life. I realized now the Egyptian Pounds that I brought is a complete waste of time. Imam Nuhu is well looked after, he's well-respected, loved, he wants for nothing, I can see that and he's also at peace.

If I give him money if the people around him are not trustworthy the money will disappear so I make a decision I'm going to give the money to this establishment I understand it is a special arrangement for long-serving Imam's over certain age to ensure they are looked after in their old age if they don't have family, so yeah the money will still be useful but not giving direct to Imam Nuhu.

In this manner we spent the next three hours with the Imam, and we had lunch with him. It was a simple lunch of fruits and couscous and lamb cooked succulent and soft but I could see he was flagging and I could see he was wandering when he could go. When I asked if it was okay to come back and visit him he told me it would be too much of a bother and that he's really grateful and happy that I made the time to come and see him, he repeated what he had said earlier that he hopes in the years that he cannot remember he hopes that him being in my life was positive it was at this stage that I lost the plot, I began to cry.

Asking for help to stand up Imam Nuhu put his hands out. I melted into it, the two observers stood there quietly watching us his attendant probably thought I was a long lost relativity, I cried, I cried for the life lost, I cried for all the happiness lost, I cried for the man that I loved, the man who stood in front of me but couldn't even remember my name, I cried for the small glimmer that short window in which I was able to reach him but that's all it was, a split second of a memory that came back of a love that once existed. I hope the man who when I thank him and I reassure him and tell him that yes he was a very positive part of my life and that who I am today is because of him.

I rambled on for a while and then realized he was struggling to stand up, I beckoned the guy who was attending to him, together we lowered him back in the seat. I knew then this was goodbye. If I come back again I think I would cause him confusion and I could sense a tensing in his body, it is clear that nobody comes to visit Iman Nuhu, that he lives his life in a set pattern which a newcomer would only upset and that's the last thing I want I thank him once more and before I left I touched his feet and I put my hand to my heart then I prostrated in front of him and touch my head to the ground, when we walked away I made sure I didn't look back, I couldn't if I did it would break me.

I would disgrace myself because I would run back to that man, hang on to him and start blabbing stuff that shouldn't come out of my mouth and I couldn't risk that. I couldn't risk this well respected man held in highest esteem in the community to be pulled down by a life he lead over 40 years ago, was there anything to forgive, no when he gets his long-term memory back from time to time I hope when he thinks about me he also feels how I feel, which is we loved, we lived our we could, I hope that bottle of Tabu comforts him.

It certainly comforted me to give that gift as we walked back and retraced our steps. I shared with Al what I wanted to do when we got to the front desk we were directed to the appropriate office.Because it was cash they initially were reluctant to accept it but because of the attached people work from my bank they made an exception and after filling all the appropriate paperwork including my passport details and you know just about every other detail they needed to know because of money laundering, they accepted the money and gave me an official receipt.

Getting into the air conditioned car provided some relief, driving away I look back at the building we're here for a couple of days, I know coming back would be damaging I don't want to go back to the hotel there's too much going on in my head I need to walk, I need to distract myself, I need to process what has just gone down as they say, in doing that I need to accept what I can't change and be grateful for what I have in Al, with this thought I reached for his hand, Al willingly gave it to me my crying is alarming the driver who keeps looking in the mirror at me, he even tells me he's sorry if my relative passed.

This driver is the distraction I need, I explain to him my relative didn't pass but it's difficult with the illness and sickness of old age where they do not remember you, ah he says yes, yes I understand very well and begins to tell us about his grandmother, his grandfather, his great aunty, he's uncle who all have the same illness we ask him if he could spend the day with us and take us around to see the city he didn't need to be asked twice, keep your meter running I said we will honour whatever it is at the end of today.

Thus we spent the day wandering around Alexandria, looking at all the usual touristy things, the museum, the markets, the souks, the bazaars, we walked on till my entire body ached, all the time Al walked quietly beside me speaking only when spoken to stirring me to where I needed to eat ensuring, I had regular drinks by five in the afternoon I was ready to collapse, going back to the car I fell asleep on the drive back to the hotel.

Al supported me as we made our way to our suite, nonetheless I noticed the curious looks from others as we walked they wondered if I was sick or just distressed. Once in the suite I stepped into the shower. I stood there letting the water at a warm temperature just cascade down. I didn't even bother to wash. I just stood there needing the water to soothe, calm me. I needed the water to restore me again, like a thief in the night Al suddenly appears beside me, sponge in hand he begins with my neck gentle scrubs on my shoulders, neck again, my back, the back of my leg he's fully clothed and he's getting wet but he doesn't seem to care he turns me around does my hair, my face, neck again, chest, torso, arms, legs, he washes me like you would wash a child, then he steps back while I rinse and rinse and rinse eventually he comes back wearing a dressing gown and he switches off the shower and wrapping me in a robe leads me out.

Drying me he leaves me on the bed and brings out one of the oils that we bought at the souk, my favourite, Bergamot, Al begins to massage me. I'm lying face down on the bed, he massaged my entire body but paid particular attention to the sole of my feet he turns me around and massages the rest of my body, the last thing I remember before falling asleep is the attention to my feet the foot rub, over and over and over the same relaxing deep tissue movements, yet as I dropped off to sleep, the bone pain my back hips and pelvis throbbed away. I dismiss my medical knowledge and give in to the bliss called sleep.

I wake with a start, I'm starving it's 11 am Al is lying quietly next to me, no noise, not disturbing me just looking at me, I smile at him, I thank him and I tell him 'I wish your face is the face I've been waking up to in my London life, I know you would have completed me' I reached out to him despite us being in a country where we are likely to be beheaded if we were found, I pull Al to me because it feels right and he melts into my arms, he's touch is light, where my need feels more urgent, then I realized what I'm trying to do is to replace what I would have wanted to do with Imam Nuhu, with that recognition I slow down this is not Paul, this is not the threesome I met in Trafalgar Square, this is Al who has demonstrated over and over he cares for me.

My tempo changes, I become gentle as well, I return his touches he knows where to touch me and gosh can this guy kiss he's the best kisser ever, he smiled, gentle, the right pressure exploring, his tongue probing I return everything he gives to me and when we did make love it was a different experience, this is what it must mean to be fulfilled, there was no anger, there was no hidden agenda, at least none I sensed, there was just the heat of two. This is the stuff of Rose & Ethel, this is what they had, the pleasure experience of totality. How can you top this feeling when somebody loves you back, there's nothing else to top how Al has made me feel, loved, wanted, desired, worth waiting for. I think for me that is the buzz-word I've been waiting for ain my life-time 'I've loved you from afar'

I am getting my happy ever after, nothing, absolutely nothing beats this as our heart comes together, the tempo changes the urgency matches, the wanting, the needing the glorious climax, I have finally met my other half, he's not where I thought, he was standing right in front of me but never in my vision as he said. We slept again entwined breathing in each other scent, sometimes spooning, that one love making is enough, there is no urgency, we connected, we're satisfied, for the first time in a long time I sleep the sleep of the dead, not once did I wake up to use the loo sick, prostate or not erection was strong and lasted but perhaps love is what's going to cure me or at least extend my lifespan contrary to what the doctors have said I sleep and I sleep well.

Dear whoever,
These are exciting times, I loved every moment in Alexandria having accepted a chapter had closed and another opened or as they say a door closed and a window opened, my window is called Al. We ate, we talked, we walked, we saw more of the city, he did not suggest visiting his people nor did he make any move to visit them alone. Al spent every moment with me, in those days I healed from my deep sore of Imam Nuhu, the stitches and balm is Al, it was a cocoon moment, I didn't think beyond the now.

On our last night I told Al about my health, never in my days did I expect his reaction, I spent most of the night comforting him, as he cried and rambled on about not being left, clinging to me, expressing his love that has been nurtured over the years, his gesture of love interpreted as kindness by me. Then came the panic talk, finding a world expert specialist. I explained the cancer was too advanced and that I had been given three months to live, another fresh set of tears and clinging on to me like his life depended on it.

I think if I had held anything back that was the moment I fell hopelessly in love with Al. Before I knew what I was saying I asked Al to marry me, Al said yes and finally his tears became happy ones. Packed and ready for the airport we had an hour to kill before the car for the airport arrived, Al was happy to remain in the room, I suggested a wander to the Cartier shop downstairs, there I bought him the signature gold ring and bangle, to the assistant Al was helping me with the ring size, back in our suite I put the ring on his finger and kissed it then kissed him, in the shop he wanted to buy me a gift, my raised eyebrow and mouthed three months made him pull a face.

Returning to England is uneventful, Al invited me to stay with him, I declined and asked instead how he feels about living across the two homes. Al is happy with this. He drops me home and says he'll be back.

Paul has called me umpteenth times, his voice a trigger for irritation then anger, I ask myself, having found Al do I need any contact with Paul, his clear dislike of me, the funmaking, name calling. I call him and tell him I will catch up with him at work. I didn't wait for his response and end the call, I did catch him saying he missed me.

Dear Rose and Ethel plus whoever

This is me Fahad, recognising how luck has finally visited me, if I had not read your letters, I would have been buried and a 40 day prayer said for me in the near future, the intensity of your love, the loyalty, hope and conviction you will one day be together is admirable. I cared for Paul for a long time, thinking he is the man for me, yet Al was always here near me. I am thankful he found the courage to tell me how he felt about me. I finally have someone to leave what I don't give to my sister.

I've gone online and found that because of the time I have left we can obtain a special license to marry giving 72 hrs notice. I will share this with Al when he returns, it will be an intimate ceremony unless Al has people he wants to invite. Tomorrow I will inform the Trust of my need to reduce my hours, it must be death in service rather than retirement, in this manner I will receive a larger sum than retirement route. I'm going to do all I can to make sure Al is taken care of. I will see the solicitor again this week to make yet more changes to my will.

Not sure what I want to do with Paul, I will have some clarity when I see him. I might use him for rough sex and make love to my Al, that sounds really nice, my Al. I am feeling tired and somewhat drained but happy and light in my mind and body for the first time in a decade. I have shared my journey in earlier writing of the trip to see Imam Nuhu, should I have gone or stayed away happy with the memories of yesteryears.

I went, I saw and I managed to connect even if the window was short. There were no sexual feelings, just a desire to get close to him, the comfort his arms gave me in my youth, the wisdom his words brought, the guidance and escape from a world of farming that never seemed enough to feed the family, much less the wider villages.

I send emails to the chief executive and the clinical director requesting a meeting Monday mid- morning if they have the space I let them know it's a personal issue and that I would like to speak to both of them first, I type the letter that will need to go to HR informing of the diagnosis making it clear I want to work until I can no longer do so. It is my hope that now with Al in my life I'm going to be in a better place. I'm going to experience what has been missing for so long in my life I hope Al brings the love he's promised, I hope that love is enough for the two of us I'm looking forward to what it's going to be like to have him around regularly, until Al when I look at the two man in my life he's nothing like either of them, nothing like Imam Nuhu and certainly nothing like the professor.

In Al I have found a man that practically worships me, worships the ground I walk on, cares about me and has done so for so many years, for that I'm grateful, again I'm grateful that I'm not going to die a lonely isolated man whose last days of life is spent having angry sex with a nuisance called Paul.

Paul is back in my thoughts, I'm not quite sure is it worth me going ahead with my plan of using him, throwing money at him, I'm not sure at this point, clarity will come when I meet him for lunch tomorrow, I'll see how that goes when I get back to work, for now I'm going to go upstairs to make wardrobe space, dressing table space. I'm going to get ready for what it was like for you Ethel when you moved in with Rose, this is my chapter starting.

Thank you once again for your letters because without those letters I know I definitely would have committed suicide. I'm where I am today enjoying what I'm enjoying because of you and for that I will be grateful. I feel incredibly tired, I tell the medic in me to calm down, yet I know finally the symptoms of advanced prostate cancer is making itself felt, known.

I hear the door, it's Al using the key I gave him, it's a good feeling I hurry downstairs despite the body pain and wait for him in the hallway he puts his backpack down, we just stand there hugging 'welcome home' I said to him over and over and each time he's response is 'it's good to be home' this is where I belong, with you, beside you, in your arms, in your bed he says cheekily, looking after you. We embrace warmly for a long time, everything just feels right, like Al belongs in that house. I don't sense the ghost of Miriam angry or disturbed it's my house. It's been my home for a long time and now it's going to be Al and Fahad's.

I show him the kitchen, Al tells me to go and sit down and watch something on TV we're both tired we've only got today to recover then back to work, he fixes food in a jiffy a healthy mixture of vegetables, lamb chops with the fat trimmed off and a sauce that I can't quite figure out but taste like sweet red pepper sauce, it's a lovely light meal as I eat I'm still puzzled about where this appetite has come from, going from eating like a pigeon because of constipation to a full-on appetite. We parked ourselves on the settee and agreed on watching the movie Shaft two. It doesn't take too much concentration and it's a light-hearted movie with lots of family traits and bravado.

I wait for the right moment and tell Al about my registry inquiry, he turns around and hugs me, it's a yes, yes to everything. I ask him about his friends, his network, who he might want at the private ceremony Al says he wants to shout from the rooftops of our love, he wants to shout about the wedding and let everyone know that we're a couple. I caution him a little bit about this.

The ceremony must be about us, our coming together, our vows, the importance of it in the face of the time we have left together, he agrees. We settled on some of the people we jointly know and a couple of people that he knows the figure of 22 guests sounds good. It won't be a problem finding a restaurant to host 24 people for a nice five to seven course meal to celebrate the day, I don't want a fuss just the commitment ceremony of marriage and a certificate to show that we're a couple, Al is in agreement, he is such an easy going person, like me lonely for a long time is all he shared.

I tell Al I plan to meet with the chief exec and the clinical director to let them know. I'm not too sure what next because I don't feel ill, I'll be requesting to work part-time if that's okay with them I'll do three days a week, when the time comes when I can't manage the three days a week I'll probably step down to two days, for now I feel good, I'm alert, my cognition is intact the intellect is intact, my expertise as a surgeon is not in question but it's time to let work know I have prostate cancer because each hour brings me closer to the grave and in fairness I need to let my employer know I'll ill, not going to tell them I am dying.

Al listens to all this without interrupting me when he speaks he simply says 'I will be walking by your side Fahad, I will be here when you need me. The rest of the evening is pretty quiet, we retire early when I walk past the wardrobe and I see Al's things hanging up it feels good, there's no longer one toothbrush in the bathroom there's two, two sets of carpets slippers, I can see creams, oils, the various he uses and finally this house that I've lived in forever and a day is a home overflowing with womanly stuff belonging to my Al, yes my Ali.

Monday dawned bright and early, bad days are always like this, in the sense of bad news day. Al and I get ready and arrive together. He heads off to his department and me to mine. Lunch he mouths, no I mouth back, always have lunch with Paul from pharmacy, Al pokes a tongue my way and disappears, I smile my way into work, dump the trays of Egyptian delicacies in the staff room, my schedule is light one surgery am one pm a practice the hospital have incase people are delayed on holiday. I have a teaching session to deliver at four. The morning passes uneventfully, email check I send back emoji to each of Paul's emails.

Dearest Ethel, Rose and whoever
Telling my colleagues I have prostate cancer was difficult, I never realised I was so liked at work, at least I hope that is what it means when two grown up men burst into tears, or it might be fear for themselves, identification they could be in my shoes. I reassure them I am dealing well with it, omitting what I want. I am given the go ahead to reduce my hours, particularly surgery time, by picking up more of the lectures. I didn't need to have another meeting with HR, a call during that meeting with instructions to HR lead Amal ended with her saying she will send confirmation of the discussion and agreed plan. I was asked if I might need any other adjustment. I assured her I didn't.

Once Amal logged off the teams call I informed my colleagues of my relationship with Al and the imminent marriage, for people who just assumed the widower did not want to remarry I witnessed the various expression and then pure joy for me that I have found my partner, Al-Fahad was used to tease me in that room, I embraced the two colleagues who cared enough about my wellbeing to just be happy for me, same sex partner or not. We did a few more moments of small talk then went our separate ways with their promise to attend the wedding. I headed towards Pharmacy to collect Paul for lunch.

We head to the dining room and Paul is over attentive I take my time, explaining my disappearance for the past couple of days, sharing the minimum, there's a relative that I went to see in Egypt he asked if I went alone, I ignored him, he then says I wish you told me I could have come with you, ignoring him I pay attention to the food, I have practically no appetite and I know it's because of the company I'm in. I spend some time studying Paul who smiles back stupidly and tells me how much he missed me particularly the sex, this fires my anger up. I have thought I would have a bit more clarity on what I wanted to do with Paul on contact, all this guy makes me feel is anger. There has to be loyalty, something Paul doesn't understand nonetheless. Do I keep banging Paul to teach him a lesson or do I draw a line on the things. I would never make love to Al in the manner that I handle Paul. Paul for me is a piece of meat.

Al is the man I love or have come to love, recently fallen hopelessly in love with, parallel they don't cross at all, the question I asked myself as I sat opposite Paul is do I really need to shag this guy and if I do what does it give me ? is it that I'm partial to rough sex or is it still the fact that I'm angry being taken advantage of, made fun of, spoken about like a piece of shit but to my face he's attentive, talking to me he professes whatever it is he think he likes about me I haven't really paid much attention and I'm not digesting much of what he says but I sit here when I feel myself hardening, so here is the deal I've given this guy 10,000 pounds in a very short period I'm gonna fuck him.

I Paul shut Paul up mid-sentense, 'let's go' you would have thought he was going for an appointment the brisk walk to the disabled loo at the end of the corridor, this time I walked beside him there's something about knowing you're gonna die soon that makes you not give a fuck about what others might think, we both going to the loo there's nobody around anyway so who cares and if CCTV picks us up happy viewing.

Once in the loo Paul knees and takes me in his mouth, I look at the top of the back of his head bobbing up and down, I feel nothing for this guy after about five minutes he looks at me and asks 'what's wrong'? My erection has disappeared and it's not coming back no matter the ministration from Paul. Telling him to leave I say I'm tired. That's why, let's catch up again soon. He asks if I want him to pleasure me. I say no thank you, practically open the door for him and push him out despite now having an erection.

I can feel it, that deep sense I need to pee so I stood there waiting for the urine to come when it didn't my panic began to rise. The truth is I've ignored a lot of things leading up to last week, on hearing Imam Nuhu is alive. I've ignored the pain in my back, hips, pelvic, ignored the fatigue, the weight loss, constipation, convincing myself it is not as bad as it used to be, the urinary trouble has been a very slight pain and burning when I'm urinating.

I know this is part and parcel of the diagnosis when I'm finally able to pass urine I see the blood my legs nearly give way from the reality, sheer horror, if anything is bringing it home to me that time is limited it is the sight of blood, the redness of it against the whiteness of the toilet bowl.

I stead myself against the wall, I flush and flush till the blood is gone. This is not good, this is not good at all. I'm seeing the urologist on Thursday but I've been told to call the department and speak to the modern Matron if anything changes drastically.

For me this is not good at all is what replays as I go through the rest of the day around 3:30 p.m. just before I went into the lecture I feel the urge to pee again I must have spent a good 20 minutes in that toilet this time no pee came I've increased my water intake to help myself because that's one thing you cannot slow down on, the amount of fluid in your system.

The rest of the afternoon goes well, Al finds me at the nursing station when it's time to head home we both take that moment as opportunity to let the nurses know we are a couple, you would have thought we're told them we'd won the pool with their whooping and congratulations and hugs, compliments you make such a good couple, it felt good but my mind is far far away, the image of blood against the whiteness of the toilet bowl. As we make our way to the car Al asks me what's wrong I assure him I'll tell him when we get home.

From the corner of my eye I see Paul observing Al I walk away and from where I was it looked like he was trying to make up his mind whether he should approach me/us or not, he doesn't. Once home I tell Al what happened and straight away he envelops me in a hug, that hug is what I've been thirsting for throughout my journey of the last 20 or so years that hug that tells me ' it's okay, I got you' The evening was a subdued one, we hugged, touched, talked, we remain connected, basically just looked at and reached for each other's often as we felt the need there is no sexual urge, just us, considering it's the second time or second day in my house our house it felt like we're being in a relationship forever, that's how comfortable I quickly became in Al's company.

There's something very vulnerable about Al that makes me cautious about how emotional I am around him, Al hasn't told me his story and I haven't probed but I know that growing up in Egypt would not have been easy for him, I wonder how he hid his femininity. I hope in the next few days or weeks he feels able to share what his life was like. I'm curious to know. Later that evening I managed to pee. This time it's not red hot blood but streaks of blood in the bowl. Al insist on having a look and I'm comfortable with that, he needs to see, needs to know, he comforts me and when he talks I realized he must have spent most of the day researching symptoms of care and support for those suffering with prostate cancer because he's saying all the right things, Everything he says reminds me of what I've read and what I know and what I'm experiencing. I squeeze his hand, thank him for making me feel safe to share.

Dinner that night was quite a feast of succulent chicken, couscous with dry fruits, it wasn't too heavy a meal, there was plenty to be had, my appetite dipped by irritation of Paul, then further by the shock of blood has not recovered and I struggle to eat much. Al is concerned. I reassure him all is well in the context of what I'm experiencing. This is what is expected, nothing I've experienced today is out of the ordinary. It's not indicating an emergency, some people suffer this for years. I've only had it today, besides an appointment with Urology in a few days I'm fine to hang in there.

I don't feel the need to go to A&E as Al is suggesting, panicking, I do my best to reassure him. Once in bed we snuggling into each other and loo and behold I have an erection, straight away I understand my time with Paul is over I have absolutely no reason to justify even talking to him or having lunch with him professionally we have very little contact anyway my disgust of Paul manifested itself in my inability to maintain an erection this afternoon.

Lovemaking with Al that night was another gentle sail, another totally consuming process. How can it be possible to love somebody so quickly, so deeply, so totally. We lay there just cuddled up stroking each other, Al puts his head on my chest, bone pains forgotten for passion. I smile to myself. It is true when you're loved up you forget the other things going on around you. We sleep well, me not so deeply but I still managed to get plenty of sleep, my thoughts racing ahead of myself, expecting urinary problems to really kick in, my main concern shows itself in that I wake regularly checking-in with my body, do I need to go pee, yet the urge was not there. I know it's either difficult trying to pee or peeing too often and so if I'm ticking the boxes of symptoms at least I don't have to tick that yet.

Thus passes the next few days, quiet at work, the new schedule kicks in straight away. I've decided to work Monday Tuesday Wednesday and be off for four days so three days on four days off. Al is planning to take annual leave one day a week so effectively the only day I'm going to be on my own will be Thursdays he has plenty of annual leave left. I'm grateful for the commitment. I'm sure one day on my own I can find something to do with myself and for the first time in a long time I think about my faith.

I think about how opposite my faith is to my sexuality but I also feel at peace because the only person that I'm answerable to is my maker/creator not society, not my family, not my culture, not the homeland and certainly not the double standard people who were there.

In England it has been a mixed experience. I have experienced prejudice. I've experienced being passed over for promotion. I have experienced being sidelined. I have experienced being used. I have experienced being treated like a second class citizen and yet I've ignored all these experiences, focused on my career. The one thing that's hard is, it's practically impossible for you to be racist to the consultant who's going to be performing your operation and because of that people who are clearly racist have checked in their racism at the door, picking it up on their way out of the ward.

I have experienced the judgmental side of people, I've experienced the negative side of people and for all the years I've lived here I know I'm still a foreigner who stands on the periphery and looks in on people who tolerate me and never accept me. I cannot tell you in all the years I worked in the same hospital when a colleague invited me home, the relationship has been strictly work-based. I know my place and for that I've been allowed to be a part of the crew. This is just a reflection of mine, the reader doesn't need to agree, it's my experience and that makes it very valid.

Al is my woman, a cook, homemaker, real wife material. You name it, by the time I wake up he's made breakfast he's even ironed my shirt. I haven't experienced this level of contentment, even when Miriam was alive, she tried but I stopped her, most of my stuff just gets dumped at the dry cleaners. I remember a time when I couldn't find a clean shirt. I have backup shirts that I just opened, for me no one is looking at me, there's nobody for me to impress other than Paul, despite him not really appearing to notice me for anything other than professional friendship. I never held back on spending money on myself so yeah for a surgeon I dress impeccably, I like to look good and I know I look good when I'm dressed. Al is dressing me, he's got out my shirt, suit, decided the shoes I'm gonna wear, he's picked out the tie. I just love this guy more. I'm grateful, I can't stop saying that I get to spend this time with Al despite the cold footsteps of death closer with each hour each day each week.

I reflect on why all the symptoms have caught up with me at once. Is it a matter of me ignoring them and filing them away or is it because my life has shifted totally from fearing living to this wonderfulness that I'm now leaving behind, Thursday will bring better clarity. Al has made it clear he will be joining me for the appointment I don't have the energy to argue with him I also want to spend as much time with him now that the Trust knows he's my partner, at least the department knows, they've agreed in the meeting Al's carer's leave should he need it to support me through any future appointments.

The next couple of days pass uneventfully. Thursday Al actually turns up with a notebook and pen making notes during the consultation, he contributes nothing, he just makes notes. I explained to the Urologist that on Monday I'd gone to the toilet, difficult peeing then what seemed like a river of blood in the urine, questions followed, how much ? How red ? How brown ?

How was it? a stream of blood or a slow urinating of blood ? Was it coming up periodically or did it just flow with the urine ?

I did my best to answer. I don't think this young guy understood what it's like to stand there, expecting urine to come out but it's more blood than pee.The average person will think they're dying inside out there and then. I do my best not to be irritable. I answer the questions, he makes notes and some recommendations. He's going to tweak some of my medication and has decided he wants to see me in a fortnight before then if when I go it's all blood. We thank him and leave both our moods heavy, even our body feels heavy and I know we can't go home yet so I suggest a walk around Westminster and perhaps we can grab something to eat before we go home, Al readily agrees.

Walking slowly makes others around us look really busy. People buzzed around, most in a rush, a few strolling and enjoying the moment like us. We look at each other occasionally and exchange smiles. Someone once told me that couples are able to communicate without saying a word. I was too young to appreciate what was said when Imam Nuhu had said it I looked at him puzzled I couldn't understand how people would communicate without opening their mouth and speaking but here I am with Al every look he gives me, every smile says I love you, my return smile says I love you right back.

We ate an early dinner at the Savoy, we needed to do something to lighten up our mood a bit. The atmosphere is good, the food excellent, the company and ambience amazing, sitting near the grand piano we could see the Thames and the usual river boat traffic. The pianist plays very soft classical music, everything felt good except for pain and blood.

It is a sober Al & Fahad that returned home. What is it about Al losing it the moment he has privacy, we walked in and he started to cry, quietly I held his hand and comforted him even when he expressed selfishness at crying. I reassured him it's okay to cry and that I wish I could because I'm sure that release would be helpful for me too. Cry he said to me and then we both started laughing as if it is possible to just switch crying on and off. To my own surprise even though it's been a long day and now it's late I will put some YouTube music on and ask Al to dance to the song he chose.

My eyes adore you is his son of choice, played. I don't know who cried more, in each other's arms we sway gently to the song. 'My Eyes adored you' he said, my eyes adored you for a long time and now your eyes adore me back. The kiss is a long extension of our mood. If ever I felt a need to live longer this moment is it but what's the point of regrets there's no point. I savour the moment, in my arms is a man that loves me. I appreciate that I could easily have lived the last few weeks, months of my life without companionship. What I have now has gone beyond companionship.

The craziness of Paul, the craziness of the Arab and the Korean Guy pushed down, what I have now is solid, it's what I've always wanted, with this I tighten my arms around Al, he understands and tightens his around me. How was I to know that last night's love making would be the last time. I am unable to get an erection again. We simply accepted it and continued to be as physical as it is possible without penetrative sex, a lot continued to be enjoyed, that sense, that feeling of totalness remained if something was to convince me about how right this relationship is. Not based on the physical but the coming together of two hearts, two strangers who wandered lonely and alone for a long time, now found themselves. I enjoy the glorious time in Al's company, a homecoming so to say.

Within a fortnight I am officially off sick. Paul has stopped trying to make contact with me. Al has taken over looking after me. I'm grateful I had time in that short window to see my solicitor make changes to my will, to ensure people I care about are the ones who benefit from my assets when I'm gone.

I now live within a broken body, my weight loss noticeable. I feel weak, I feel tired of taking medication so that I don't become impacted because the constipation has worsened and I'm either trying to wee, manage to wee never feeling that I've finished. It's a terrible feeling, I stand there with the urge, nothing comes, no sooner do you sit down that the urge is there again.

Al has no shame he's bought me a bottle, he puts my dick in the bottle and he says just wee if you need to leave it there even if it doesn't come, it's going to be your new best friend. This brings a smile to my face, a gesture of how much he cares about me and wants my dignity to remain intact. It is clear Al's desire for me has not dimmed.

I'm on pain patches now and also more liquid Morphine to use if pain overwhelms me, the word palliative care has come up. Three months they said, six weeks to three months why is everything closing in at four weeks. I wonder if the trip to Egypt accelerated this but I doubt it because without that trip to Egypt I wouldn't have experienced the happiness that I have in the past month. The passing of blood is now normal in fact if I pee and there is no blood it's unusual. I am monitored closely by the experts. Nothing new has been picked up. The other comfort is my daily call with my sister.

Dear Ethel and Rose

Today I introduced Al to your tin of letters. Divided into three bundles. Ethel the letters you were reading to Rose, then the letters that you wrote but didn't send. Rose, the third bundle is the letters that I have written to both you and Ethel, later adding to Whoever. My hope is that when I'm gone your letters and mine won't be forgotten in some dusty corner or thrown away.

Al has been telling me a little bit about himself. It's been hard to hear what he's been through. Al has started writing his own letters, it's interesting that he addresses the writing which he shared with me to Ethel and you Rose. It gladdens and lightens my heart. I continue to read your letters, some for the umpteenth time in that it speaks to me of one of the greatest loves I have come across. When I'm gone I hope it gives Al strength and courage as he rebuilds his life.

The wedding never took place instead we said personally written poems at a dinner with close friends at the Savoy we had notified them ahead of the delicacy of my health and delighted to say they pulled all the stops out for us I know it's money that's buying that level of dedication to our party but it was money well spent we had a wonderful time. We asked our guests if they were able to, to give a donation to a prostate care charity. I know that every single one of them gave something and that comforts me. Do I sound like a dying man, well I am, that's why I'm writing this final letter.

To note this is the only letter that will be written and sealed, it's really important for me that Al doesn't read this letter until I'm gone, because in my final days I came to realize a horrible truth. That while I was imagining myself in love I didn't realize I'd been set up. Al doesn't love me, never did, he is a conniving horrid human being who is simply on an assignment.. All along I am the one played.

I found out Al and Paul are partners and have been for many years. You will wonder about my proof of this. First sexual encounter with Paul I knew there was a possibility that Paul though married only had the work hours window, based on how quickly he would give his excuse when we did meet for a bite after work, to say he needs to get home to the wife. It crossed my mind he might be screwing someone at work, his reaction to anal sex too accommodating for want of a better phase. At no time did I tell Al about Paul, no secrets just irrelevant.

I check my memory over and over, I've never even seen Paul and Al talk and so the possibility that they knew each other much less had a relationship and are lovers would never ever occur to me. Let me tell you how I knew something was amiss. Al persuaded me to allow those who really care about me to come visit, apparently they are asking to. Too fatigued to keep saying no thus began a two-week period where every other day somebody popped in to say sorry to hear you're poorly. I still haven't told anybody I was dying.

Paul was the last visitor I expected, I also wasn't told he was coming. I didn't even know, as I said that Paul and Al knew each other. The giveaway and I would not have noticed if it wasn't that I raised my head quickly while we were drinking tea. Al offered to get some more biscuits, I put my head down to take a sip, changed my mind, lifted my head up and caught the look, the exchange that broke my heart and sent my world crashing.

That look told me everything I needed to know that Paul and Al are not strangers, they know each other, that Paul and Al have been exchanging information about me, that Paul and Al all along were in on this together. What is the modern word, sex scam, find a foolish old man, preferably one on his last leg and take him for everything. My complete and utter foolishness in thinking that I had found the love of my life !

Keeping my mask on I pretend detachment, let me help you clear up by Paul had him and Al hugging furiously in the kitchen, a low murmur of not too long now because I was listening hard to catch anything said. Lying back with my eyes closed to the observer when they came back in the room to snatch further touches and even brief kisses all the time believing I was asleep, the final nail in the coffin is the slap on the ass from Al to Paul at the door and the quietly spoken, 'can't wait to be with you'

As I said this is a sealed letter because yet again I made contact with my solicitor this time for a home visit as I was too tired and weak to make my way into town naturally I asked the solicitor to come on a Thursday the only day I was on my own for the final time I changed my will everything absolutely everything I owe to my sister and her children to do as they see fit. Someone said revenge is a dish served cold, mine is so cold it's frozen for best effect.

I will be a liar if I say this didn't affect me, it absolutely broke me and probably accelerated my demise. I accepted Al's embraces, sweet words however fake and massages. I accepted his kisses and his gentle hugs. I accepted the way he ministered unto me and took care of all my needs, earlier I had transferred twenty thousand pounds into his account to keep us going. I learned to create a mask of love when all I now feel is betrayal, anger, disdain and possibly hate. Hate is such a difficult word even in such difficult circumstances.

I think of all the things against me all my life, culture is against me, family mustn't know, hide it at work, hide from friends who will turn against you, felt like the whole world is against me then I manage to find someone who I believe gets me, cares for me, is on the same page and they turn out to be a scammer. These young gay men or bi-sexual men getting together to pick on older gay men to scam them out of their wealth, get money out of them for sex favours, I had nearly become a statistic.

The second fact that confirmed that Paul and Al had a relationship, and had done so for a long time was when I was in the shower and Paul used the WhatsApp app to call Al. I was lying in bed and looked over to see Paul's picture, it wasn't so much the picture it was what was written across that picture. The word mine in capital letters, can you imagine yet these two despicable creatures allowed me to sleep with them, allowed me to believe as far as they were concerned that I cared for them and I did. I fell so hard each time.

Paul I could deal with but Al's betrayal is hard, even if I had lived for more than three months he doesn't deserve a penny of my wealth. All processes were in place to ensure he's not getting any of my wealth, the solicitor had been very clear Al cannot challenge anything when I am gone, going as far as taking the poem I read to Al at our dinner, taking dates of when we got together etc. The solicitor also suggested a need to move into a private Hospice, ensuring the day I leave for the hospice is the day Al leaves my house. No if or butts they come to pick me up for the hospice care, Al must leave, my solicitor has instructions for that day and has a locksmith on standby the moment I confirm both Al and I have left the house, naturally I would encourage Al to move his things back to his place prior to my move date, the lock is to be changed once I leave.

I look back at my life and I've never felt such incredible sadness, a feeling of being cheated, why me ? What have I ever done to those two to make them home in on me, is there a sign across my forehead that says how desperate I am to be loved, that says how desperately lonely I have been, that made me a target. I wonder when their relationship started, I wondered who tutored who to allow me or came after me, seduced me. I wonder who's the lead in their relationship, my guess is Al for Paul to have allowed me to be intimate with him Al must have given consent.

What wouldn't people do for money, how I wish my happiness ever after did not blow up in dust. I wish I'd died in ignorance because at least I would have died happy. I do believe it's the depth of my distress that is accelerating my passing. Oh well, if I can't fight them I will find somebody who can and the pen has always proven to be mightier than any brain. The ten thousand pounds given to Paul is small change when I look at my entire estate.

The fact is neither of them is going to get their hand on a penny that belongs to me. In my case it'll be victory in death. I've accepted that, reconciled myself to it all, as we say ' it is well' with no legal wedding and having stayed with me for a few weeks Al is not in a position to claim partnership, my written instruction refers to him as a work fuck-buddy.

Dear Paul and Al

I'm writing this specifically to you both, one may be stupid but no one is stupid for life. Big mistake coming to the house Paul. That Thursday I realized you are a couple. I have to say you managed to shock me. I realized how naive I have been thinking that I had found a partner first in you Paul and then in Al. I overheard you talking about me to your wife when we went for the first meal that faithful Sunday, it wasn't until you came to my house I realized you and Al are in a relationship. I put two and two together and realized when you said you were talking to your wife you were speaking to Al.

Well nothing secret stays secret forever the biggest mistake you made Paul was taking me for an old fool coming to my house, riding on the back of colleagues who truly cared about me to come, you see a thief is always a thief and what gave you and Al away was just a look, the moment I saw that look I knew that you had both set me up and that not only had both of you been in a relationship for a long time this was your plan to use me and acquire my wealth.

As you read this I'm sure by now you've realized that you both have ended up my pleasure item. Paul I felt such contempt for you after I heard the way you described me on the phone making fun of me that the only nature of sex I had with you was raw content sex but I don't expect that you would pick that up and you thought that was passion. You deserve an Oscar. Believe me you sure can act. Every single contact I experienced with you was anger and disgust filled. Not for one moment were you sincere in your dealing with me, I just wondered why it took you so long.

I guess a death sentence of Prostate cancer emboldened me to call you, thus giving you the go ahead you needed. A simple look gave you away. Let me give you a piece of advice. There's a saying in the homeland of my country of origin that says 'a youngster can never have so much clothes that he would have as much used clothes/rags as an adult' that's exactly what's happened to you both believing in your excellence at pulling the wool over my face. You both could have ended up relatively wealthy, comfortable for your lifetime with the money invested well but for the betrayal.

Even as I'm dying thoughts of you two triggers pure unadulterated anger, disgust at the sort of human beings you are. I hope you take time out to reflect on what you tried to do, how wrong it's gone because in a homophobic world I as a gay man have enough problems without men like you picking on me, on us. I hope mine is a lesson that you've learned. For revenge I briefly thought about contacting your wife but then that would put me on the bottom rug like you two.

All I can hope is that whoever that woman is she finds you out one day Paul and leaves you, goes and leads the life she deserves. This letter to you and Paul will be kept separate outside the tin of letters, it'll be available for you to pick up. I have asked that the tin be returned to the ward and handed over to the Modern matron for its drop off at Patients Affairs office. I know I no longer have so much energy or strength to continue personally writing and I don't want to dictate through a third party so once again and for the final time.

Dear Ethel & Rose
I'm counting on you to light the way, please come and get me. I hope wherever you now reside is a fun place for us where we can just be ourselves where we're not just in Plain Sight unseen,

I really hope we're seen there, we can love and be loved, we can be free and expressive, not judged by our sexual preference.

Thank you once again for pulling me back from the brink of suicide

Love Lives Always, from the depth of my heart
Fahad Abudul-Waziri MD FRCS (Eng)

Like a fly on the wall I watch events unfold the afternoon I am taken to the hospice. Al is all over me like a rash. He seemed puzzled days before when I told him he needs to move back to his place he wants to stay with me. I share with him I'll be going to the hospice in 72 hours. He is surprised that he is not aware of it. I only need to keep up this charade for a bit more, his next shock will come when he is not allowed to visit me, I doubt if I will last forty eight hours. I realise I am not napping but drifting in and out of light unconsciousness. With the confidence of a fool Al clears his things back to his place, he is puzzled when the solicitor turns up with a locksmith as they are loading me into the ambulance, strike one.

I gave my mobile phone to my solicitor and thanked him for his service. Al insisted on riding with me, I pretend sleep most of the journey, I am settled in quickly, I wonder how Al plans to get back to London from Sevenoaks, the private ambulance crew are kind and give him a ride back, with multiple kisses and a promise to be back in the morning, assurance he will be here everyday, Al departs. The moment he leaves the hospice puts the plan I requested in action, within an hour I am on my way to Lower Mead Sevenoaks's most private and exclusive area, in this quiet village is the cottage I have chosen to spend my last hours, equipped with private nursing and medical team of six nurses and two specialist Urology consultants.

I wish I could have had the pleasure of seeing Al being told my stay at The Heights was just for the check-in and that my final destination is not to be disclosed as per my instructions with him to be signposted to my solicitor if necessary.

Dear whoever,

My final thoughts as I am too tired to write, too off my head in an induced euphoria of four hourly doses of Lorazepam. I want to reassure you I am at peace, I have reconciled myself with the poor outcome I had, I want to let you know there are good people out there, loving and capable of real engagement in a relationship without ulterior motives, men and women who thirst for the fountain of relationship fulfillment. Don't be afraid to try, Ethel and Rose found each other, I found Imam Nuhu, Paul and Al found each other as others have over the centuries. Be you, I have managed to be me, I accepted the rough years and embraced the brief period of happiness however tainted it became, shine your eyes properly and do your research, hopefully you will find your missing jigsaw piece. This is goodbye from Fahad.

Death is strange, it is true what they say about out of body type experience , I saw Iman Nuhu clear as if he was in the room, he stayed and kept close to me, sometimes he spoke other times he just held me to comfort me. That wonderful smell of Tabu, the feel of his crisp white bellowing material. He spoke gently telling me of things that had passed, things to come and the middle passage whatever that is. The more I responded to him the more sedation they put in the IV, to settle me.

Iman Nuhu was later joined by the Professor, I was unhappy about this but Imam Nuhu pointed out however I feel this man also loved me and loved me deeply. When they were not talking to me they talked quietly together about the one common denominator: their love for me. Finally in my vision the path between my house to Imam Nuhu's residence, this time Imam Nuhu and the Professor walked either side of me, steading me, smiling reassuring at me, telling me to be careful, look where you are going, it was daybreak, and as we walked on the sun rose and rose in the sky.

I swear I saw the silhouette of two women holding hands then waving to me before turning to walk ahead of us, the sun seemed to be dropping out of the sky to meet me as it neared it got brighter and brighter until I had to close my eye, walking holding the hands either side of me, I felt safe, knew I didn't have to look where I am going because guiding me are two men who gave me priceless love. The last comment heard by my ears before totally shut down 'what a lovely peaceful way to go, that serene smile on his face, a beautiful goodnight'

Dearest Ethel, Rose & Dr Fahad

I am whoever. 'Mo-tunde' but everyone calls me Tune. I am daughter to Bayo and Titi, little sister to Tola, Lola, Fola, Bola and Kolarin. Mum and Dad were able to come to England as my grandmother had mum here on one of her buying trips, she was a fabric dealer who came to Liverpool Street wholesalers at least four times a year. On hearing of Margaret Thatcher's intention to quietly change access my parents hurriedly packed up their teaching jobs and landed in London.

Access to social housing was dead easy if you took what you were given hence North Peckham became home. Neither generally talk about the transition so I don't know how easy it was but they left what I think is better security in terms of jobs, their quality of life, particularly in terms of how well they were doing as a young married couple to ensure in the future their children could have British status and access to reliable education. It wasn't easy for them in terms of integration into the community here.

Both my parents have strong Nigerian accents, even now, so a job teaching in England was out of the question their English was fine but not for a classroom in England so Dad ended up finding work with London Underground as it was for people who came over in that period, Mom got a job in a local supermarket, they worked hard, worked long hours. Dad due to his education, hardworking nature, dedication, calmness eventually became deputy Station Master, with this they decided it was time to start having a family and the children's started rolling out every other year total of six children, the interesting thing is so many children and somehow they managed to pack all into a two bedroom flat on the fourth floor of a high rise council high block, well they did, we lived there happily relatively cocooned in our world. We didn't lack anything, the atmosphere was generally okay, we had laughs, we enjoyed school.

We are content; the only niggling aspect of our household is how religious our parents are. We have to toe that line. Everything had to be linked to Christ if you had a good day it was thanking Jesus. If you had a bad day it was Jesus we come to you to conquer Satan and how he tried to ruin today and so on and so forth. Either way I just followed the footsteps of my parents. If they wanted us to go to church, we went to church, it didn't mean because I was sitting there I was listening but I went through the motions.

I will describe myself as neither a believer nor a non-believer, I will say I am a watchful wait, as the youngest child I would say I probably would have got away with murder because I was the family joker, the one who would ensure everybody was happy, bubbly, I would do all the funny dances, mimic all sorts of different accents that I heard at school in the playground and generally relied on as the family jester.

In our house the older child looked after the junior. By the time the eldest was ten she was being left to look after five younger siblings with each one delegated a task, role or duty by Mum. We would be in that house and nobody would know, that is how good we were the deterrent to be anything otherwise a statement by mum ' if you make noise police with social services come to get you I won't look for you, they can have you, if you can't behave yourself and keep quiet while we are at work.'

The one thing that was plentiful in our house was food and that was by virtue of mom working in a supermarket, the staff had access or at least first choice, first pick of all the food that will be expiring, with an additional 10% off member of staff status. We ate like kings and queens you name it, beef, turkey, fish, chicken, sausages, burgers, deserts we normally would not have access to. I know our diet would have been different if Mum worked elsewhere where she had to pay full price for the food she brought home. One of the negatives is that she'd come home from work ladened with all sorts, chicken, fish that we had to prepare that night because today is the expiry day and so the one smell you could count on when you walk in the front door is always the smell of food.

As a couple my parents cared about each other, you could see it in the way they checked in with each other or sit quietly together, perhaps reading the Bible together, even fall asleep on the settee holding hands in the middle of watching a movie, we knew there was love, we observed kindness, they were good role models, occasionally my father would raise his voice but that was after mum had lost hers telling us do this, do that as we turned into teenagers and didn't listen so good. We never mixed with the local kids, it was unheard of for us to be hanging out playing in the local park, instead we would go to interesting places such as London Zoo, Chessington and seaside day trips.

One thing that did not exist in our house was violence,not in talk not in deed, neither of our parents ever hit us and so we grew up really open to new ideas happy eager excited to take our place in the world, quite naive because we were as I said quite cocooned, if we were not at school we were at home, we were at church, the people we mixed with were the people my parents mixed with so we naturally mixed with their children. We were not exposed to the outside world. The programs that we watched on TV had to be family viewing, no swearing, rapping, no outrageous dressing, just so you know the moment a gay artist/performer came on that was cue to change the channel.

I would say I practically danced and enjoyed my way through primary school it was such fun as the youngest child, my older siblings looked out for me, again the type of protective care where someone is always asking me, are you okay, do you want anything, do you need anything, why'd you look like that, why are you crying, what do you want, come here come and have a hug, let me help you do your hair, are you struggling with that let me give you a hand ,so I have nothing to complain about in terms of my upbringing apart from the feeling that we practically lived at the church. As I was pretty much left to my own devices I watched people a lot, this is probably the reason I ended up working as a nurse because of my observational skills.

I'm the only person I know who would catch people exchanging that one look, who would catch that quick discreet gentle touch of the hand of two people that do not appear connected but clearly have something going on. I'm the one who would notice something that others are so busy, so wrapped up in themselves they wouldn't. If you are having an affair a relationship, pretending to be something you're not I would be the first to know because I was constantly observing people watching the dynamics, watching how people came together, the body language, listening to what they say, try to figure out if it aligned with what their body language is saying. I grew up very much a lookie-lookie of what's going on around me.

Secondary school was no different, I began to realize the nonsense girls might each talk about when it came to boys, rock stars, pop stars was of absolutely no interest to me. I realized that I like girls for themselves, I like being in their company, when it was a mixed company of us girls and boys I still gyrated towards the girls. I was interested in what they had to say. I was interested in how they looked. I was interested in how they carried themselves. I was interested in everything female.

I look back and won't say I was one of the it or top girls but I fitted in there I certainly wasn't the bottom rug and so when it came to socializing I was included you know we're going here, we're hanging there, can you ask your parents if you can come more often than not I wasn't able to but when I did catch up with people at school they would fill me in with all the gossip and because I was sitting with the girls sometimes our body touching just slightly, might be the shoulder, the leg, knee, anything I was happy to listen for hours not so much about the dribble they were talking about because I was next to a girl. I liked it, that was enough for me and no I am not a creep.

As for the actual sexual awakening I don't know when that happened but after you start attending school dance, local dances, even the supervised dances the boys believe they can touch your chest via that sneaky little hug, I realized it did nothing for me and so if I could dance with a girl I thought that was great because as we danced we held hands. You know how it is, we'd practice and form new dance moves and that meant holding, touching, pushing or at least coming into contact with each other's body. That was nice for me it didn't scare me at all, what scared me from a very young age is Sodom and Ghomorra, hail and brimstones of hell preached in church every Sunday.

If the girls realize that I like them, would they turn against me ? would they become nasty ? would they still be my friends ?

what would happen if they knew I liked them. This question started from that really young age. It's what it is and by the time I was in my late teens it was not a matter of whether I like girls I knew that I wanted to be with a girl. I had zero interest in the opposite sex you name a girl in my year and I could describe her to the detail that she herself was not aware of. I just looked and observed and quietly longed for a girl partner. Did I find one hell no I know what would have happened if it got out to my parents that I like girls and so I behaved myself I learned how to conduct myself.

I learned how to use my eyes to drink what I wanted but to keep my hands to myself and my mouth shut when it came to discussions about who do you like and what do you like. By the time I was fifteen there were a few girls in my year who had come out as lesbians but that was such a different time, it seemed, it was the fad of the moment to access so much. Inform the school you are lesbian the school is all over you like a rash, to get additional support needed or not, with support girls who wanted to move out of the family home at the age of fifteen and go into the social care system because there was tension at home since the gay reveal.

It was a really confusing time for me because I had no one. I was too scared to say I am a lesbian yet there girls who were coming forward and saying they were lesbians, some were being removed from the family home and put in hostels, given money not just pocket money but loads of things by social services but then they seem really damaged in the sense that the ultimate rejection from their family it didn't matter what social services threw at them the damage that needed to be repaired wasn't. Someone said they were all abused but none of them ever mentioned it so I can't make any comments on that.

I saw them change, I saw them go from happy go lucky young female to looking weird, dressing weird, the language changed, swearing like troopers, then the self-harm behavior, you could see where they scratch their wrists and I think a couple started using illicit drugs and so again when I think about the preaching in the church the Sodom and Gomorrah and remember the way my parents behave when we're out and about and come across a man who is quite feminine or there's anything about him that just screams I'm gay, oh the way my parents react !

I did not dare not even in my wildest nightmares to give any impression that I was nothing other than the daughter they expect me to be, which is to go to university get my degrees, get my qualifications and then bring a nice boy home, get married, my own home, children as in start hatching like a chicken in this manner the cycle begins and continues.

I hate myself in terms of my appearance, I am five foot nine inches, striking but for the wrong reasons, the amount of times I have been approached by talent scouts to model, nothing could horrify me more, make-up and girly nonsense, I never gave the cards to my parents binned them as soon as I turned the corner, now if they wanted me to model men's or urban outfit I would be so up for that. Nobody at home looked at me to express any concerns, I remained the good girl, youngest and the sunflower of the house.

I lit up any room I walked into. In church I am in the choir. I helped whenever it was needed. People see what they want and people make up and accept versions that are comfortable for them so as the model daughter the model sister the model pupil the model church attender the the model child of God the model a-z.

I went through all the motions and did everything that was expected of me. I was well-behaved in our community, people complimented my parents about us, we certainly were not one of the fifteen year olds getting pregnant, being given a council property. We focused on our education our parents couldn't tell us enough how much education is power, education is key, how much you will never be able to claim your right unless you have the educational foundation so with that imprinted in our head, in our heart and at the tip of our fingers we all left home with one focus every day to be the best at whatever was asked of us. Life remained relatively predictable and easy and you just had to do as you were told, do your chores, attend church, be nice to relatives when they turned up, such as give your bed up for the duration of their stay.

My life really began when I left home for University. Even sixth form did not prepare me for leaving home. Universities are a city made up of so many different ethnicities that I wonder how we do it. Imagine standing somewhere and having all sorts of different languages spoken, it will make you realize how bottom of the rug English language is because you have students who have command of six, seven, eight languages and they slipping from one language into the other so fluently so smoothly so easily that the English students who only speak that one language are in awe, even somewhat nervous they're not the top dog believed.

You can see it in the little bit of freshers week I attended. Their initial bravado of being the locals, you know this is our England calmed down very, very quickly faced with people who had come from far away countries, not only could they speak English fluently, I mean the Queen's English to French, Cantonese, Italian, Japanese, Portuguese and to listen to them yes English is the introduction language but the next thing is where you from ? I'm Brazilian and language changes, where are you from ? I'm Italian and language changes.

It was lovely to see that aspect of the university but as I said University is like a city, it has rules, languages, laws, it has guidelines that you have to follow.I had no issues following them the most amazing thing is the fact that I am away from home and for the first time I get to decide. I decide if I went to church or not, I decide what time I went to bed, I decide what time I ate. This opened a whole new world up for me. The only thing I had no control over was the lectures. I had to turn up full stop, to be honest I had no problems with that I only had to think of the North Peckham Estate, education is my bus pass out of there. Apologies for the long introduction. I wanted you to know a bit about me, my background, my home life and the things that shaped me.

I am the Modern matron here. Dr Fahad's your solicitor dropped a tin of letters off as the agency staff were not sure of the origin or purpose it was brought to me as instructed. The entire usual ward staff remember Ethel and Rose, and your passing, they were not around as it was a team building day. We also know Al and you are partners. I have delivered the letter addressed to Al, thinking I might need to be nearby to provide some comfort. I was alarmed to hear a long string of profanity from him and quickly departed. It is three months since we were informed of your passing, none of us attended your burial as it was done according to the rites of your belief, the same day we heard you were put in the ground.

Dr Farhad, your picture is displayed at the nurses station with a remembrance book. I wish you could read what people have written, not only were you respected, you were most loved, your kindness, patience, helpfulness and acceptance of others is a continuous theme in the messages.

The day I gave Al your letter there was an incident with him and Paul right outside Pharmacy, it got heated and physical, lots of accusations back and forth, the police were called and both remain suspended, today I heard that Al has resigned and Paul dismissed, behaviour unbecoming of a chief pharmacist.

I started by reading your letters Dr Fahad, I have also read all of Ethel and Roses letters, the tin has been my constant companion since it came into my possession the week you passed. I have read and reread the letters, finally I have clarity, your letters have craved my path. I would like to share a bit more about myself.

First I am a lot younger than all of you. I just turned twenty eight and have limited life experience, got an education as expected of a child of immigrant parents. The mantra in our house is 'do you want to live here ? is this where you want to spend the rest of your life, face your studies, your qualifications will be the voucher that will get you out of this demonic estate we live on' I can say I never failed an exam due to my level of anxiety about not ending up a broken person trapped on an estate with such toxicity. I made it out of there, never returning after I completed my nurse training, securing a job even before exams results were out. I agreed to share a flat with two other ladies. The arrangement is good, I have no complaints.

Reading your letters has given me confidence to put what is in my head and heart on paper. I knew I seriously liked girls in my late teens. The foolishness of boys drove me crazy. I wanted to be a boy and couldn't relate to the foolish reactions of girls and boys to each other. These were lonely times. Was I different ?

not really just that all the groping the boys did during slow dances did nothing for me, I am built quite boyish so the effort to cup my breast is generally a waste of time as there was very little to cup not even a handful.

I was also silly tall hence the pool of boys who had the nerve to ask me to dance is minute. But let me and a girl hug and my juices would flow, I would come alive and not want that hug to ever stop. As you can imagine I had to be careful, coming from an over religious household, church attendance Wednesday, Friday and Sunday, I often wondered if my family single handedly killed Christ based on the length of time we spent praying for forgiveness. I went through the motions and worried more about what would happen to me.

My salvation came going away to University, I had the common sense to apply for a place as far away from London as possible despite my parents insisting there were better Universities I decamped to Warwick University without a backward glance, to my delight my parents put me under the care of Christ and did not visit until my graduation, you can guess I stayed to do my Masters, I was the child that gave them no problems, I was seen as sorted and on the pathway to success and independence, next step is employment and bringing home a husband.

In freshers week I met Jiya, her name translates as radiance, light, sunshine, she was nothing of the sort, I have never met someone whose name simply did not fit, she was a small nervous ball of tension, over alert and ready to exit as soon as the noise got out of hand, her Indian accent is something to behold, yet I knew she and I had something in common, so I set out to befriend her.

The key to befriending an asian is excellence, we first became study buddies, I was aware of her scrutinisation ensuring I was education focused, no drugs, alcohol or any other misuse of illicit substances. The freshers week was not for us and after the first few events I told her I had no plan of attending any of the remaining events, Jiya has thought it was compulsory, I made fun of her first generation mentality and told her no one can force you to do anything, you are here to study not make friends.

Jiya gradually began to let her guard down, telling me about her life back in India, introduction to the food, movies and even some items of clothing she would bring back for me from weekends home. As our friendship progressed she went home less and less until like me she was on campus even during the breaks as long as she did not miss family zoom she was pretty much left alone with plenty of praise for integrating successfully, not sure one friend is integration. We did everything together and gradually began to stay over in whichever room we found ourselves, squashed in a single bed, top to tail or occasionally someone on the floor, we became totally comfortable in each others company.

I wonder sometimes if I was a predator or groomer ? I befriended Jiya because I was attracted to her. I worked at building the foundation for a relationship and knew the moment to test it out. Without checking with her I booked a coach ticket to go home, found her in her afternoon free period and told her I needed to go home for the next few days as my Mum wasn't feeling well. I have no doubt a seat is reserved for me in hell for this. Jiya offered to come with me, I declined her studies and all, then pointed out my family will be freaked out by her worship of the various Gods she believes in, religious hassle was enough to make her stay back.

I knew I would be away for the weekend, more for my Mum's birthday as a surprise, heading back on Tuesday. Jiya kept in touch to the point of obsession, I answered each text and call, each time I told her I missed her, got the same back, by day three she was saying I love you come back soon, I responded the same, I'll be back soon.

Going online I change my return coach to ten pm arrival, it is a short walk from our accommodation hall. Knocking on her door a little to 11pm the door is flung open I'm dragged in for a massive hug and naturally the first kiss, that night we clumsily explored, two female with similar attraction but nil experience or guidance, so we wrote our own book and rules noting what each liked, ensuring what we did not enjoy was not repeated, vibrator was one.

The warmth of another human against your skin cannot be explained, we are two consenting adults. That first time Jiya and

I were intimate we were both just short of our nineteenth birthday, adults in lots of ways but incredibly naive in other areas. We had no idea the pressures, needs, unexplained jealousy and general nonsense that comes with relationships. If you have ever had an Indian woman in your arm you will get me, the caress of her hair, enveloping you in the fragrance of coconut Vatika oil. Her amber skin smooth and glowing, teeth white against the darkness of her lips, eyelashes that make you think of a pixie fairy, curves in all the right places and lips that begged to be kissed whenever she spoke.

We didn't realise once we crossed that threshold into intimacy things could never remain the same and that a healthy relationship involved downtime, me time, that it's okay, we didn't have to live in each other's skin. How I wish we were like open western lesbians, perhaps our outcome would have been different. It would have been helpful to get some guidance and support from older wiser lesbians but no we hid in the shadows like two criminals when it came to our sexuality, again in Plain Sight but unseen out of fear, our friendship and closeness seen as two bookworms who topped in all areas of studies, an area that began to disintegrate during our fourth year at Uni in which I suspect we both opted to do our Masters so we would not have to face up to her return to Birmingham and mine to London.

The worst decision we made was to flat share a one bedroom, perhaps if our parents were visiting we would have been more cautious. To my 5 foot 9 is Jiya's incredibly petite frame of five foot four we made quite a striking figure when out and about, Jiya with hair down to her waist, while I wore mine in a low Afro.

We had a lovely elderly landlady who lived downstairs with the top of her house converted into the self contained flat we rented. The new experience of sharing a flat is incredibly exciting, we created this amazing personal space for ourselves everything about the flat spoke of us, from the little knick knacks, cushions, we picked up together and created an amazing lovenest, we did everything together we went to lectures together we came back together we ate, slept studied together and this was a heady time for us, we simply believed that life would go on like this for the one year we had left and that nothing would change in our naivety.

Life changes will come, nothing stays the same, I wish we had somebody who told us that it could have helped us prepare for some of the rocky roads that lay ahead. The first sign of trouble and we didn't know the sign was that we didn't identify spending time away from each other. It started with little irritabilities, why did you put that there ? Why did you move that ? led to the first argument, of course living in a one bedroom flat where could we go ? We didn't have friends outside of each other.

We couldn't go home because for nearly three years we've managed not to go home regularly except on the odd occasion, so even in an argument or misunderstanding a place that felt full of warmth suddenly became like a freezer. We didn't have anyone to intervene, thus we found we went several days without talking to each other.

It felt really really strange, extremely damaging, impossible to concentrate on dissertations or courseworks or meet deadlines. The first couple of times we found our way back to each other within a couple of days we apologized, talked it over, reflected on what had gone wrong and vowed to try harder but this didn't last long. Two hormonal women stuck in the same goldfish bowl swimming round and round in circles was never going to have a good outcome.

For the first time we struggled to meet deadlines, struggled to stay focused. There was so much going on. We had a pink elephant in the room and not addressing it every day brought us closer to parting and yet we were not able to talk, behaved like Ostriches our heads in the sand pretending that that day in June would not come, course and rental finished 30th of June and whether we like to or not we had to make decisions.

What do we do ? both try and get a job in the same place, rent a place and try to carry on living this way, is it mandatory she return to Birmingham ? all this we found impossible to discuss. The last place I want to be is North Peckham. I knew from the time I came to university I wasn't going back home yet for a couple so close we still did not sit down to ask what happened to our love ? what happens to being together, what happens to the physical side of our relationship, what happens to the psychological support we've been for each other ?

What happens ? Well what happened is the ultimate betrayal, where Jiya flatly denied every accusation that was thrown at her but I'm getting ahead of myself I'll share with you the final whistles of our relationship.

The period preparing to submit assignments, dissertations and studying for exams kicked in.I didn't know this but as part her culture her parents drove down with her two brothers to see her when they arrived we were both at the dining table paper spread everywhere laptop on working quietly when the doorbell went, I stuck my head out the top window, I met four Indian faces staring up at me. I immediately told Jiya your family is here as I went to open the door, greeted them respectfully and stepped out of the way so they could go upstairs. I went back upstairs and put some additional clothes on, greeted them again and said I would give them some privacy and I left the flat.

I went down the road where I sat in a cafe, carried on working on my laptop and kept an eye on their car parked in front of the house. Their entire visit lasted three hours. When I went back to the flat something had changed, had shifted and it took effort and so much time before Jiya would disclose what had taken place. Her entire family expressed their utter displeasure at her sharing a flat with a black woman, what was she thinking, we were not to be trusted. I would lead her astray, I'm bad for her health, bad for everything that is to do with her.

She was told spiritually I was bad to have around her as well as for her physical health. They then went on about other things that I don't understand linked to religion and caste. Worse than all that as a black person I was beneath her, beneath them and she shouldn't have agreed to share a place with me. She would have been better off flat sharing with an Indian like herself of the same caste or at the very least flatshare with a white person.

I just stared open-mouthed at Jiya. This can't be the same person I've spent the last three and a half years with. What did you say? I asked quietly. What did you explain to them about our setup ? I couldn't get a word in, she said you don't know my family, you don't know my brothers, I'm scared of them, I'm really really scared of them because my brothers went through this flat with a fine tooth comb and they kept going back to the fact that we're sharing a bed and that at the very least we should have two single beds so I'm just as freaked out as you. I didn't know they were coming, on my, the storm had started.

I asked her what she meant by a storm, what storm has started ? Jiya looked at me, shook her head and for the first time since I met her shut me out completely. It was that look, the look she gave me that told me the death kilt of our relationship. Jiya looked at me like I was a subordinate to her she looked at me like one would look at a hired help, home help, a housemaid, Coolie she described back in India that was seen but not seen she looked at me the way one would look at a black person that they didn't care to have around them.

I have never felt such utter sense of hopelessness the past three and a half years evaporated like smoke. I looked at the woman in front of me, this delicate five foot four that I would give my life to protect. She looked at me like I was a used piece of dirty tissue paper she needed to discard and discard very very quickly.

I shivered, and couldn't explain why I was shivering other than the shock of the last three and a half hours. I don't know this person in front of me, this isn't Jiya, this is some person left behind the real Jiya taken home, replaced with this hard as nails individual accusing me, saying awful things to me, I pushed her into the relationship ? I bullied her ? she's forgotten we are equal partners. I never forced her to do anything and when I try to tell her that she gives me another filthy look so I back down.

What is the way forward Jiya ? this is March we are here till the end of June, we've got important exams coming up, we've got deadlines to meet, how are we going to spend the next 12 weeks ? Is it doable ? If you don't want me near you I don't have an alternative but I'm happy to sleep on the couch. I don't have anywhere to move my things so we still have to share the bedroom wardrobe space. I won't come near you, I will respect the stance that you're making.

Please don't make my life miserable because I have absolutely no intention of making yours miserable, the words you said and used this evening I will not forget, I cannot forget and I reiterate it now I will try my best to keep out of your way but please don't treat me like I'm a piece of shit because I'm not whatever the prejudice going on between Asians and other Black races, it's not my battle to win, I don't have the strength, and I won't point out how overeducated Nigerians are.

Jiya burst into tears, I can't do this, I can't do this. What can't you do, what are you being asked to do, I've asked nothing of you, being a part of each other's life I haven't made any demands I haven't asked you to change yourself so what is it you can't do ? finally the truth.

The family came to inform Jiya of her wedding arrangements at the end of July. Jiya will be marrying her cousin who has just arrived from their homeland. I stand there frozen like a statue. I need to make sense of this afternoon, you, your family don't like black people but you will go home and marry your cousin or is this not where you approach the welfare authorities and ask for help. What do you want Jiya, we can relocate, we can get lost in England, we can go abroad. I know help is available because we're classed as a protected group.

Wrong answer for her, an alarmed look. Different approach straightway, I'm trying so hard to understand what you're going through and to know where I can come in, help or stay out, the venom from you towards me because of your family's visit is incredibly hard for me. I can take anything from anyone but not from you. I don't deserve this. I haven't done anything to make you treat me this way. In response she gives me yet another disgusting look, picks stuff from the dining table and slams the door to the bedroom.

When I see people crumble to the floor in movies I think great acting but that's exactly what happened to me my legs gave way and I found myself on the floor. I sit there hugging my knees rocking back and forth for comfort that didn't come, what do I, who do I go to, who do I have to go to, the one person that I can go to is behind that door, my life is falling apart. My hope is turning its back on me, my future is leaving me.

I asked myself again, did I groom Jiya or just recognized a kindred spirit who did not have the courage like me and together we found the courage. Jiya has grown the same way I've grown. I remain polite, I remain gentle, I remain humble. I see everyone around me as an equal, your cultural background, your pedigree is irrelevant, what you bring to the table, that's what commands my respect, you the person.

This new Jiya in the flat with me I do not know but she must have existed all along. For a moment I wonder if Jiya used me to get through the past three and a half years. Could this explain why we never had penetrative sex, for her wedding night in which the hymen must be intacta, unspoilt or hell to pay, our relationship guaranteed the bleeding that's expected. Has Jiya always seen me as someone beneath her, not good enough, while I saw my lover, partner, soulmate, did she just see a slave, something to be used and discarded, her pleasure now over.

The visit from her family has only accelerated June because while I've been stupidly wondering about June and how we're going to circumvent that period her relatives visit today signed sealed and made it very clear once the studies are over she is expected to do as she is told. I feel like a canoe adrift in rapids without a paddle. I feel like someone who's been dropped in the middle of the Sahara desert with no compass or supplies. I feel like the bumbleweed we see in Western movies, blowing aimlessly wherever the wind takes it.

I've lost all sense of direction, no dreams, no hopes, no more Jiya that's for sure, so Tune-tune who likes girls is sitting on the floor in a one bedroom flat thinking what now? It's the cold and the ache in my bones that made me get up and the fact that it's dark and it's been several hours and neither of us has moved. I can't hear any movement in the bedroom she hasn't put the light on.

I get up and go to the kitchen. I make a cup of her favorite cardamom chia, knock on the bedroom door, I put the cup on the bedside table and turn to walk out. I didn't even see her get up as I reached out to shut the door. She uses her left arm to push it back and her right to grab me. Jiya is crying, mumbling, talking, clinging to me.

I stand still. I don't put my arms around her, it's not my place anymore. Words tumble out, the apology, fear of her family, the respect, doing as you are told, she admits as a family no contact with black people, the general belief is that black people are bad. They don't know any black successful people, the black people they come across are not exactly Ambassadors for black people. I listen to all of this as it pours out but that's all I do. I just stand there with my arms by my side while she hugs me and talks.

For the first time in three and a half years I have a distressed Jiya. I'm not responding to her and it feels strange, it's as if my heart is gone solid steel. I know part of it is shock but I just stand there and look at the top of her head, normally I'd be caressing, holding her to me, reassuring her telling her we'll find a way for whatever it is she's feeling or whatever is happening, not this time. Her family instructions get rid of me based on my skin color.

Jiya doesn't realize the amount of danger she's in if they were to think for one moment that there is something other than flat sharing going on with us. I looked at her and I realized how much danger we're both in. Danger lies in the backgrounds we come from, their expectations. Our families refuse to accept anything Western that doesn't align with their beliefs or their culture.

For the first time since coming to University I feel unsafe and I wonder if Jiya's family are going to turn up again. I have a feeling they will. I don't know when but clear in my head her brothers will appear again and soon. That scares me because I know what I'm capable of if I'm cornered. I will defend myself yet how can I defend myself and hurt Jiya's family member.

This situation is impossible. I feel the hotness of tears roll down my face as Jiya continues to touch me all over. I stand there, eventually she drags me to the bed and tells me to join her, I do, I just lay there quietly fully clothed. The wetness of Jiya's tears soaking through my t-shirt as she tries to kiss me, I tell her no, I don't think it's a good idea. A lot has happened today and we need to take some time out to digest it.

You've said some hurtful things, I'm sure I've said some hurtful things back. We need to get some rest, let's see how we feel after we've had a good night's rest.Thankfully she stopped trying to be intimate. I wish I had a good night's rest, for over three and a half years Jiya slept on me and it's never been anything but pleasure but tonight It feels like a lump of concrete is pressing down on me there is no pleasure, no togetherness, there's no coming together, no fulfillment, nothing other than a pressure on my chest. I let Jiya stay there. At some point she rolled off me and wrapped herself in the duvet as she normally does. When her breathing steadies again I get up quietly picking up the spare duvet. I continued my sleep on the settee, I might as well get used to the new arrangement.

The morning brought a fresh set of drama.
A wide eyed Jiya came out to the sitting room demanding to know why I left her in bed, without waiting for an answer she slams into the bathroom, has a shower, gets dressed and departs. I sit there wondering what happened between this time yesterday and today. We've gone from living a quiet peaceful life to what feels like a war zone because four people came to visit without prior notification and with their visit our world falls apart.
Jiya is back within minutes raving, I can't do this, I can't function, I can't think, she goes into the bedroom and lies down in the fetal position. I don't move from the settee because I don't know what to do. I don't know how to react. I don't know what to say and I don't understand the situation as it's new to me.

Forty minutes later Jiya sits next to me, we need to talk, she said it like I hadn't said that all along. Can we talk now ? no I said and suggested to her that we meet at the park, one of our favorite spots this afternoon. All right that I can do she says and this time there was no slamming the door, she packed her stuff again, gave me a quick hug and departed.
I ran my bath a little bit hotter than I normally would, got in and laid there, several times purposely slid all the way in only coming up for air when my lungs felt like they were going to explode. My head above or underneath the water I still couldn't

think it felt like my brain had been filled with concrete. No one told me life could fall apart so quickly but I have to survive, this is now about damage limitation. What became very clear yesterday is there is no future with Jiya. The love that was birthed here, lived here, will die here.

Love ends in June, me to London Jiya to Birmingham where marriage to her first cousin awaits. I'm not being evil but the statistics for disabled children from those unions numbers are high. I remember watching a documentary about it. To help myself I go online and begin to look at jobs, something that I thought I didn't need to do for at least another two months yet I am CV ready and begin to send it off left right and center to London but nowhere near home I don't want to go back home. I also go on the students notice board app and place an ad saying I'm looking for jobs in central London and people to share a flat with if they're interested please make contact.

I gather my head back enough to go back to my work. I don't remember. I have not eaten anything since yesterday, it wasn't until my head started pounding with a migraine that I remembered that I hadn't even had a drink since the evening before. Oh well if life is to go on I need to nourish my body. I couldn't tell you what I ate because I didn't taste it, having never felt such levels of distress. I thought about calling one of the crisis line numbers that the University has pinned all over the place but am I in Crisis ? no, the bottom line is I'm dating an Asian girl, nobody knows about us and now we have to stop. It's as simple as that. The sooner I swallow and digest it the quicker I will probably be able to pick up my pieces and do my best to move on, achieve my grades, get on with my life but the next twelve weeks are clearly going to be a nightmare.

The Nigerian in me is drawing on the resilience of my ancestors, if one road closes, find a detour but don't be distracted, don't lose sight of the destination. Why am I not crying, creating drama with Jiya, it creeps in on me slowly, Tune: men don't cry. Men, what sort of lesbian am I ? If we had mixed with others I might have clarity around my own identity, does one relationship really bring full identity. Where do I fit in as a person, certainly not doing this walk with an Asian, I will never look at another Asian woman.

I comfort myself with the bounce back we are so capable of as a race, never say never motto. Today I agree and accept I am broken but not unrepairable, the anger at being told I am not good enough by a bunch of illiterates niggles me. Her father and both brothers with their red mouth from chewing tobacco and yet my presence is treated with disdain. There is no point dwelling on how deeply Jiya is loved by me but already a wall stronger than that of China is being built as I get myself ready for what lies ahead. I thank the ancestral spirit that guided me to immediately accept what I cannot change and plan forward.

The weather for late March is beautiful, for students long locked up indoors for the winter the park is relatively packed, it wasn't hard to find Jaya she was sitting where we generally sat around the same spot. I said hello and sat down, we looked at each other from a moment and then I looked away I chose this open space for a reason and the reason is that wherever you are sitting there are people within earshot of you, I needed that to ensure that our conversation didn't erupt into a shouting match or a crying scene.

Jiya I said: I want to thank you for the last three years, I have never met anybody like you and I have never felt so complete. I thank you for the good times because that's what I'm going to keep and take away with me. I thank you for the exposure and opportunity to be a part of your life and know more about your culture. I thank you for learning about mine. I thank you for liking, loving me enough to explore with me on this special journey that we've both been on.

I'm not going to say too much but this is my way of actually seeing goodbye. Jiya it's goodbye in the sense that if we're not both cautious you will be in danger… she tries to interrupt me, don't say anything yet ,don't interrupt me please, let me finish, let me tell you what can happen if we continue to live the way we are. We are at risk, your family turned up yesterday without giving you any prior notice. Can you imagine if they turned upon where'd been in bed asleep, the way we sleep dead to the world in the buff, what if we didn't hear the door and our landlady let them in ! I know that would have been the end for you, I don't even think they would have let you continue with your studies. I think you will be straight back home and the wedding two days later so please listen to me very carefully. My decision right now is with you at the center of it.

Your well-being, your safety not now but the future. I don't want you to go back to Birmingham broken, you have to begin to develop your own resilience, you know what lies ahead and I suspect even when you came to university you may have known that after your studies you will marry your cousin. I'm not saying you purposely kept that type of information away from me, it's just something we've never talked about so here's what we're going to do after I've said this I'll keep quiet.

We will live together for the next few months, I will sleep on the settee, you will have the bedroom, we will continue to split the bills as we've always done. I will need to come into the bedroom to have access to my clothing, bits and pieces but the bedroom is yours, it's your space. The sitting room will become my space, there might be occasions when I might be asleep and you would want to sit in the sitting room and watch something, we have to agree that on those occasions you leave me be. Watch what you want sitting at the dining table. I don't see a problem coexisting under that same roof with you. I do think the kind of awareness that we didn't have before we need to have it now.

I can guarantee you that your brothers will be back. I just don't know when.

When they come back I want them to find a situation where they have absolutely no doubt about you. You may think it's crazy for me to be saying things about honoring but you need to be really really careful because you're the one who has to go back to Birmingham. I love you dearly. I would always love you yesterday, forever but the reality is now and the last 24 hours reality tells me that the greatest love that I can show you is to let you go and let you be. I'll keep quiet now, I wrap up.

'So you're saying no more sex ,no more touching you, no more sleeping with you, no more being intimate with you. What are you saying because I don't hear you, you're telling me we're going to live in that flat like strangers, is that even possible or have you lost the plot completely?

Yes I'm scared of my brothers and yes I'm scared of my parents because I have to do as I'm told but I can't ignore you, I can't pretend I don't feel what I feel for you, even now I just want us to get up go back to the flat make love and block out everything that happened in the last 24 hours. Instead of you telling me you feel the same, you're talking about the greatest love you have for me is to let go of me, have you eaten too much jollof rice or is it my curries that have gone up your nose somewhere and it's affecting your brain? don't you understand I need you!

Your plan is not going to work. It doesn't sit well with me, it's not what I want and surely what I want must count so have another think and tell me how we're going to move forward for the next three months. I have accepted that come the end of June I'm going to Birmingham to begin the second stage of my life and the quality of which I know because one of the reasons for marrying cousins is so that you can never divorce, that's why usually the cousin comes from the home land.
You marry them whether it's a boy marrying a girl or a girl marrying a boy and you can't leave them because they are family. It's your Aunt's son or your Uncle's son or daughter whichever but that's the reason why you're marrying close relatives to make sure we don't leave, we don't divorce we don't become westernized. Can't we work something out, couldn't you move to Birmingham? couldn't you come and live in Birmingham. I'm sure I can cope with being married by spending time with you, couldn't we do something, say something Tune just say something for goodness sake!
Jiya with respect for what we share you're not making sense, you're not thinking straight. I'm telling you that we actually don't have a choice but to change and you're coming out with all these wild suggestions, what do you think would happen just for the sake of it, if I get a job in Birmingham, come and live there you'll play being married and then what? you'll make time to come and see me once a week, once a fortnight, once a month and you think that's a quality of life for you or me.
You need to stop, just stop. I'm trying to hold it together and that's what you need to start doing okay. The main thing to

remember is that there is no third party you're not cheating on me and I'm not cheating on you there's nobody else except your family and so we need to tread carefully going forward. Jiya, one of the reasons I asked us to meet here today is because I know if we try to have this conversation in the flat it will not end well so while we're talking and we've got people around us we both will not raise our voices as we would attract attention.

It's also to ensure that we can stay focused on what we've come down to the park to talk about. I suggest everything else we do we carry on as we've done, there's nothing wrong with being study buddies, we cook, we eat together but when it comes to sundown and intimacy that's not going to happen. Let me reiterate this to you whether you believe me or not your brothers are coming back and when they come back they're probably going to be even harder on you then this visit.

They are wondering how you can live with a black person so comfortably, what's been going on for three years and nine months with you. I will do all I can to help you to adjust but please remember this is a period of adjustment for me as well. I've never been in love before. I've never met anyone like you. I've never been loved back like this and to know that it's not even going to end slowly it's got to stop right now is hard for me too. I thought about counselling and I thought perhaps we could access counselling separately so that we will have a safe space to talk but that's up to you.

I'm going to share some news with you and it's not because I've gone and done anything behind your back but it's because I recognized that I need to begin to plan my life. A life that does not include you so I'm going to share this with you with the hope that you'll start doing the same thing. I spent mid-morning today sending my CV off, applying for jobs and I've also put an advert to see if anybody wants to flatshare in London.

That's me, I'm all talked out. I don't know if you have anything else you want to say before we head back to the flat. I get a mini rant in response, what's the point, what can I say that's going to make a difference, can we at least discuss at the end of each week how this is going because if it's not going well and we need to make some adjustments we're going to need to be able to discuss that.

Jiya, it's still me, I'm not a different person, it's still Tune. I have a non judgemental attitude, you know my approach to things is always positive, it's about finding a way forward, it's about finding a way around things, it's about getting things done, it's about not losing focus of what lies ahead. What we need to achieve, of course I'll talk ,of course we'll talk, we'll reflect on each week as it passes and if there are adjustments that we need to make of course we'll make those tweaks but what we cannot do is turn back the clock to before yesterday when your brothers and your parents came to visit.

I need you to accept that because it's just going to make the transition that we're trying to attempt easier for both of us. I'll say it now, I take no prisoners, I love you, they will always be a place in my heart for you but we need to move on. It's been a wonderful, wonderful time but like sleep we need to wake up and this is our wake up moment. Raising up I extend my hand, let's go get something to eat, we start the walk back to the flat. We walk through the park like two strangers distance between us if you observed us you'll know we are together but not the giggly two that would walk down the street and talk heads together, always talking about something, looking at something, pointing something out, this time we walk back each careful to ensure no contact, no physical contact that is.

We didn't see the car at first until nearly at the flat and I thought it strange that it had a Birmingham number plate. It was parked literally by the cafe where I sat yesterday but where you could see the house. Still it didn't register that apart from it being odd it might have anything to do with Jiya and I, as we walk past the Asian guy in the car looked away so that I couldn't register his face all I saw was the back of his leather jacket as he leaned backwards in his chair as if he was trying to get something from the back of the passenger's seat. All that took my attention really is the Birmingham number plate on the car. We go in and fix food and eat in a relatively tense atmosphere. The peaceful sitting at the dining table holding hands, leaning in for quick kisses, touching of legs, rubbing of knees, the quick hug or a deep kiss, all that is missing, we sat at the dining table like the two students we are and just ate our meal.

It took me the second week before I could say I had solid concrete evidence that there were two alternative cars with Birmingham number plates. Two cars that took it in turns were watching our flat. I swear I saw the men in the cars taking pictures of either us or just Jiya because of the movement of someone quickly putting a camera down when he realized you're looking straight at them.

How do I tell Jiya to be careful, who are they? My guess is they've been sent by her brother or alternatively her husband to be but if he's new in the country I doubt he can set this up a fortnight after we first had an unannounced visit. I knock on the bedroom door open the door and sit on the ground in the doorway 'Jiya there's something I need to tell you I say'

Rather than remain on the bed she jumps up and comes to sit next to me on the floor, this woman still has hope that something might break in me and we'll get back to the intimate relationship we had. I told her to turn the bedroom light off, she did, then I led her to the window and I showed her the car and the man sitting inside. I led her away and we went and sat back by the bedroom door.

Jiya there's been two cars taking it in turns watching the house. I can only say either us, or watching you. Watching our coming and going and that's from the day after your family came. I've never noticed those cars before, what brought them to my attention is the Birmingham number plate so your brothers or your parents pulled enough strings to say here's the address, sit there and watch what's going on. Need to know what's going on, who comes in, who goes out, who you see. With that Jiya creeps back to the window and is there for a while just staring at the car parked just up the road.

Very Softly she begins to cry, it's me they're watching not you, they're not interested in you, they're concerned that with education I might break away from what's expected of me within our culture, within our family, within our community. That I might run. We've had it before where from Universities girls or boys haven't gone home to marry their cousin instead they've asked authorities for help, they've disappeared into England, they've been helped to stay off the radar so I think it's me they are watching to make sure that I'm doing what's expected of me, my routine is the same, I'm going to my lectures and maybe even to ensure there's no male coming to see me or me keeping company with any male in terms of not mixing with the opposite sex or having friends outside of our Asian identity.

My auntie is quite a wealthy gold merchant, it wouldn't surprise me if she dispatched those two goons for want of a better word once my brothers and my parents reported back to her. I'm sure it's nothing to do with you. I'm not going to do anything, anything I do will put me in danger because if these guys take a bad report back and say they are concerned, trust me Tune I'm gonna be pulled out of Uni the same day, it will be to hell with the Masters, you're coming home and that's it. So this is what I'm going to do. I'm going to make sure I give these guys no cause to make any kind of unusual report back to whoever told them to come and keep an eye on me. I'm also going to make sure that I play dumb because the moment they realise I've made them that also can be dangerous for me.

I thank you even when we're not together you're still looking out for my welfare, my well-being for that I thank you Tune. I love you, with that she moves away from the window, gets into bed and curls up in the foetal position under the duvet, a sure sign all is not well. I get up quietly close the bedroom door, we are done. Jiya is in for a life ahead she might have very little control over. I pray her cousin is kind to her and her to herself. She seems so vulnerable. Looking back, that was the final moment of separation. The fact she is being watched contributed largely to that with no more attempts to get close to me. Like I warned her earlier her brothers did come back. It was a month from the first visit, a saturday afternoon, Jiya was asleep in the room, I had fallen asleep studying. Neither of us heard the doorbell or perhaps they did not ring it.

The landlady let them in, the first I knew the landlady was gently shaking me telling me Jiya's family were ringing the bell with no response hence rang her bell worried something was wrong maybe she was sick and couldn't answer the door…. yeah right ! This time her brothers and just Mum, eyeing me like one would a vermin, I say a polite good afternoon, turn my back and carry on sleeping. When they walked into the bedroom I heard Jiya yelp and smiled to myself, on this point I am so right. The conversation is intense, Jiya raised her voice briefly then must have thought better of it and started crying instead. I hear lots of comforting murmuring, the entire visit lasted less than last time, satisfied they departed but the observer car remained and doubled as their second car when the family came back for the move to Birmingham.

With the new regime, final submissions, exams, the weeks flew, no time to think. I responded to all around me automatically. I must have done something right because not only did I secure a job pending my results but I also found two amazing boy mad young women to share a flat with in Fulham. The interview for the post was done online. I made sure I booked a study room for best outcome, nil distractions. I am winding down, four precious years of my life ending. I am a young adult, experiencing more than some who are twice my age. I have lived a life I can never share with my family. How was I to know life has a way of exposing you when it's ready.

Jiya left first as I suspected no sooner did she finish her last paper she was whisked away. I kept my goodbye polite and disinterested in front of her family. I thanked her for being a good flatmate and wished her well for the future. I watched from the window, she didn't dare look back except to give the landlady a hug. This was well tolerated by her family, I don't need to be told a hug from a gala-black is not welcomed. Thus closes a chapter of my life, onward and forward to London, no warning that what I hid will soon be splashed across billboards and the internet.

Dear Ethel, Rose and Dr Fahad,

I have settled back into life in the capital city well. My parents have learned to accept I will not be living with them now or in the future, they even seem somewhat proud that I have left Peckham. Fulham must be the great height though renting a three bedroom ex-council flat is not the pinnacle for me, Yet I thrive, I love my job, my colleagues appear to like and respect me. I get back what I give. Flat share is neither here nor there, it is a good co-existence once we agree the ground rules. Initially there was a lot of traffic in the girls bringing back their men, once we agreed they would keep whoever is with them to the limit of their bedroom and use of the toilet they seemed to calm down. I had become quickly fed up of coming back from a busy shift to find people sprawled on the settee, meaning my decompression place became my bedroom.

I settled very quickly into my life as a nurse. I'm supportive of others. I do my job and I'm reliable. I'm described as an asset. It's a good feeling. I found my niche in life and I'm getting on with it, my colleagues find me approachable and quite often people share their difficulties with me it doesn't take long for me to have the unofficial agony go to person, it's not unusual for me to have people who want to talk to me outside the work space, I do my best to accommodate.

A particular colleague approached me one day and asked if I had time after work. They needed to talk, I said of course and after the shift waited for her. We grab a coffee and we sit out on the steps leading to the garden space at work. A very nervous colleague tells me her story. She's Ghanaian, she comes from quite a religious background and she talks about 'Soupie'

It's a nickname for a lover, in this case a same sex female lover. My guard goes up immediately. Where is this conversation going? I listen as she carries on. She wants to attend the quarterly LGBTQ Trust meeting but doesn't have the confidence to go on her own. Would I be kind and accompany her? It's open to everyone, not just LGBTQ colleagues. I keep it low, I keep it slow. I asked her why me? she said because everybody feels comfortable with me and if there's anyone she's going to ask for support it definitely has to be me. I tell her okay, that's fine I don't have a problem accompanying her to the meeting we exchanged numbers, she sends me the details before I get home.

I don't feel anything is off in this encounter or this conversation this isn't about me it's about her she's younger than me, she's not coming on to me, she clearly feels she can relate with me as an African like herself, she is just looking for some support, compassion, acceptance and validations particularly with an older figure that you can go to who just says as it is. I made a note in my diary that the reason this part is really really important is that there are times when we need to learn how to say no, however much we want to support or help others.

On the faithful day I finished my shift and met up with her. I've never been to an LGBTQ meeting even though it's an Organisational Trust one. I'm staggered by the number of people there, the place absolutely teems with people, it looked and felt like an all nations assembly. Food, drinks, sandwiches, wraps, you name it all spread out. We help ourselves and sit down. I'm not quite sure what exactly the meeting is about, I am mesmerized as I sit there munching my food kind of half listening to what's going on around me, drinking in the scene of people free to mingle.

The meeting covers everything from well-being to work to life target performance. Career conversations to career progression to health conversations, wellness, self-help conversations we listen to speakers, I was impressed, I was very impressed. Of course my colleague was very grateful, she also stated that she feels having attended the first meeting she's okay to attend future meetings and gatherings.

Well that's it for me I walk away no second thought about the evening. I've supported a colleague. I'm still in the closet. I don't have to address my needs. I'm cool where I am, until 72 hours later and my face with her sitting next to me is on the Trust magazine online,clips of the meet-up are on social media. There is my face larger than life, sitting next to her amongst smaller pictures. People see before I do and the first I know of it is a phone call from my hysterical mother crying and screaming.

I struggle to understand what she is talking about in between her ranting. How could you ? How could you let us know this way ? How could you do this to us ? Have you thought about the effect on us as a family ? it's all over social media, it's all over everywhere I look ? Who is that girl with you ? it's in Metro free magazine. What are you doing and putting your face on Gay meetings, why didn't you tell your bosses you can't go ? are you promoting gayness and so on and so forth. There are some things that we don't realize are a blessing in disguise. I wasn't ready to come out to my family but I knew if I did not take this opportunity there would never be another one and I would continue to live my life a lie. I calmed my Mother down, and said that I would come and see her at the weekend.

From my mother's hysterical reaction to the most amazing acceptance, warmth, camarada watching out for me at work, people from the LGBTq community who had never spoken to were saying hello to me, it puzzled me for a moment, until I realized that actually the LGBTq community were reaching out to me, owing me, saying this is 'One of Us' making me feel that I belong and yet I hadn't even acknowledged to anybody that I'm gay. Yet they knew.

The visit to Mom at the weekend was a mixture of stupidity, at times complete comedy, other times hopeless. You could tell how sheltered my mother has been, sitting there holding the scriptures using them to talk to me to encourage me to reconsider, encourage me to recognize that Adam and Eve not Eve and Eve, followed by do you have a girlfriend ? Have you slept with someone ? How do you know you're gay ? Have you slept with a man ? what's the difference that makes you gay and so on and so forth. I sit there quietly because I understand the enormity of this meeting and I say to my mom 'mom can you just reflect on the sort of child I have been, that you raised, did I ever come across as feminine ? Have I ever been girly ? no mother.

I see myself as a strong male, I think like one, I act like one, it's who I am. I'm attracted to women. I'm no longer scared of who I am. No, I haven't had a long-term relationship and yes I have had a girlfriend and no I don't have a boyfriend. I'm not interested in boys' mum. I haven't slept with a boy and if you need to know I am still a virgin so you can try mum and work that out yourself I'm not sleeping around I'm not promiscuous. I just happen to have met a girl at University that I really really liked and that confirmed to me that I like girls. She's an Asian Mum. We hid who we are for four years until we finished our Masters and went our respective way.

I thought I was getting somewhere, Mum did most of the talking, my Dad was quiet, more exposed due to the nature of his job. Thinking I was getting somewhere my mothers next statement floored me and reminded me of the danger I am in as a Nigerian, no less Jiya's if her sexual preference was to be known. I know a Pastor that can help or maybe you should go to Nigeria for a while, various suggestions, different things tumbling out of my mother's mouth, a woman desperate to not be ostracised by her society, culturally or in the church.

Nigeria !!! 14 year jail term for being gay. I have no doubt the treatment for me not to be gay would be sexual intercourse with male, we have heard of it from victims who managed to get to the safety of the West. I tried a different approach: we have gay Pastor's mum, no, no, no, no, not in our church, not in our religion, not in our belief. I am met with this barrage. I quickly dropped that approach.

I try something else, I tell my parents how much I love them, reassure them I would never put myself at risk, I say to them I am gay, I know I'm gay this is not me exploring or trying to find my identity I know my identity already. I will never purposely do anything that will embarrass you but I am who I am and I need you to let me be me. My siblings sit there at the dining table just looking on like it's a cinema but I'm grateful to them because they must have recognized at that moment that what I needed is touch, reassurance and I love you without having to say it.

I don't know if they'd communicated this to each other earlier but I had four siblings come up to me pull me up and envelope me in a hug, with that both my parents begin to cry and they get up and they also hug me and somehow it feels like it might be alright in the end but I know this is just the beginning of the storm.

Gatherings when it comes to our culture it's not so clean sailing. I also have to deal with my siblings whispering in my ears 'Gay pinup person, our own billboard Tune, from a difficult beginning the visit appeared to end on a positive note. I left feeling yes I'm a part of this family no one's turned their back on me and I still retain my identity. Extended family will be navigated when the time comes, it will be weddings or funerals. I have no intention of turning up at birthday parties.

My wellbeing as a gay Nigerian lies in keeping a low profile, living a quiet life away from the limelight and they just might forget and move on to other topics. I must ensure I don't ever end up in Metro, Timeout and splatter around the Trust buildings ever again.

Work is where it gets interesting. The invitation and inclusion began to happen probably too fast for me and so I slowed it down, careful to only accept invites to places or events that I felt would actually help me grow. I accepted an invite from one of the doctors to a golf tournament. I know nothing about golf. Charts Hill Golf Club not too far out in Kent. That charity tournament became an interesting journey for me because that's where I met the woman that I remain with till today. I learned that happiness is possible. I learned that the road can be bumpy. I learned that times when mountains will seem to spring out in front of you. I learned that times where the ground will give way under you. I learned times when you feel good and times when you feel so bad you're crushed.

I also learned that like a flower, like a plant, we can rejuvenate if we're watered and cared for but most important of all I learned that when you least look for it you can find treasure beyond your wildest dreams, let me tell you about Tolu-Ibadan, even her name excites me.

On arrival at the golf tournament I quickly found the Doctor who invited me to say thank you. A nice junior doctor friendly despite his poshness. I said I know nothing about golf yet the gathering is chilled, it's friendly it's a happy crowd. I noticed her before she noticed me and the reason that I noticed her is because she could have been a black Jiya the same cute petite shape the same strange full head of hair but still that delicate air around her. I walked past as I was going to the ladies, our eyes met and we smiled.

When I came out I don't know if it's a coincidence but she was waiting for me, she said hello a smile lit up her little face, her eyes twinkled. I returned the hello and introduced myself. She's an Oncologist, not a surprise as most of the crowd appear to be Medics of one sort or the other, NHS or private health care based. Tolu-Ibadan is easy to talk to. She speaks proudly of her Nigerian heritage, I'm Ibadan she says as if that guarantees exemption from goodness knows what. I am also from Naija South I state.

Neither of us have lived there but visited thankfully when we were too young to see the land as anything other than magical in comparison to being cooked up in a flat for me the size of the houses, rooms, the garden space called yard felt like having a field to call garden.

In no time at all we were in deep conversation, I introduced her to my friends and her me to hers. We literally spent the rest of the afternoon together and when everything was over and we went into the reception in the evening naturally we continued to gyrate towards each other, when she asked if she could meet me again I said yes. Giving her my number was one of the best things I ever did. Tolu-Ibadan is kind yet feisty, takes no nonsense yet can be sweet and soft or hard depending on what the occasion calls for.

She is light years ahead of me in feeling comfortable with her sexuality, six years older than me she is clear about what she seeks. Loyalty, faithfulness, nil hidden surprises, she even checked I am not Bi masquerading as gay. This tiny very feminine woman packs such a punch when it comes to life. Despite me taking the lead with Jiya, I am happy for Tolu-Ibadan to take the lead, make decisions, be happy and content. She keeps me in mind and considers my likes and dislikes.

The first few years have been heady. Have we settled into a routine, no, every time feels like a honeymoon. Relationships are extra sweet when there is money and that we comfortably have. Tolu-Ibadan's parents turn out to be loaded, her father described as a Prince Merchant and mother a shipping magnate.

I was simply presented at their London flat a minute walk round the corner from Park lane then their house in Barnes. ' Mum Dad Tune-Tunde my partner' that was that. No preaching, no drama, a welcome to our home. By the end of the meal gentle teasing. After coffee we played games, there was a lot of noise and laughter. Their staff travel around the world with them. At the house in Barnes I realised as an only child Tolu-Ibadan had led a life we read about in books, private school, piano lesson the whole shebang, yet she's grown into a well rounded adult no hidden bad habits what you see is what you get.

For the first time since Jiya I am filled with panic I might lose someone. Not the affluence but a new contentment, a feeling of safety, the looking forward to finish work just to get back to Tolu-Ibadan who had delicious meals waiting, who greeted me with warmth, touch that made me quiver and want more, we share long welcome hugs, when I say long I mean entwined and content to remain so for a long time. There is nothing more complete than the warmth of someone you want, that is the magic, I want Tolu-Ibadan more, does she want me everyday she demonstrates it, the hidden notes, the texts and the endless emojis, all saying, you are on my mind.

The topic of wasting money on two rents came from Tolu-Ibadan. Relaxing one evening she brought up the map of the London underground. We need a location where we can get into London within half an hour, plenty of green and places to eat and hangout. We poured over the map unsure we added British rail, almost immediately we decided on Blackheath. Enough places of interest with the health itself the park and then into the Cutty Sark, plenty to keep us busy.

We begin house hunting in earnest, it is the first time Tolu-Ibadan speaks of my family to me, a no go area for me and our precious relationship as I was too scared of something being said that would make Tolu-Ibadan's world and mine collapse. At this point she makes it clear both families must be there for the first day in the house. I ask if it's necessary and she insists even if it's the only time we must follow the tradition of prayers and well wishes done when moving into a new home.

Tolu is ridiculously proud of her Ibadan heritage, a well balanced woman living comfortably between several cultures courtesy of forward thinking parents. I finally found my other half. She's upper class trying very hard to pass herself off as working class but all you have to do is listen to her accent and you realize that you're talking to a really polished woman from a very good background.

My life changed immensely in her company. I start to experience events and sports activities that would normally not occur to me. Tolu-Ibadan took me skiing. Fair enough I spent the time on the beginners slope trying to learn how to control these two long sticks called skis but it was a wonderful time because in the evening we would sit in front of a fireplace drinking hot chocolate or beer and just talking, the fact that we were the only black persons in the group we stood out for all the right reasons. I was there with my partner and my partner was very much there, visible with me and totally in love with me.

Switzerland, Austria, Vienna, the cities that normally if I was to visit I'd have to plan, weekend or quick four day breaks, here a quick three night break, there with friends, without friends, doing our own thing. A whole new lifestyle opened up for me. While on a trip to the famous IceHotel Jukkasjarvi in Sweden with the aim of watching the aurora Borealis Tolu-Ibadan proposed, I said yes, yes so fast, I should have guessed because it was a leap year but it was yes all the way and so I only had one partner before Tolu-Ibadan. I didn't know too much pain and when I think about Jiya I think about her with fondness.

It's such a shame Dr Farhad that you didn't have your happiness ever after but I hope that wherever you are you can take comfort from the fact that I found my happiness ever after. Tolu-Ibadan is everything one could hope for in a partner. She's loving, she's considerate and she really does make me feel complete. As for the LGBTq Community it's become impossible for me to stay in the closet as I remain the BMA poster face of NHS LGBTq group for the Trust. My work life is good, I cannot complain, I don't know where all this is leading me but when I think of life without Tolu-Ibadan I panic, that's how I realized that I'm that Ethel who has found her Rose. I pray my Rose is not hiding too many pickles. I hope that unlike the difficult, toxic domestic violence relationships that we hear about we don't join the statistics. Out of respect for my parents I have ensured I live a quiet life, yet the new house and wedding will draw them to our circle however briefly. All I wish is for my mother to see people and not sexual deviance.

Dear Ethel, Rose & Dr Fahad

I've been lucky in the sense that I haven't had to struggle for years before I was lucky enough to meet Tolu-Ibadan. Your collective letters shared so much pain, loneliness, that intense feeling of isolation that you carried with you but for you Dr Fahad that feeling of never having at the end of life achieved or be blessed with what you wanted so much, that sense of belonging, to be loved to be held, to be of importance to someone without its involving giving something material. Basics of Marslow's hierarchy of Needs.

Such luck Tolu-Ibadan spoils me. I've never ever known anybody like her, she's just the best ever, she gives me the best and in turn I make sure that I am the loyal committed partner she deserves. For our engagement her parents bought us a property. I later found out the flat was previously owned by a Dr Fahad…you! I marvel at how life just keeps going in full circles without us realizing it.

How did I find out it was your flat ? Well one day shortly after we moved in Paul and Al turned up and rang the bell. I immediately recognized Paul from the pharmacy and the fact that he no longer works with the Trust so it figured the Arab looking guy with him is Al the Egyptian. I think both had come to check out what happened to your flat, just in case you forgot to dispose of it and they could make a claim.

Tolu-Ibadan and I answered the door and explained to them that we bought the property and moved in recently, adding it was a steal at 2.7million, Tolu-Ibadan looked at me but said nothing knowing I will explain my odd behaviour once they left. The lame response from them, both explained a friend of theirs used to live here and passed away, both wondered what happened to his flat and who lives there now, if it was relatives they wanted to give their condolences.

I stood them in my mind thinking utter rubbish. Dr Fahad of the two of them Paul looked really rough, he looked like someone who is one step away from being street homeless, he just looked so neglected. Both looked stressed and came across as a shady pair. I have no doubt they are on the lookout for another victim. You know bad news gets around superfast we know Paul's wife threw him out, also Al allowed him to stay with him for a while but looking at them today that arrangement looks rocky.

I'm still astonished by the fact that we ended up living in a property that you owned and what astonishes me more is without anyone of us knowing you or your story her parents bought that flat the day it went on the market with the intention of giving it to Tolu-Ibandan but once they knew that I am a fixed part of her life and that we intend to marry they added me to the deed of the property.

I tell you Dr Fahad we're going to look after this property, we're going to fill it with love, we're going to fill it with hope, fill it with contentment, we're going to make it a home. I hope this brings you some comfort. We ditched the thought of moving to Blackheath.

Tomorrow I'm finally going to take the tin of letters to patient property. I've added mine to it. Ethel and Rose's letters I have tied in a pink ribbon. Your letters Dr Fahad I have tied in a purple ribbon.

Purple in my culture signifies royalty. Tolu-Ibadan and I have decided that our letters are going to be our favourite colour which is neutral so we're just using a very very pale gray ribbon. There is hope in me that somebody else picks up this tin, reads our letters and adds theirs to it. Life is about experiencing, living, feeling but most important of all giving account be it good, bad or downright ugly because from a documented account can come comfort for someone else, these accounts can light the way, can enable someone to end a bad relationship or give them the courage to start a new one. Sharing how to be patience, yet be fast when it comes to self and ownership preservation.

To whoever:
The main thing is to please remember we are someone's child, someone's brother, someone's sister, someone's loved one and like you we have a right to love and be loved and to have access to all the opportunities that you have and may take for granted, protected group or not.

So I say this to the stranger that happens to be reading this, Be you, find the courage, always be YOU in PLAIN SIGHT.

Tin of letters taken to patient property today at 11:10hrs

Third Race (bonus read)

James Parry-Kay was trained and conditioned to lead.

His leadership style may be difficult for you to stomach but it works, tried and tested time and time again.

No mission under him has failed, there will be no failure on this mission either, despite the knowledge it's a do or die situation, safe return is as low as 30% with everything including terrain against a positive outcome.

Gathering his chosen specialist crew a collection of skilled man killing machines if and when required are capable and ready to take back Sector 8 and restore much needed order, there is no longer room for disorder.

The year is 2046. Man has not changed. The order has.

Sectors

Watching the new group glide up and make their way into the building some hurriedly others slowly almost reluctantly I feel the rush of power, that muscle awakening that comes with the knowledge you can make or break, the crushing without thought for consequences, why not I smirk as I watch JW Wilson slide out from his electric cruiser, straightening himself he strides across the car park purposefully long strides of a man whose time means counters, counters that is not to be wasted. Dressed immaculately and groomed to perfection he enters the building no doubt in my mind he will make me earn counters he is paying for what is politely recommended but between the lines is instruction to attend. What can make a man like JW Wilson make time to attend a closed support group for those whose partners are referred to as 0.5 meaning they became unwell in the last five months and the outlook is bleak. Maybe he is more clever than he is given credit for.

JW Wilson of the formal Wilson Oil, Gas and electrics is not a man to be found at the Five Way sector base in Sidcup, it is not a part of town you would expect him to drive through much less stop and park up. Think of Vienna, Casablanca, Monte Carlo, think rich boys play ground and you'll expect to find him there with the usual escorts masquerading as hospitality host/hostesses at the beck and call and occasionally with mutual consent between the sheets of the powerfully rich, well that lifestyle no longer exists, this year is 2046 a lot has changed. At 6 '1 in his late fifties, a not unattractive man with a grey streak at the temple his cold grey eyes will stop you in your tracks. JW certainly known to love the finer things in life, he did not get where he is without making a few enemies. History wise the British public know little to nothing other than he is old money who married well and has done the Wilson business no harm, locking the file marked JWW away I make my way to the room where I am awaited.

Gone are the days of tacky exhibitions of wealth, I walked briskly along the quiet corridor walls painted duck blue so claimed the calming colour chosen by me to give that false calm. Rosie falls silently in step with me as we make the short walk to the glass bowl, it doesn't matter what part of the room you place yourself you can be observed from outside. It was purposely designed in this manner again to increase that sense of all is well. Pausing for a nano second I gather my thoughts as I push open the door.

The atmosphere is mixed, some visibly tense, others fearful but JW inpatient, he looks at me when I walk into the room and dismisses me as admin or cafeteria staff coming to refill the urn, focusing his attention on Rosie whose blond curls bounce as she walks across the room where she takes a seat in the corner. When I clear my throat to get everyone's attention JW demands to know where D R Monice is, looking at his solar powered watch he declares ' I haven't got all the time in the world'

I smile at the others in the room and clear my throat, the majority of them smile back nervously. Not sure where JW plans to go or what he needs to do but clearly with the rich some things never change even hanging on to the pretence of their own importance. He deserves to be ignored in a setup where all has crashed and electricity is the only reliable commodity dependable, with the loud mouth in front of me owning a huge chunk of it and thinks that will continue to be the case in the short future then yes by all means JW is free to feel very important.

I am Dr Richard Monice, the lead in the 0.5 partner programme. Pointing to the chairs arranged in a semi circle I invited people to sit down. I would like to welcome you. I say keeping an eye on JW, he records the fact I ignored him for now too overwhelmed by the fact I am full black no doubt. No surprise there, when was the last time you came across a black psychologist in the old UK talking less of present day London Sector one? rather rare like the Kooinon diamond a very precious commodity indeed but black I am and there we have it.

I launch straight into the house rules pointing out Jo Polston who is sitting in the corner will be taking minutes which will form the basis for feedback and summary of all discussed. I shall go through the motions so these newbie's do not smell a rat so to say. Rosie is present to offer immediate one to one should anyone get to that point of distress needing that level of input, this ability to talk and be detached I concentrate on, I look round the various faces attaching name to face from the database held based on the amount of blood on their collective hands. I assure all present it's a closed group no new personnel will be joining, the group will start and finish with the same six people present.

As a warm up exercise I ask them to pair up with the person seated to their right, each sharing three interesting facts about themselves with the stranger who will then introduce them. JW looks outraged and takes another look at his once expensive watch, the rubbish the rich hang on to! turning to his right he looks down his nose at the woman beside him with such disdain, staring at her like one would a bag of rubbish waiting to be collected by bin men, he tells her to start. I watch the two other couples talking politely, laying a foundation of sorts, bonding with a stranger who they believe has something in common with them. Politely calling people to attention mindful of JW's beady cold eyes on me, I ask the first couple to introduce themselves.

Adam introduces Susan, a 55 year old teacher who took early retirement to look after Tom her husband of the same age who suffered head injuries in a car crash leaving him totally dependent on others for all his needs with his speech limited to yes no and bizarrely the ability to sing the John Lennon song Imagine over and over. Susan misses the brilliant Mathematician she married. While Adam spoke Susan hung on to his every word, nodding along trying hard not to cry wringing her dainty handkerchief. I am not fooled by this show of femininity.

Susan takes up where Adam left off, 'this is Adam age 41 married to Maggie, Maggie is diagnosed with clinical depression, they met when Adam was 21, Adam got his first job in the same bank where Maggie a few years older was already an established successful banker, she took him under her wings they feel in love and married soon after. Maggie kept one secret from Adam fearing he would leave her; she played down the intensity of her depressive episodes. Maggie tried to commit suicide many times over the years some serious overdose requiring hospital admission some not so serious.

Fed up with her failed attempts Maggie jumped out of a fourth floor window of a nearby block of flats where she knew no one nor had any connection with other than the discovery from her office desk she could see this block of flats in the distance. She didn't die but the trauma to her body means nil speech, nil ability to care for self. I forgot to say Adam is a Judo double black belt. Susan and Adam smile at each other and the group, ice broken and ready to hear what others have to say. I nod at the next two ignoring JW knowing very well JW expected me to let him go next.

Sam takes up the conversation introducing Matt who is an electrician married to Tessa age 58 a former bus driver who suffered a stroke. Matt now lives with a woman he considers a total stranger, her personality so changed by the stroke resulting in intense aggressiveness who when frustrated by her restrictions such as poor mobility will turn that anger on herself, Matt or the house. Matt has had to call the police on several occasions. Tessa's stroke is the result of an unhealthy diet peppered with kebabs and other greasy wrap meals.

Matt picks up the thread 'It is my pleasure to introduce Sam who is 51, a surveyor married to Cindy an artist /photographer who was able to hide her mental health issues for a long time as she was often working away. Cindy has a diagnosis of Schizophrenia. Sam's world revolves around long hospital visits when Cindy is an inpatient. Unable to work as a surveyor Sam retrains as a security consultant pulling on the skills learnt when he was in the forces , his world now narrowed down to the few occasions he is able to work providing ex-naval seal officers via agencies for those needing movements between sectors who could afford the price, this way Sam copes with the loneliness of marriage without the regular presence of a partner.

Turning to Betty and JW I smile a cue, Betty rather than speak looks at JW who waves her on. This is JW Betty states, he's married to Wini who suffered a stroke and is now totally dependent on carers for all her needs. Her speech is limited to grunting and screaming which she does every waking moment. JW heads what is left of the family company, they have no children.

Clearing his throat JW begins to speak the American in him peeping out via his speech without him recognising it, Betty is 39 and married to Jim a jeweller who suffered head injuries during a raid at his store with catastrophic results of a brain bleed. Today Jim needs total care with frequent fits and communication limited blinking his eyes. Betty is able to work from time to time but this is few and far between, they have a fifteen year old son who lives with Betty's sister up in sector 14 so he can have a resemblance of a normal life. On this cheerful note this is us JW rounds up.

Thanking everyone for sharing I suggest a quick coffee and toilet break for 10 minutes then head out of the room, stopping next door to observe the group member I pop on the ear phones and tune in to each person's conversation, this is no run of the mill group each of the six participants have been identified as high risk making them very suitable for the work we have in mind, that We is the order of things in the year 2046 . Each of the six express delight and surprise; they have martial arts in common apart from sick spouses. As expected JW is stand offish and walks across to ask Rosie what else she does. Rosie confuses him with conversation around mindfulness, he gives her that look Psychologist can expect when they talk Psycho-babble.

I look at the six people of interest, I know not one of their partners will be alive in the next few hours which will tie in well with the four weeks which is the exact time needed to prepare them for what lies ahead. The world no longer has space for long term sickness, the system is constantly weeding these out, steadily quietly so as not to alarm the most ignorant of you. People die every day. The six about to die have the perfect cv to get past go. I will not second guess how they will react but everything works for the good of the nation. I double check everything is on track for Matt the oldest of the group at sixty to get the call his wife passed away five minutes before we are done with today's gathering.

    Walking back in the room I put people in two groups leaving it up to them who joined who, explaining the Hierarchy of Needs, I leave them to complete their triangle as a group and as individuals, walking quietly between the two groups I remind them of the purpose of the group their journey to where they are today, their current circumstances, the need to identify what self actualisation is for them and barriers. While the other five unsuspecting women and men think that and put pen to paper JW is uptight and spends too much time glaring at me, he can sense something is not right but can't at this point work out what it is. His body language is massively passive aggressive, I can see he's not yet sure how far he can push things.
    Two calls come in simultaneously, Matt gets a call to say Tessa passed away while Adam receives a text to head home as Maggie has deteriorated rapidly. Pointing out to the group this is one of the criteria for attending to have support in place before the end of life of their individual partners. As planned and hoped by me the group ends in a mixture of alarm, for some distress for others compassion.
    The arrogant JW tries to say something that would fit in with the tone of current events, while his actions showed he couldn't wait to get away, proven by the fact he was the first to leave. I gently reminded the group to look at what we've done today and think of how they want to incorporate them into everyday life. All six will snuff their partner's out if they could get away without being observed, their acts of concern don't fool me.
    Logging on BSSR system within a system which you have no knowledge of but most certainly has full knowledge of you, if you are a person of interest. Bringing up the information we hold on Matt I marvel at an electronic genius masquerading as an

electrician. A man who has worked for foreign governments who has designed and installed systems in Presidential offices, homes and maximum security bases.

His mobile tracking system used by Billionaires World Leaders, the excellent track record when the eldest son of the President of United States was kidnapped, not only was the location known within minutes he was quickly found in a crate on a cargo plane waited for takeoff to Russia at La Guardia, the entire drama lasted fifty five minutes without anyone outside the tight circle around the President knowing.

Matt's rap sheet reads like teflon, nothing sticks, a suspect in incidents and accidents associated with electronic malfunctions, plausible occurrences in everyday life, an exploding fridge that burned the house down is his first wife's grave, electronic malfunction of the car driven by his second wife on the motorway engulfing her in a massive fire ball ends that life before meeting Tessa. Matt had the common sense to move around Europe always abroad wherever each incident took place, returning but moving house regularly.

His business partners did not fare any better when boardroom politics reared its head, of the four partners, two are dead the only one alive is probably alive because he resigned, did not demand any money and moved to the then Country of South Africa. Ex-Army with his various self defence skills I am going to enjoy breaking Matt.

Flicking to Adam who spent time at Her Majesty's Feltham accommodation how he pulled things back together to go on to study and emerge with a degree in Accountancy baffles everyone but us. Running riot in his teens it was just a matter of time before he came to police attention, aggressive and ready to fight at any opportunity he maintains till today his friend had fallen over while drunk and hit his head on the pavement killing himself, as it couldn't be proven Adam was done for breaking the jaw of one security guard and leaving the other collecting disability allowance for a broken leg which Adam had snapped in three places, all for the sin of trying to break up the fight between Adam and his friends.

Years later we recovered a grainy video clip showing Adam first strangling his friend then shoving him backwards creating the head injury needed to cover his tracks all at the age of fifteen. Adam I am sure has no idea of the existence of the clip, next to that on the system is a clip of him while an army cadet before he was kicked out, always a sore loser.

2046 is a reminder of how things now work, just in case you are under illusions things will get better as the years roll on, think again. Let me put you in the picture. We now live in sectors and deal in counters. Starting with the population of England, drastic drop. Look for the disabled who are unable to contribute to the new world and you need to go underground to the very edge of the Isles created for them to live with any relative interested in supporting them, most relatives who tried this soon moved back into the sectors, their commitment and sentiments vanished, faced with the harsh terrain and isolation.

Allowed to live are the genies trapped in malfunctioning bodies. Note I said allowed to live.

Elderly homes no longer exist, children's wards are closed, no intake as modification has been made at the embryo stage, the sexes are well balanced, same number male female ratio born each year. Unemployment no longer exist there is no room for benefit claimants in the new order, cemeteries are no more, all get cremated no space to waste on rotten flesh with family ties kept to a minimum, once the child is on solid food they join the Crest were all children are assessed and put to training for what they excel at by the age of five based on ongoing assessments and observational studies from the moment of birth.

There is no immigration, we do not welcome or refuse it, travel is limited back to the top tier and for the benefit of the people rather than personal gratification, the cheap all inclusive droves heading to holiday destinations obsolete. What survived of each country has been on lockdown since the incident of 2038 that reshaped the world, with the usual weather forecasters getting it wrong with their conflicting report of hurricane, volcanic eruptions, meteor showers and several weeks of unexplained total darkness with the Sun's absence presumed on holiday, they failed to predict the unexplained sinkholes each the size of a county. The Atlantic, Indian, Arctic, Pacific Oceans folded into themselves initially reduced in size with the result continents were shifted closer, whole islands were lost, too many to count but then who is counting.

The worst affected is Europe who no longer have borders and who's waterways after causing severe flooding that took uncountable lives now lie nestled together a terrain totally changed. Sierra Leone nestles on top of French Guiana while Nigeria kisses the tip of Brazil. Canada has all its provinces shuffled like a card with Greenland now a mainland no longer isolated. Australia's Eastern tip sandwiches Madagascar with Malawi on the other side, I do hope you are getting the picture.

England is now reported an hour by sea from Canada only four men made it back and the nearest tip of New York a mere 25 minutes away has only been achieved twice in twelve years. I tell you this because it is what we want the crowd to believe. The truth is those who went either did not return or I suspect turned back at the first sign of trouble. None of those who returned brought back the various proofs asked for, either way they were dead within days of their return, the solution to a loose mouth.

Spain, France, Italy Greece and Turkey are all crushed into the top end of North Africa. Russia Mongolia, China continue to struggle, where the collapse took place a chunk of the central part of each country broke loose and swung back picking up countries like Japan, Philippines,Taiwan Malaysia, Indonesia, Papua New Guinea bringing them to rest in the Pacific Ocean finding itself in a hot climate with Bangladesh, Thailand, Cambodia and it's tropical weather a new neighbour, do you get the gist?

That one day in 2038 showed us we have not conquered nature or environment. The amount of death by drowning is what brought the declaration for all bodies to be cremated. No birth certificates, certainly no death certificates are issued. The useless things that paid accolades to wealth and affluence quickly went away, following the disasters the Third Race rose up to take on its purpose and commission that which was officially born in the 1950's but had since 1960 been quietly pushed.

I work, shape, supervise and serve the Third Race. Though the Third Race is in charge I am acknowledged as a director.

Away from the 0.5 work I am the fixer. Let me enlighten you about the third race. After the second world war the rich and privileged foreigners who travelled to the West for their studies realised they needed to do something so the world population no longer remained black or white.

If it was left to remain thus it is only a matter of time before the next holocaust this time on a bigger scale than what the Jews experienced, with African already cut up and controlled the wise fathers and elders who saw the warning got together and agreed the need to infiltrate the blood of the very people who see themselves as a superior race. Taking a gamble knowing even the most racist will hesitate to eradicate his own kin.

At the initial gathering were black men who all went on to become Presidents and Kings, the interesting thing was a few Asians were allowed to be part of this think tank. The idea is simple, create a third race that is a combination of us and them. Invest in that offspring's education ensures they understand the future so that at no time does the third race die out. Marriage and alliances must be carefully planned so that the third race is kept on the strict growth path needed to become a strong voice in the next hundred years.

Did this dream succeed? you bet it did big time for the blacks or else I won't be addressing you right now. The asians failed miserably, most had one child with a caucasian then scuttled back to their community. With no acknowledgement of the child and no investment in the education, the message got lost in translations as it was more of a novelty for newly arrived Asians to have a caucasian girlfriend the vision, drive and one off gora offspring they faded quickly.

The simplest instructions bore fruit. Every young black male and female had to date a non-black and must have at least one child, the mixed race child then married one of each race, ensuring neither reverted back to their previous full ethnicity. Leaving allowance for the diehard who would never even make friends with someone outside their culture such as our dear friends from what was once our famous shop in Welling Kent that was marched on, so for the likes of blond blue eyed Rosie there are a few exceptions or are there?

The quiet manner this was done is pretty staggering, each African returned to their country and encouraged what was seen as mixed relationships or mixed marriage, the mission though was marriage or no marriage get them pregnant, if they attempt a termination take them to court, the 3rd race already had the staff in place for any eventuality that might crop up. Millions of mixed race children were born all over the West, quietly welcomed, nurtured and tutored endlessly. Majority were allowed to school in the West up to age ten then sent back to motherland such as India, China and Africa for secondary school and training.

Returning to University in the West with one mission, disruption to the education of the opposition. As expected the men were able to keep the women out of education while the black women built to withstand that bit of extra load simply got on with the pregnancy graduating in their specialist fields, while their western counterparts were happy to be given social housing and benefits. Gradually the balance of power shifted like the sands of the Sahara quietly and unnoticed until it had encroached into the fibres' of society just like my journey.

Fish and chips, McDonalds, KFC, Fried rice munching me got the shock of my life when rather than stroll off to my local Crown Woods Secondary school as I had hoped because my parents seem modern and quite westernised, well instead of the twenty pounds a month pocket money I dreamt about I found myself at a boarding school in the homeland, a name it took me a year to pronounce properly. Lord what a day! Yet it took very little time to settle in as the clever elders had made provision for most of all we had back in the West.

The school is set in acres that made it seem we were in a settlement of our very own mimicked what we have today only we didn't know the vision then. Apart from a few tears we were all so busy watching programmes like friends, league football, comedy open mic the first week felt like a holiday camp. One night during dinner it was simply announced school proper will be starting tomorrow am. Wake up alarm is 05.30hrs. For the first time I felt uneasy, very uneasy. I didn't bother with the TV or movies on offer. I was in bed by 20.00hrs.

A ringing no different from a fire alarm began, the noise so loud it cut through your nerves, the ensuing panic is something to behold, I sat up in bed quickly pulled my tracksuit on, wasting no time I quickly wore my trainers and followed the mad crowd jostling to get out of the dormitories. It is dark with no sign yet of the dawn to come, following the person in front of me I pushed and shoved like the best of them. People are already in tears, some are shouting and babbling away in panic and still the alarm rings on and on. As we poured out into open ground I saw an unbelievable sight in my eleven years of age.

It seemed there were several thousand people all jogging in a clockwise direction. Pouring out to the field we joined the mass of bodies and still the ringing continues then just like that it stopped, that first day I tried to prepare myself for the alarm and tried to figure out why it went off, the only thing I noticed is once the final bodies had joined the slow jog and we looked like a slow moving galaxy the alarm stopped.

At various intervals stood people I will later label minders, in the middle of the field stood the instructor who from time to time would shout out change directions or instructions such as left, right, newbie's like me simply copied what the older boys and girls did. In this manner we spent two hours staggering and sweating. Those who had run out in flimsy wear initially crying about the chill now moaning about not having enough material on them to absorb their sweat. This was the norm for seven years, Monday to Saturday two hours of exercise at dawn with everyone quickly realising the faster we get onto the field the sooner the alarm is silenced. Breakfast followed at 08.15hrs with everyone in their classrooms at 09.00hrs.

The education itself was strange with a mixture of world and homeland history approach combined, without us noticing we were gradually split up. By the age of fourteen I was in a class with only a dozen others. At some point we stopped bothering with Western television as entertainment, mainly watching the news and meaningful events happening around the world. In the classroom we learnt all that was expected of us, outside the classroom was a different matter.

The focus activity during my first year was martial arts, this was not learning the basics, three hours every afternoon was devoted to this activity. I learnt dexterities I had no idea was possible. I built up upper and lower body strength that by the end of the 1st year when combats took place in the dark I had developed a third eye and inner ear that helped me to locate opponents no matter where they stood or how quiet they thought they were.

I fought hard with some inner warning system always on to remind me nil room for failure. Over time some of the opponents who lost had simply disappeared while others assumed they had been moved elsewhere. I knew there was another explanation for their disappearance though I was unable to articulate this at age eleven.

The following year saw a shift to the intense studies of animals, identification of, locations specification, uses, pros and cons. Usefulness and understanding animal life. Dissecting or recognising unattached body parts. Tracking, trapping, preparing storage and transporting. We travelled wide and far. This was the only period a few of us returned to the UK during the summer holiday. We stayed in farms in Minehead and Exmouth roaming Exmoor and Dartmoor homing our skills, living off the land with minimal instruments or instructions, some seeing it as fun adventure but I knew better.

We learnt to ride horses bareback, drive a pony and cart, outrun a pony and cart, plan a route and arrive ahead of the horse and rider. Build makeshift water ramps to cross streams, handle knives and shooting rifles with confidence yet were firmly told this was simply survival not military training. By the end of summer I could trap kill skin and remove all evidence of the kill restoring the area to how nature presented it. Age 14 I was able to go for three days without any form of nutrition if needed.

Returning to studies saw an unhealthy focus on plants, we travelled extensively that year moving around the homeland spending time in specific locations with tutors, all local uneducated but with a knowledge that would make any western pharmaceutical giant dance naked in the rain with glee. With the aid of interpreters we learnt, we mixed, we located and identified what each was used for, the contra indications, the amounts, the methods and where to find the plants, we harvested and dried seeds we would identify and describe without seeing.

We ate them, mixed them with water, used them as food, sedatives, cures and to maine. We spent weeks in the middle of nowhere, digging, plucking and learning how to breed and cultivate. We learnt which plants provided us with essentials like food, we marvelled at all the west thought it knew when it knew nothing. The rain forest region people knew the most, I felt like a walking encyclopaedia of plants and animals. Studies towards GCSE continued alongside martial arts. In-house we were taught about the plants in the West.

In my fourth year we were taught survival, land, water, heat, cold, mixed weather like the deserts. Water living took place, we stayed on water for endless periods until each of us experienced land sickness, something we had never heard about. We learnt to understand currents, tell the time by the ebb and flow, meet all our needs in and on water. Not all fish and things in the sea are edible is an understatement. The fear of sea snakes keeps me alert, these slim swimming vipers are only interested in dangling feet, many lost their lives this way, I only had to be warned once.

We learnt to dive and spear fish staying underwater for long periods, and no we have not developed gills. Try not to let your imagination run away with you! This is serious stuff. From avoiding death by sea snake to digging myself in sand for the night to stop me freezing to death in the desert breathing through a bamboo pole the same as you see people do in water.

That summer we were brought back to Europe taken to Chirinda in the middle of nowhere in Russia surrounded by snow and not much else we continued the survival training under the guise of summer holiday the locals were none the wiser. Everyday an expectation to use skills learnt to acquire even more in areas that initially looked bleak but teemed with animals and plants which I was ready to identify and state their usefulness. By now I knew there was a mission and hoped very much I would qualify. A total no-no is emotional attachments, we worked, lived and learned alongside our female counterparts while both parties remained a-sexual.

GCSE year brought a focus on electronics, pulling apart, rebuilding, learning the elements, making communication instruments from scratch, learning to improvise. Building solar panels. Mixing modern and old learning the morse code and on a laughable level the local communication systems wherever we were. This year was a mixture of communication modes. Learning to send water based messages with natural plants that grew on the water side, sending each uprooted plant downstream added up to communication like we were standing next to each other.

Rock messages legible only to those who know what to look for and how to read it, tree messages seemly animal scratches on tree trunks, leaves and branches bent and knotted by the wind meaningless to some clear instructions to me and my fellow learners. In this manner we all sat our GCSE examinations with every single person in my cohort landing A+ in all ten subjects.

Sixth form saw a change in my group, by being attentive I was able to see the skill mix, everyone has a statement of future studies we now had just about everything represented from engineers, builders, town planners, electronic experts, medics in the sense of first aiders who were just that bit too skilful to be just first aiders. Plant, Environment and animal leads, Infection experts and nutrition guides. The ones that knocked me for six are the diagnostic giants. By feeling you looking at various parts of your body they arrived at accurate diagnoses that were confirmed by specialist doctors every single time.

Those two years were spent consolidating all we had been taught. With everyone heading back to England the last week of August we quickly realised each group will be attending the same University, finally the evening before departure the lead of each group was announced, I made it as the lead for Canterbury University, we are heading home.

Seven years is a long time to be away. I left Witherston Heights as a child and returned as an adult skilled beyond my age. The few days spent at home were not easy I was restless bored, wired and needed to be doing something meaningful, when my dad suggested I mow the lawn I approached the task like one in a drug induced coma that is until I bent to check there was no obstructions under the blades and saw the plant message, I wondered if the years in the homeland had induced an illness but no....message was there before my eyes the instruction was clear Chislehurst Caves at 13.00hrs. I said nothing to my dad and destroyed the plant formation as taught letting the plant return to its natural way. Suddenly mowing became a pleasure with me on the lookout for any other instruction.

Arriving in Chislehurst above the bungalow building declaring Caves and Cafe open was the second instruction fashioned out of the low hanging branch and leaves of the innocent tree at the back of the building, to the untrained eye was a tangle of foliage, to me it stated proceed to the cave with the bunk bed sleeping display, standing behind the rope looking at the display not sure what to expect is another message in the sand at the foot of the woman holding a baby while appearing to be talking to a man.

Again nothing of interest unless you are looking for it and able to make sense of what looks like an ordinary hard floor with some loose sand. With instructions to keep my lamp on the right side I slowly follow the crowd, in the middle of caves that had algae and water marks from previous centuries, the next message stares at me pointing me in the direction of the flintknapper, in the grainy ceiling of this I find the next instruction, heading to the echo chambers there are people stationed all along waiting for the experience of how dark it gets in the caves with instruction to all remain where we choose to stand and switch off our lights I read the final message which looks like luminous nothing on the ceiling.

There are fourteen of us leads present there if we read the message right. Make no contact, do not acknowledge each other. Await further instructions and with that I complete the rest of the tour, nil new messages or instructions. I love the affirmation. It feels good. If folks were more alert they would have wondered why there were fourteen young men on the tour none of whom appeared to know each other as could be expected in a group tour, really someone should ask themselves since when did Chislehurst caves become so popular with young black men.

Time leap forward with me receiving several messages on some days and nil on others. One of the most enlightening occasions was meeting friends of my Dad who smiled patted me on the back stating 'you are one of us we have all confidence in you' if that is not confirmation and validation of my position I have no idea what is. In the period between getting ready for University and the actual departure I attended a lot of functions at social clubs, function halls, parties, church gatherings and nightclubs, not once did I ignore an instruction. Within moments of arrival my contact will make themselves known. The night before my birthday I got instructions to prepare for my first impregnation.

Late afternoon I was directed to a part of town I am unfamiliar with, walking through Battersea park I waited for my next instruction, looking around me I see the message on the footpath telling me to have a seat at the park bench, no sooner did I do so that a blond woman with a small dog join me, her conversation confused me as it lacked intelligence or at least the sort I am used to, as per instruction I talked with her and accepted her invitation to coffee as we headed towards the road, she lives across the park and within minutes we are not having coffee but sex, it is strange I knew what to do.

Once done I wash and leave heading back to the park as instructed , a new instruction lite up as I walk along, a woman approaches in the distance, 'destroy specimen' still visible as I trip her up drag her into the undergrowth breaking her neck in the same effortless way, I am back on the path and on a bus heading back across the bridge in minutes. The last instruction before I got on the bus was to get a haircut and shave. I jumped off the bus in Edgware road, once grooming was completed I headed home to depart for my digs in the morning.

My first sexual encounter and instructed killing experience was nothing significant to waste time thinking about.

Kent is an interesting place to study my focus the first few weeks was to identify brethren with message and signs guiding me towards each individual and those before me leaving a path to follow using forums such as international students evening we quickly gel, quietly and in a friendly manner asking if folks wanted to change rooms portraying noisy dwellers we were able to acquire one wing to ourselves. We quickly settled into a routine, starting the day at 05.30hrs as taught we put in two hours of exercise, outsiders who tried to join soon dropped out.

Some cited they found it odd we didn't speak, just exercised. A deadline of three months to get our drivers license had us all scribbling for driving lessons, every single one of us met that target with the majority purchasing a car immediately. I am pumped.

Each member joined the gym every evening Monday to Friday. An hour and half was spent on material arts again those who showed an interest hung out with us briefly then moved on. For the exercise and Martial arts there was no visible leader. We simply got on with things as instructed once finished each went its separate way, the discipline installed never far.

Every other weekend was spent in animal plant and survival skills with the ignorant folks referring to the exercise as 'going for a ramble' the other two weekends we headed to areas the instructions identified with the words 'Plant' these were usually to nightclubs, discos, parties, wine bars and occasionally pubs popular with students. Here we planted sometimes each sleeping with as many as six women before the evening is over.

If you are racist or uncomfortable with who you are you might feel intimidated at the sight of several dozen young men all suited and booted. This never lasts long, with us nil drugs, nil alcohol, just a bunch of studious law abiding young people focused on our education and the answer to your prayers as suitable partners for your child. Shortly after the first quarter we were given instructions to begin planting in Kent, starting in Tunbridge Wells we moved swiftly through areas such as Tenterden, New Romney, Deal, Dover, Felixstowe, Margate, Broadstairs, Canterbury, Whitstable, Faversham, Isle of Sheppey, the Kent Downs, Ashford, Sittingbourne, Maidstone the list over the three years four months at University is endless.

We studied and obeyed successfully littering Kent countryside with our sires. The instructions were the same but different in the numbers you were set to achieve, I was given a number of between ninety to ninety-five, the logistic meant a lot of night club attendance this was the easiest route as the local girls were delighted to be rumbling with students from prestigious universities, at the end of my studies I had successfully fathered a hundred and five children, babies were born it seemed every few days with no alarm raised as the carriers are spread evenly up and down the Kent countryside, as taught I kept meticulous records of whoever contacted me to say they were carrying my child.

By begging them not to end the pregnancy encouraging them to proceed with the help of the state which was more than ready to help girls who couldn't keep their legs together, providing them with money, housing and whatever else was felt they were entitled to. With no recommendation needed for the fathers presence the children were registered with my name but not my attendance. Playing the poor student image I gave each the same sub story of my parents mustn't find out yet. Of the number of women eighteen were University students like me, it was a success and building brick towards our aim to create a second tier of educated but non-professional women who having messed up would follow my guidance to educate their child to the hilt.

The icing on the cake were those who had two children stupidly focused on having the same dad for them now they've started. To the naked eyes these were reckless days, to those of us in the know mission on track, it was not all rosy many a times the message will be to take out a female who was beginning to ask too many questions or fancied themselves detective because of the explosion of bio-cultural children, knowing there is a dependent child did not make any difference I simply presented myself confirmed I am the daddy and asked Social Services for help while I completed my studies.

The children are quickly placed into foster care, for English grandparents an unwanted problem out of sight, occasionally a sentimental couple will rear their heads the death of one of them quickly shifted the attention away from the 'give me my grandchild scenario' the soft knock and opening of the door snaps me out of my remembrance.

Rosie comes in and informs me Cindy has been located in sector three the area of Hereford to Shropshire hills, I give the nod for the elimination to go ahead adding Sam should be notified immediately of the discovery of his wife's body with the cremation taking place tonight, adding Tom Jim and Winifred's death should follow in the next eight hours. These will be much easier as it requires administration of relaxant into the IV lines used to administer medication, all three will simply go to sleep peacefully. That message to bring things forward was written clearly on the side of JW's car for me to receive on his arrival.

Pulling my coat on I make my way out marvelling at the sight that greets me never sure how my forbearers knew things would change on this magnitude I stand looking at the terrain the water lapping up to what used to be five ways on the A20 the beginning of the sectors or London as it was formally known. Movies in the past have shown great desolation the reality today is the opposite it would seem the earth and its original content land and sea wanted to return to their previous form, sick to death of man pushing water back to build ridiculous self indulgent edifice the land protested at the constant vibration digging and dynamiting both elements decided to push back at mankind at the same time. A man-made disaster totally avoidable if we had lived peacefully with nature.

I remember the instructions to begin to move inland specifying the middle belt.

With the meticulous record keeping it was easy to see to this, the children I had created and ensured I kept in touch with, the house prices in London and its surroundings made the step on the property ladder almost impossible so selling the idea and the uptake of it required very little effort. In my forties I remain unmarried, not sure what I would do with a wife if I was instructed to acquire one. One instruction I did follow to the letter is the propagation, per annum on average I sired one hundred and sixty to a hundred and seventy two children.

Each of us chosen for the third race project achieved the objectives set year after year. Choosing carefully and getting the balance of professional intelligent highly educated women and the riff raff local babes who in the future would be used in the everyday manual functions when there is no longer a demand for hair, nail and tanning salons.

I kept information on each and encouraged regular communication and friendship without face to face contact. With the help of the old whatsapp I kept in touch with the offsprings, sending the same message to all a message of friendship, encouragement and focus on an identified useful career. All listened grateful to have an identity that set them apart from those whose fathers did not want to know them nor hid the fact.

The act of making sure they married the required other was more tricky but again the need for identity made it easy with the subtle hint of what I would like to see each individual while steering them away from being too white or returning to full blackness. From time to time a white combination will give birth to a child dark as the night, with blacks giving birth to blond blue eyed, there are no accusations of affairs, we all knew and accepted at one point most now had black blood.

In the distance lay the empty abandoned homes and skyline of London, the landscape changing continuously no guarantee the buildings semi submerged in water will be there at sundown, the water levels remain stable but land shift activities continue deep under the water. Some days whole areas will resurface covered in mussels and other crustaceans. On these occasions those foolish enough continue to row out to this silent world, hoping to recover what I have no idea and don't care, many regularly don't make it back.

Based on the current knowledge of each sector submitted England has been shaved back on all sides leaving the middle strip we occupy, now who would have thought it possible. Do not get any wild ideas about strange creatures coming out of the deep. It's nothing of the sort; those daft things only happen in the movies. Whole communities and cultures died together the same way they insisted on living together, not mixing, not moving further afield all clustered in the same postcode.

That amazing London shopper's paradise multicultural stew pot vanished overnight, the nearest to a new capital starts and spreads from the edge of Sidcup bypass with the former

Chislehurst School for Girls the new headquarters and residence for the Royals and top previous government personal that survived, they like to put on the same show but behind closed doors know who is now running things and recognise their total dependence on us.

    The master plan taught and engrained in our mind is the same worldwide. The building up and stockpiling of tinned essentials started a decade ago under the guise of the Asian corner shop and Afro-Caribbean shops, canned salted and dry goods were ordered and stored for my sector, with Leeds Castle providing the perfect location, every five years the entire stock was quietly rotated and sold with fresh stock put in place.

    Every single space is now occupied by those of us lucky to be left behind, there is no overcrowding with each sector broken down a to z in zones, each zone has people in place making it a check and balance system between the third race with no one disrupting the order of things and events. Food and other materials are shared out according to what you deserve or have contributed, it is no longer a world of people wandering in and out of supermarkets consuming and consuming. Everyone gets a meal a day with nursing mothers and young children eating three times a day. The biggest pleasure I get is seeing the reward of all the planning that went into place.

    Think of essential staff, the third race makes up 95 percent of the personnel. The top tier of doctors, dentists, surgeons, heart specialists, orthopaedic experts are 99 percent from the third race. The middle tier of farmers and growers, rearers of livestock, controllers and distributors of nutrition to each sector is a 30 percent representation of the third race in the driving seat, years spent at Agricultural Universities, knowledge gained put to use, nothing or new events frazzling those who have been prepared all their life.

    The bottom tier is made up of the lookie lookie generation, those who had grown up looking on while their parents collected benefits for every event in their life nil contribution to society other than production of baby after baby after baby. In the new England as we no longer say United Kingdom these are the manual folks cleaning, cooking, running errands, rebuilding, learning new skills finally doing more than sucking the air and waiting to collect benefits.

We no longer have prisons, all those who survived and remained in the prison walls were simply served their first and last meal of castor oil seed laden bread and milk. In the remaining middle belt over two hundred thousand people were quietly got rid of. Who was to protest, no one was looking for their relatives in prison too preoccupied with their own survival. In this manner valuable space to house people was freed up and down the country.

JW's name remains known as his commodity Electricity production was not too badly affected. With no safe reliable gas work everything has reverted back to electric, surrounded by water we have no problem generating it. All the petrol and diesel cars dismantled now line the coast packed and weighed down with rocks to act as a breaker should the water levels rise.

There is no currency exchange, all the gold and diamonds hoarded by the rich are not fit for purpose, no one is selling and none are buying. At the first sign of rebellion folks are taken to the water edge, put in a boat and set adrift; it soon corrects the foolishness of other minds. Some of our BNP and British League friends who made it across in the chaos tried to get something going, this quickly pitted out into quiet acceptance and real fear when it dawned on them they really are the outsiders and a minority in their views and beliefs. After all the numbers for them are low while the third race accounts for huge numbers.

People are free to move around the sectors utilising the vehicles that leave twice a day making it easy for us to monitor movements, most venture out and return quickly as they have no right to food or lodgings outside their sector provision. One look at the fragile landscape and a witness to sudden sinkholes soon puts an end to bravado and foolish wanderlust.

Taylors sew endlessly, the amount of clothing you are entitled to like food depends on your output and contribution, builders check and carry out repairs during daylight hours, when water levels appear stable and areas are identifiable those in the know expert divers go out together and retrieve tools in work buildings bring back valuable metal tools. Fishing boats do not stray far from shore testimony to witnessing boats at arm's length away unable to return to shore, twisted and bashed about by currents we still do not understand.

In the current climate food is plentiful, the genetic modification allowing simple crops like cabbage to remain fresh for three years as long as it remains in the soil. Animals are carefully reared with one strain of cow dedicated to producing fatty meat. In the first wave of panic dogs, cats, rats, snakes, giant lizards kept as pets all vanished if it moved. It was quickly used as nutrition until we stepped in and brought order. The no pet rule was not really needed as most had eaten them in the face of hunger and uncertainty.

Our Asian counterparts played ball while the Chinese amongst us needed nudging in the right direction, if you live in England you had to be a part of the new regime to try to be anything else simply put you at risk, those who had got the foolish idea of behaving like the Maroons in the history of far flung places like the Caribbean soon wised up to the danger that surrounds them, loneliness and isolation the best corrective teachers.

The new era is the electric era, gas remains unsafe and unreliable with many lives lost in the early days with uncontrolled surges followed by explosions. Travel between sectors remains based on the electric charge of the cars and vans available.

For survival and continuity of the programme people are matched up and encouraged to reproduce; they are given dates and times to ensure each year we have arrivals of new infants within a two week period unlike the chaos that previously reigned with people getting pregnant willy nelly. If you are not pregnant in the three month programme you are removed and returned to the specialist list until deemed suitable for another cycle when the time comes.

Life now has meaning. Babies are born round the clock over that fortnight period, the baby receivers then have approximately just over five months before the next surge of arrivals. All mothers express milk which is then stored centrally with no child dropping below their birth weight or needing formula which is in precious little supply.

Electricity has meant we have been able to listen in on the outside world, if they are also listening in on our conversations we have no means yet of knowing how other areas are fairing but round the clock we have a designated team sending out messages as well as trying to make sense of the conversations they pick up, I know others survived if they followed the programme the way we did each continent will have its third race in place and all the personnel and expertise needed to take things forward.

It gladdens me to tell you the new age for extermination is sixty eight for men sixty-five for women who like Trojan horses are hard working disease and problem free up to the date they are sent to live on the Isle, a distant cluster of land no one had returned from to give a report. It is sold to them as the next tier in the new order of life. As there are no intimate ties folks simply get on the boat quarterly and set sail. Occasionally there are repeated sightings of fire burning in the distance that looks like domestic fire, this line of belief is encouraged. I know it is nothing of the sort, more likely the gas explosions we experienced in the early days are still rearing itself.

I hear Rosie before I see her, my listening homed to perfection over years of training, this woman is the nearest thing to me having feelings, she is my first shire, as her mother had only an eight black blood I wasn't surprised Rosie is born blond but thankfully brown eyed, the current success with the breeding programme lies in her suggestion of exchanging those of childbearing age with other sectors and vice versa it also meant in-breeding by accident has so far not happened with the meticulous records kept by each sector and the central holdings which is in sector one.

Rosie does not speak, her presence confirms all activities have taken place successfully, I now have six grief stricken but no partner ties people I need. It is time to go over the information we hold on them that makes them perfect for the work at hand.

Returning to my office I pull out my keyboard marvelling at how quickly man adapts faced with situations that require immediate adjustments. The biggest bonus is the reliable supply of electricity, this means we still have TV though it shows all the programmes stored on the central system.

For now there are no new programmes, all repeats ,nor is there a choice, we have one channel which is interrupted only to insert read only news which is strictly warning sent in from other areas, a sudden land shift or sink hole appearance are newsworthy, otherwise folks are watching programmes through the ages.

BETTY

Pulling up 39 year old Betty's information I sat back to reread, born to a lesbian couple she studied natural medicine, her first few relationships were with women until she met Jim and moved down South to be with him, he encouraged her to follow her dream of Architecture and accepted her dual sexuality. During and after her return to University Betty did well to hide her other persona, the call girl lifestyle, a very beautiful woman with thick auburn hair she made hundreds of thousands of pounds each year tax free via sugar daddy website links often telling Jim she is away on study related activities abroad. Guzzling the finest wine and champagne meant her body cried out for the excesses when home leading to an alcohol dependency she hid and managed well. Her career pathways smooth with fast promotion supported by the fact she gave both sexes what they demanded.

Jim, a ridiculous six pack all toned fit man, just hit the bathroom floor giving himself a hefty whack on the head courtesy of the marble flooring and suffered a cerebrovascular bleed. Six days in a coma, time quickly brought home the fact the stroke he suffered has taken away all functioning activities leaving a cabbage of a man to call a partner. This did not deter Betty from her lifestyle, courting, escorting world leaders, senators, members of parliament and anyone with wealth remained amongst her clientele.

Betty became a serious concern when the special branch clocked up the fact that she was sleeping with top officials from

America, Russia, Syria, Iraq and other heads of European Countries. Taken in by special branch she agrees to wear a complete set of diamond jewellery, the necklace hid a full functioning video camera with the earring and rings voice activated listening devices the best and virtually undetectable.

During her active years Betty collected valuable information that released, would have all the various countries going to immediate war against each other with the first casualty being Betty the collector as she was nicknamed by special branch. Super power security, trade, monetary secret alliances were all recorded. During this period Betty was given five solid years of combat training as she continued to appear in the midst of rich powerful men who are all drawn to beautiful women. Giving the impression of average intelligence and keeping her mouth shut several thousand hours of recording was made via her trademark jewellery. Seen as a high class hooker by the world powers she never needed to use her combat training.

She was decommissioned when she met and married Jim, though she was no longer gathering information for the government she continued her lifestyle when able, her personal best remaining sleeping with six men in one day, during a world superpower meeting in Vienna , quite something! walking away with over eleven million dollars just spreading her legs in the finest hotels in Vienna. Money meant the best. Betty was able to pay for the best of health care, often disappearing to Switzerland for a working week that included a full health check.

Nothing about her presentation today would remotely make you think she is anything other than the suffering wife of a 0.5. Betty's knowledge of natural medicine and architecture plus her dual sexuality would be invaluable in the not too distant future. Apart from petty issues such as riding the then London underground without a ticket there is very little in terms of a criminal record.

MATT & Batt

Minimising Betty's information I pull Matt's up. Impossible to read about one without the other hence notes sit together as they are so intertwined. Age six Matt is pulling apart portable radios and other electronic devices reassembling them without instruction or ability to explain his skill. Matt was repairing larger units such as TV fridges, microwaves and cookers by the time he was eight. Age ten he rigged up the electric supply so his family paid nil bills to date wiring things up in such a manner the entire street paid a slight increase on their bill that was never questioned. Years later he explained he simply rotated the home paying each week without fail.

Matt in year seven at school made friends with Batt's who went on to be known as the HYM murderer. Between Batt's sick fascination for exploding small creatures in the microwave and Matt's ability to quickly repair them their friendship lasted a seven year period before Matt's family emigrated to the USA in that period most small animals in that area vanished with the local pet shops questioning the endless purchase of rabbits birds and kittens. Batts parents died when he was in his early twenties with him making headlines at the age of twenty seven for what was labelled the HYM murders.

To understand Matt you need to know Batts.

Batts, a sadomasochist is responsible for the death on record of fourteen homeless young men targeted around the Trafalgar square area offered shelter and possibility of a job at the breakers yard in Erith where Batts worked. Batts greed lead to his downfall, he allowed the young men to use his address claiming housing benefit for renting one room, this money was paid with checks done continuous on an annual basis by which time the young person had long disappeared, when they didn't turn up for interviews and contact was made with Batts he stated they had moved on a plausible enough respond.

Evidence of the presence of the young men cohabiting with Batts was found but no body, it is believed he crushed these bodies with the scrap metal cars sent to various parts of the world as metal. The scrap yard gave blood, brain tissue, body fluid and various bits of organs as proof the missing people were once there in the investigations that followed but yielded no bodies.

Batts was convicted on the evidence of the one that got away, a young man from the back streets of Bradford who had fallen out with his family while visiting relatives in Birmingham travelled down to London on the spur of the moment, missed the last train and settled in to spend the night wandering the bright lights of West end was mistaken for homeless by Batts and invited home, thinking fast on his heels he agreed and jumped on the night fifty three bus.

Arriving at the house he is given a cheesy pasta meal to eat while Batts jumped in the shower the bitter taste of the cheese put the young man off after a few mouthful, scraping the rest in the bin he washed the plated and was asleep on the settee from the effects of the few mouthful he ate.
Waking up an hour later to find himself naked and locked in a mental cage in the middle of a basement having watched enough gruesome films he knew he was in deep trouble hoping the man had taken it for granted he ate the entire food laced with sedatives thus would expect him to be unconscious for several hours, he quietly and quickly worked the lock on the box. Batts first mistake was not padlocking the box confident in his tried and trusted method.
Standing up from the confines of the box the pain hit the young man, seeing the dry blood that had dried down his leg his first thought was he had been sexually assaulted but touching himself he quickly realised the mad man who had offered him a room is totally insane as he had cut off the haemoid that clustered round his back passage testimony to his refusal to waste time eating vegetables and roughage as advised in his younger days. Pulling his clothes on and using a wad of cotton wool to catch any further bleeding he heads quietly upstairs armed with a baseball bat.
The first blow dislocated Batts shoulder and certainly woke him up. The next blows rained down making it clear he was in real trouble, quickly negotiating to give the young man all the money he had on him apologising and crying with promises never to repeat the incident and stressing it's the first time, he hands over close to three thousand pounds as a further blow that knocked him unconscious the young man dresses quickly and lets himself out of the house.
In the early hours of the morning he was back on the night bus heading into the city and was at London Victoria train station for the first train to Birmingham. Ironically it was this same morning

Matt arrived from the USA for a surprise visit, when he got no reply from his numerous phone calls he heads over to Batt's letting himself in with the key hidden in the window ledge, within minutes he had called an ambulance, at Greenwich Hospital the story was Batt's was mugged not realising how serious it was had gone home.

Within days of his discharge he told Matt the true nature of what happened to him, such was the rage of these two in the remaining ten days of Matt's visit from the United States two women and three male met their death at the hands of this duo, with the microwaves now bigger and of industrial wattage there was a constant aroma of roast dinner from the property. These were then taken to the breaker yard in cool boxes.

The revenge deaths and the pleasure of having his friend around appeared to appease Batt's who after Matt returned to the States quietly returned to room letting until seven years later a vigilant benefit officer expressed concern about the yearly tenants who simply vanished and didn't reappear in another part of the country as would be expected. The benefits fraud investigation team rigged up a camera in the house opposite, nothing of interest was gathered until a new officer suggested looking at three years worth of surveillance as one rather than nothing to report each year. Watching the tapes on a fast forward showed the young men clearly spent about six weeks in the property each year then they disappeared, in between there were other young men mostly arriving at night but never exiting the house.

Things quickly unravelled after this. Batt's loyalty to Matt is something to behold, up until the incident he maintained he had always acted on his own. Matt's name and their friendship during their youth remains on the record. A few years in prison Batts told a new cellmate of Matt's visit and the victims used to appease his rage at the time. Matt's response of course put this down as the rant of a mad man encouraging the police investigative contact to ask if he was involved in the killings that occurred why had Batts kept quiet. Had the police been more proactive and looked into Matt's affairs since that period it would or should quickly uncover behind the facade of marriage and dedication to

Tessa lies a sadomasochist voyager whose first wife's death can only come from a horror magazine.

MATT

Matt met his first wife Lori just after he graduated, head hunted by IBM he was sent for further training having been spotted and monitored during his last year at University for suitability to join the elite team of genius who were the real defence system, a small collection of electronic wizards who worked for the American government but their names never appears on official paper. This core group lived in a twilight zone, if America was friendly with your country these guys were used by your Presidents and the Billionaires who could certainly afford their fees for private work.

Many are the children of world leaders who were put to sleep, operated on via the oesophageal with trackers implanted deep within the chest cavity using high tech materials that mimicked the bone structure and did not set off metal dictators nor stand out in x-rays meaning their parents slept well, very well indeed.

On the down side many are the men and women in the top five percent of power and money that divorced each other based on the same tracking system, planted on spouses to expose fidelity.

At sixty Matt has the body and build of a thirty five year old male, still looking in his prime he has none of the flabbiness or health complaints of men his age, the last female the lead sent to entice and sleep with Matt reported he was physically very fit, no slowing down once he got her in bed, it needed the excuse of needing to take a pee for her to get away from his constant attention.

With Tessa his wife who had grown grossly obese as a side effect of all the medication cocktail needed to keep another cerebral vascular accident at bay and the mobility that no longer allowed her to do the circuit training she enjoyed so much one wonders if the aggression towards Matt is the knowledge she knows he's screwing around. Tessa with her upper body strength developed from years of driving a bus packs a mean punch when she is able to land one on Matt something she would not have thought about and not dared if she knew the circumstances around the death of Matt's wives, at least number one wife Lori's death was quick.

Lori with her beautiful petite figure and peachy complexion tugged men's heart wherever she went. She had that effect that made every man want to do something to make her smile, protect her, please her and make her comfortable, all without her saying a single word. Lori had a gentle nature and never imagined the horror that awaited her at the hands of a man she fell head over hills in lust and love with. It started slowly buying her toys to try out grooming her until she began to accept his taste and let her guard down even when she felt uncomfortable such was her need for Matt she ignored the warning signs. Matt the predator kept his sadistic other self under wraps until the last seventy two hours of Lori's life.

A wealthy woman in her own rights Lori's business of hospital dry goods supply meant a very comfortable lifestyle with a Country home an hour's drive from New York. Here they spent weekends with friends alternating which friends they invited. Her crowd were more quiet, wanting to relax and do cultured things like poetry reading or a violinist to play after dinner while Matt's friends played the car key game, had sex all over the house and made enough noise to wake the dead up.

Gradually Lori began to prefer Matt's crowd, convinced by all it was such a lovely time together. Her friends alarmed by the Lori's who now isolated herself from them and had very little conversation to share when they did manage to see her apart from the latest kinky going on's, having tried their best to reason with Lori and be a part of her life they eventually gave up, none of them had ever like the Englishman as they referred to Matt even though he had lived in the States for a decade he is still considered a foreigner.

Lori gave Matt the American hold and control he craved, with their combined earnings they wanted for nothing and moved freely in the social circles they wished as to be expected of a man like Matt behaving himself at home meant a need for release, should anyone care to investigate their country home held nothing less that the corpse of eleven female and two male, the male unfortunately each time accepted a lift from the respectable looking man driving a very expensive car, his offer to drop them off further along the route they want as it will be dark soon, if he can drop by home to pick up his credit cards sounded innocent enough, until once they got in the house which again was easy enough once they saw the property, except none ever left.

The last guest he took back had been tiresome taking unnecessarily long to die in the water tank he has specially for that purpose, taking sick pleasure in the fact his future house guests are bathing in water tinged with the last dying moments of a nameless faceless being. Matt enjoyed the water tank, it was easy to relax his victims talking about his age pushing home he is older then he looks, talking about nonexistent physical difficulties and aches soon appealed to the compassionate nature of most. Driving into the garage which like the gates once closed sealed you in, Matt accessed the house through the connecting workroom linked to the garage.

Once inside the house he would point as he disappeared making a show of saying 'feel free, I feel safe with you' help yourself to a drink, the guest bathroom is that way and head upstairs. It didn't matter which small bottle of water or juice the person chose, they were laid out on the floor within minutes of a sip. Matt took great care to inject through the top of the drinks no one ever suspected the drinks had been tampered with after all they unscrewed the bottle breaking the security seal themself.

Matt, having undressed, simply took the unsuspecting person and dumped them in the water tank, the freezing water and short acting life of Rohypnol soon revived them. The sadistic devil Matt simply sat there staring at his victim while they struggled and begged for their life, totally mesmerised by the victims last moments, something about drowning excited him, the way the body loses its fight and slips effortlessly under the water.

Matt would watch while the body floated gently round for anything up to several hours. He would then use the hook he kept specially for this, hooking the body to the side he would lift the body out without any difficulties, a plus in the manner he carefully chose his victims, he hauled the body, taking the clothing off, he would smother the body in honey, then let himself out the side gate.

Thus begins a five mile hike to his favourite site, comfortable in the knowledge his nearest neighbour in any direction is twelve miles away and like him are city dwellers who may not have time to visit their property in years.

Matt had chanced upon the giant ant hill while out learning the terrain years earlier, he had nearly become dinner to a young bear himself, making a rapid u-turn when he came upon the bear he had just enough time to see the bear was tearing bits off the anthill. That very moment he decided to return daily to leave a chunk of meat at the base of the ant hill to his delight each time he returned to check the meat had been devoured. The perfect place to leave his victim once he was finished with them. Not once did he ever find the bones of the bodies he left on the ant hill, not even telltale dark ground soaked with blood. L

Like all good things once mastered Matt quickly lost interest. The only benefactor from his acts is Lori who foolishly thought the rampant sexual sessions was a sign Matt had missed her when she's away. Had she an inkling his arousal was based on the length of time it took each victim to die Lori may have had a different reaction to the barrage of sex.

Matt simply tired of Lori, unlike those who would separate and divorce Matt used his electronic brain to bring things to a permanent end. Booking business trip to Washington several months ahead, on one of his return from their country home, having loved her beyond her senses and left her sleeping soundly ensuring she drank way too much alcohol, Matt rigs the shower, loosening the electric wire ensuring it is exposed slightly touching the metal waiting for the final ingredient to make it beyond deadly. Knowing your partner's habits helps, unlike him who would run a shower before stepping in Lori runs the shower while under the water having set the temperature.

Kissing her bye he drives to the airport knowing by the time he lands in DC he will need to return straight home to what is left standing of their house, he is not expecting there to be much body parts to bury.

Bad things and times go smoothly, Matt's name is announced as the plane taxis to the terminal, making himself known as requested, the cabin supervisor take him aside to say there has been a horrible blast at his home address, he is needed back in

New York, they are unable to say if anyone was in the house at the time of the blast, no body identified in the fire. Matt returns to New York on the same flight, using the turnaround time to cancel appointments, all the while crying beautifully and frantically calling Lori's number, calling their fuck buddies to ask if they've seen or heard from her, strange thing as they only get together during their self satisfaction parties.

Minute body parts fragments of teeth and ribcage are the identifying pieces that someone was in the house at the time of the blast, the icing on the cake is the thirty million life insurance policy settlement he received, within eighteen months Matt has wound up his affairs, spending a week hiking in the grounds around the property, sighting no signs of human bone goes ahead and sells the carcass of a property a tidy sum of seven hundred thousand dollars, Matt moves to Washington, the pain of his loss cited as the reason to move base.

Connie, his second wife suffered a worse fate, a buyer for a major men's wear outlet she travelled in and out of the United States at a dizzy rate as required by her job. She had a lot of bonus for Matt to want her, an only child whose parents died well before Matt came on the scene. Connie had married young and divorced young. With no man to clutter her life she rose to the pinnacle of her career and held sway there, her choice of buys dictating men's wear for that season without the men realising it.

Connie had friends in high places on the international scene, as would be expected of someone of her nature; she was a very private person who collected assets the way one collected shoes, a multi-millionaire in her own right, a mixture of inheritance and good investment.

As with Lori it was the English accent that got her, heard in the most unexpected of places at a food shack in the park, the conversation and confusion was around pop or soda meaning soft drink, asking if she could be of assistance she pointed out depending where you are in the states all fizzy soft drinks is referred to as either pop or soda, having ordered his bitter lemon he engaged Connie in conversation and the rest is history. It doesn't matter how much single people say they are fine on their own, along comes someone who reminds them of their loneliness and bam a relationship kicks in.

Connie was easy, lost in the conversation about various corners of the world; she enjoys Matt's accent and Englishness; she agrees to dinner. When he takes her to Ambar, an Eastern European restaurant in Capitol Hill, she is impressed no end that he had been listening when they had spoken about favourite food. On that first date she decided Matt will be a safe bet, after all the English men are portrayed as gentle folks, she is smitten by the end of the first month again the fact he works in the corridor of power giving her a false sense of well being.

Financially she has no concerns not once asking herself why he would leave his online banking page open while he pours her a drink. Believing she has met an equal she falls hopelessly in love, sex with an English man is not bad. The love of parents and that inbuilt radar parents have which enables them to warn their child 'you are with a lunatic' is not available in Connie's case.

The sprawling mansion in Alexandria a mere twenty six minutes drive from DC is home, the flat Matt is renting is easily given up after six weeks of not staying there, Connie's suggestion. With them staying in her property in the area popularly known as Chevy Chase neighbourhood Matt fits in well in his opulent surroundings. Matt is careful to ensure they live a quiet life, holidaying abroad or at home depending on what Connie wants. Matt makes love to her twice a day like clockwork, at the weekends he continues his ministry, slowly testing the water, not introducing his taste to Connie. One weekend he made love to her six times and watched her reaction of shock and concern she might not be able to keep up with him, this not being a norm for her.

At that moment Matt knew he had made a terrible mistake, he couldn't imagine spending life having regular sex, if Connie knew the sort of in-vivo images he pulled up to enable him to get an erection in order to touch her she would run a mile. One night he gently attempted to enter her from behind, Connie was quick to move and correct him about the wrong hole, that one single incident sealed her fate. The nearest to kinky Connie came was the two of them slipping into the water tank in the loft ignoring the Jacuzzi or small pool, holding her and supporting her weight he made love to her, this is the only brief moment he would feel the real him steering.

Connie spoils things when she insists on emptying the tank and refilling, the thought of free swimming semen too much for the mild mannered Connie.

The next day Matt began a recon of the house and its ground, what was there that would give Connie a death that would raise no suspicion, they had been married three years when Matt decided on how Connie will exit the world. While Connie lived in blissful thoughts of her husband whose physical need for her had not diminished, a man that was happy to join her for a few days on some of her trips, who smiled at her first thing in the morning and told her he couldn't imagine life without her before they slept, 'I love you' always the last words she heard as she drifted off.

Nothing in his behaviour gave Connie concern, if she called he answered, she knew his movements and delighted he didn't hide any facts about himself, freely leaving his mobile phone laying around the house and giving her his computer access number when away a ruse he wanted her to check some details for him.

Encouraging Connie to take a few days off, they spend that time visiting favourite restaurants, movies with long walks in and around places of interest. Matt books a work trip to Kuwait to update systems he had installed for one of the Billionaire families there. He will be away for four days over Easter, Connie is due to fly out to Hong Kong two days after him. Connie's death would need no equipment or electronic work. The night before he departs Matt cooks her the traditional roast English dinner with side additions like cheesy cabbage, caramelised parsnips, Connie ate her fill, topping up with Matt's homemade apple pie and vanilla custard all nicely washed down with glass after glass of wine. Such was her pleasure she didn't notice her husband hardly drank.

By the time dinner is cleared away she is merry and loose, quickly agreeing to Matt's suggestion of making love in the water tank she giggles her way to the bedroom to return naked to the stair access where a naked and visibly excited Matt is waiting. Matt's heavy breathing is mistaken for excitement by Connie.

Lifting Connie in the coldness of the water sobers Connie slightly, swimming around she waits for Matt to join her and stupidly asks him if they are going to make love in darkness when he drags the cover of the tank across.

Matt leaves a small space for light to penetrate through knowing Connie will naturally swim towards the light, he uses the expanding walking stick he bought for this purpose to prod her back when she comes to the side all the time the tank is filling having being turned on manually, Connie does not like the new game and says so, fear not kicking in until she realises she is having to tread water to keep her head above a water level that has kept rising. Matt simply stayed silent, his only response to poke her with the hook to stop her each time she tried to climb out of the little opening.

Three years of bliss flash through Connie's mind, she pledges to understand what she has done, what has changed, what she can do to make things right. She speaks love, she gets angry, threatens, Matt simply pushes her back in the water where she has been sick several times, probably from sheer fright, when he is happy with the level he turns the manual switch off. Connie is getting distressed, the coolness of the water making her weak, her fear making her panic and the silence of the man who claims to love her deafening. With no neighbours to hear the commotion she's making Connie realises she is in deep trouble and begins to pray out loud, this finally gets a reaction.

Matt speaks as if Connie is not there, he talks of his childhood, his adventures with Batt. Moving to the States, work, meeting Lori and the pleasure of Lori's death. Connie fell into his lap when he wasn't looking. The horror of being married to a woman who thinks sex is a man on top of you gyrating away. The frustration of no pleasure in almost four years, the need to wrap up this chapter, move on and find a likely minded partner. The promises that poured from Connie's mouth fell on deaf ears.

It took four hours for Connie to die, such was her determination to talk her way out of the situation in the end the coldness of the water and fatigue took their toil. Matt removes the cover and lets out water until it's back at the level expected, he then wipes his print off the manual tap, with that done he watches the floating body for a while.

Four hours later he calls Connie mobile just before takeoff and leaves the usual bull shit message of loving and missing her. This time there will be no phone call to ask him to return home, in forty eight hours he will make a call to the police and ask them to do a welfare check on his wife, concerned she hasn't answered the phone.

As with simple uncomplicated plans it all goes smoothly, the Police asked the usual questions which Matt answered honestly, yes we regularly made love in the water tank, occasionally she goes up on her own for a dip, time of death is estimated somewhere late morning of my departure, a verdict of accidental death is recorded. Matt being Matt remains in DC for another three years, loaded in money terms he carefully plans his return to England, he has enough money to retire.

Arriving back in England he finds the lack of structure to his day crippling, within a month he quickly enrols on an electrician course and finds work with a leading Electrical firm. Matt meets Tessa at one of the adults-only private parties in the Kent countryside. She is feisty and kinky and matches Matt's energy and drive to take things to the next level, agreeing to choke and other strange sexual practices that would have the average person calling the police and pressing charges. Matt has found his soul mate. Her work as a bus driver meant she had upper body strength that enabled her to hang suspended for their strange games longer than you or I would last before crashing to the ground.

Whenever Matt made new suggestions she happily went along, often bringing home unsuspecting individuals who found themselves faced with an angry man, quickly agreeing to allow him to join in the fun. Fun that regularly required some to seek hospital treatment, still Matt manages to stay under the radar of the police or concerned citizens with those who had crossed his path preferring to distance themselves, too embarrassed to make a formal complaint. The fact Tessa spread like butter did not make a difference until she had a stroke two years ago. If there is a trigger for Matt to return to killing it is an aggressive woman, stroke or no stroke, well now he no longer needs to worry about getting rid of Tessa. I have taken care of that for the bigger picture that is about to emerge.

SUSAN

Changing the screen I pull Susan's file up, Susan who has a shell of a man who's only ability after a nasty car crash is to sing the words of 'Imagine' over and over. All activities of daily living needed doing for him. An IT specialist who recognised in her teens the world was going to be made small via computer keyboards also acquired record keeping skills before deciding to train as a medic. The change of direction came at a time when those around her were beginning to ask if she was alright, noticing her vagueness from time to time. With a new background in health Susan finally finds a word for what is wrong with her, self medicates and hides her psychosis well from the outside world. Tom and her had been married for 20 years before the accident that turned him into a 0.5.

Susan is significant to the programme because of her multiple skills, the down side of course her mental instability if she doesn't get access to the maintenance dose of Modecate her body must have on a monthly basis. Newer drugs have not worked for her, just this low dose of 25mgs monthly. I am aware she has stock piled enough ampoules yet continues to use the hospital supply. A restless patient who once barged into the clinical room just as she was about to inject herself in the thigh did not get a chance to say what he saw, encouraging him to come in she trips him, landing fully on his face his head bouncing off the tiled floor he lasts seventy two hours in ITU before life support is switched off, her secret safe.

Susan who was brought up in care, the long term foster placement has no idea the long line of schizophrenic forbearers she comes from, each time adoption was tried the couples who took her on soon returned her, a destructive child it was clear there is something unpleasantly different about little Susan. Late teens with the deadly combination of drugs and alcohol playing a part, comes the age old question: what came first the voices or the substance misuse? One of seven siblings none of whom she is aware of Susan was lucky with the Lawton family who took her in. She was neither loved warmly nor treated coldly, they were paid to look after her and gave her a decent enough childhood.

The first time Susan heard a voice she was alone at home lying on the floor in her bedroom watching TV, the voice was loud and clear 'don't go to work tomorrow' she rolled over and looked out the hallway, no one was there, thinking it was a fluke she carried on watching the fashion program that is a must for all seventeen year olds. It is Friday night and she is looking forward to her Saturday job at the local post office, her job was to look after the greeting card section and ensure the main areas are clean and tidy, topping up the various forms members of public helped themselves to not bothered if they left half a dozen lying on the ground.

Brushing her teeth while half asleep that night she heard the voice again ' don't travel' looking around she shrugs it off as picking up conversation others were having.

That Saturday the post office was robbed resulting in several members of staff needing hospital treatment from being pistol whipped and the public who were waiting to buy stamps traumatised. For her troubles in going to work Susan was punched in the face and thrown unceremoniously into the boxes that contained her stock.

As she laid there having being doubly incontinent and heard the voice loud and clear, 'I told you not to come to work, if you will let me I will look after you and keep you safe from now on, just remain lying where you are they will not touch you again' curled in the foetus position she stayed thus for what seemed like hours in reality the robbery took six minutes. The male voice who became her guardian angel took up permanent residency with Susan that day.

She did not share his presence with others as instructed by him but guided her he did. What to eat when to eat, when not to eat, who to talk to, which way to seat, who not to talk to, who to avoid, when to sleep, when to be on watch, which drinks and food are safe which is poisoned who poisoned it what poison was used, who loves her, who hates her and wants her dead. What to wear, when to wash, if the water is safe, who is watching her, who plans to hurt her, who is trying to take away her soul and on and on it goes.

Subtle at the beginning the quiet voice of reasoning in the background. Susan appreciated the food advice the most, on the tubby side she found herself losing a few pounds without even trying all on the advice of the kind voice that only had her wellbeing at heart.

Approaching her final exams in sixth form she glided through while others panicked, told when to study and when to sleep Susan followed instructions to the letter, waking sleeping, going to lectures studying, eating, mixing with others always under the say so of the voice. With no vested interest in her the Lawton's let her get on with her routine after all it didn't disturb anyone and she was no problem really. Because of the voice Susan recovered quickly from the post office incident, the five thousand pounds compensation she put in an ISA account as advised by the voice.

Without adverts being placed in the local newspapers to announce a job vacancy the voice guided Susan to the local library, when she enquired she was not only told there was a job going as the post office incident was well publicised Susan was offered a job there and then by the well meaning manager Stuart who would later be Susan's first victim.

Susan passed with flying colours and was told which University to apply to, by now Susan would quietly ask the voice a question and wait for an answer, as she is not animated nor speaks out loud those around her put her behaviour down to vagueness. The day Susan turned eighteen the praises started, ' you are beautiful, special, chosen for an amazing future' the change these praises brought was overnight. Susan walked tall, her confidence soared, out of nowhere her language changed, her spoken English like one who had been privately educated, she dressed smart chic but conservative and stood out for all the right reasons, Susan blossomed under the tutelage of the voice.

The first clash with the voice came when social services enquire, now eighteen, if she is interested in making contact with her birth parents; they have a duty to support her and provide all the assistance she needs. The voice told Susan not to look for her parents, with her new found confidence it felt right and Susan was slightly irritated, for a few days the voice stayed silent, this didn't bother Susan who was up to her eyeballs with information released by the adoption agency, to her disappointment there was no letter on file waiting to be given to her at the age of eighteen, but she learnt her father lived in Bermondsey and her mother in Beckenham.

That they are separated did not bother her as when both were contacted they said they would like to meet her. The option of meeting at a contact centre was turned down by both, the meeting to see her birth father was to take place at his flat. Her link social worker would accompany her with the provision for counselling put in place should Susan need it.

The voice continues to guide Susan in everyday matters but falls silent whenever her parents are mentioned. The process of setting up meetings with both parents took a matter of weeks, Susan was told her parents' health is delicate. How delicate they are would hit Susan like an arrow between the brows. On the faithful day of meeting her dad, the voice started at six in the morning ' you don't have to do this, there is still time to change your mind, the outcome will not be good, it will make you sad, they are not people you want to meet, they are beneath you, they will hurt you, your life is in danger, you are going to be hurt and I won't help you if you don't listen to me'

By two that afternoon when they are in the car heading to their destination the voice is ranting, loud and angry almost incoherent. Susan has a headache that is so bad she sees lights swim in front of her eyes, the social worker puts it down to the stress of the moment. The voice warned Susan all the way in the lift then fell silent the moment they rang the bell to her dad's flat.

The door was opened by a toothless old man who Susan wondered if by chance is her grandfather or an elderly relative. Pulling his dressing gown close underneath a pyjama pair that didn't match, the toothless grin invited them in, passing him he smelt old slightly malodorous, now in the sitting room is a middle aged rather attractive man, they all sit down, all the while Susan continues smiling warmly at him.

The social worker speaks first shall we all introduce ourselves, the untidy old man's voice comes from somewhere far away, Susan shifts in her chair to look at him, did she just hear what she thought he said' hello love I am Kevin, my mates call me Kev, I'm your dad love' and him here is Terry me social worker to be here for me like meeting you after a long time as it is'

Susan manages to shut her mouth as nothing comes out each time she opens it, she catches the two workers exchanging glances. Finally she asks 'what happened, why were you unable to keep me'

Kev speaks of how he met Nicole, Susan's mum at the Olde Rose and Crown in Greenwich, they got together but it was difficult times, she worked as a cleaner and while he was a kitchen assistant at the local hospital. There was also a small problem with the drink, it's the reason why we couldn't keep you, you were taken away the minute you were born, you had too much alcohol in you from your mum's drinking. We couldn't look after you, it was the same with all the other seven children whisked away by Social the moment they were born.

The social worker got an order from the court that meant your mum had to have her tubes tied. We loved each other we did but the drink, it does funny things to you, you wouldn't believe I'm forty eight years old would you love, I feel eighty, I've lost all me kids, my home until they gave me this flat, I lost three of me toes from frostbite when sleeping rough, I ain't been too lucky love but I have you now, maybe my luck will change. I can't stop drinking love but I don't drink as much as I used to. Susan just stared at him unsure what to say.

Kev continues, I was twenty and your mum was twenty four when we got together, we had a baby every year it seemed, I guess each time they took one away she simply got pregnant again within three or four months. She's lovely, your mum, everyone likes her, you look like her, so beautiful. We lost touch when she went to some place in the country for a detox, they said she shouldn't come back to the same area. I moved around a bit me-self.

Tell me love, can I get you a cup of tea? I smile a yes please, while he's moving round in the kitchen, I look round me, what a horrid place, cigarette butts over flowing, the ceiling dark from the constant smoke, the place looked like it needed to be cleared out and everything started again, I note with disgust the way the carpet stuck slightly to my shoe, looking at the carpet I wonder how this man Kev can live like this.

If this is the long term outcome of drugs and alcohol I concur. I can't wait to get away from here, I have seen enough. Kev comes back in with a mug, his hand trembling, anxiety or withdrawal. I take the dishwater looking tea, steadying the mug. I feel slim underneath the mug and wonder how I will drink this without throwing up. Bringing the mug to my mouth I place my bottom lip inside the mug thus avoiding open lips to the rim. It was not a bad cup of tea but the environment made me feel sick then angry, embarrassment and other emotions like regret.

As expected because of my distress the voice came, comforting reassuring me I can get through this meeting as it will be a one off. The voice told me the right things to say resulting in Kev and the two social workers tearing up, telling me what a wonderful special person I am.

I have no idea what I said simply repeated what the voice said to say. I looked at the prune faced man sitting next to me and wanted to put my fist through his face. How dare you not do something meaningful and constructive with your life, how dare you spend your life drinking and stoned out of your mind while others work hustle and feel stress to bring food to the table for their families while you live in a haze of the next can of cider. I cannot possibly be related to this repulsive man, I look at him long and hard and thankfully see nothing to visibly link me to him.

I need to leave, forty minutes of small talk is enough, he can't remember anything meaningful, can't tell me about extended relatives, his parents or his childhood memories, the alcohol has scrambled his ability to recollect events, to hide the fact he is struggling to remember my name he calls me 'love' Departing I give him a hug and inform him I am going away to University so he may not see me for a while.

Back home I stand under the shower. How can that wreck of a human being be my father? Christ! what an earth is the mother going to look like. Best to get it over and done with I think a week later as I head to Beckenham with the same social worker who softly warned me my birth mum may not communicate much if she is having a bad day. I wanted to laugh out loud on a bad day, I have had a bad day since I met Kev.

We drive into the grounds of a beautiful home a stone throw from the old asylum. A typical nursing home has butter colour walls and flower prints framed pictures to hide the smell of disinfectant. We are led into a conservatory where a woman who unfortunately looks like me is led out, I mean looks like me when I am in my late seventies. Dressed in one of those awful nylon easy wash dresses with daisy flowers she ambles towards us, smiles sweetly at me but says nothing.

We sat down to the tea and biscuits provided, this is even worse than I imagined at least Kev could talk, Nicola is a carcass of years of serious self abuse or victim at the hands of those who encouraged her to drink and take drugs. In front of me is a woman who is in worse shape compared with Kev, she is here but no one is home. Not a word out of her, just the occasional smile from eyes that did not connect with anything in particular.

The person supporting her shared she had been knocked over by a car while drunk and had hit her head on the kerb during her last alcohol binge five years ago, as a result of the injuries to her brain she now needs care round the clock, as if to validate the point the lady had just made, my mother was incontinent of faeces, or maybe it is her normal toilet routine but the smell enveloped all four of us as the nurse asked to be excused to help my mum clean up.

When they returned ten minutes later I was ready to leave. I look at my mum for a long time, tow years older than Kev, what a bloody waste, why should the state use my taxes from my Saturday job to look after my birth parents, what have they done for the country, why should people destroy their own lives and then be supported. I feel nothing for the two foolish selfish weak waste of space individuals that brought me into the world.

In the background is the comforting voice, gently telling me I will not turn out like this, not under its watch, not with its guidance. I smile sweetly at my birth-mum, she smiles back with vacant eyes, then finally says something meaningful ' where are my little ones? I have no answer. Walking out of that home I fantasise about becoming a powerful person in government, I will make it tough for those who use drugs and alcohol, they will not receive priority and will need to sober up or starve, the state certainly won't maintain the habit for them.

Well I have had a glimpse at the two individuals that are responsible for my arrival here on earth. The wish to be responsible for their departure crossed my mind. I don't want any clown turning up when I am successful to embarrass me. That is why I have written six letters, all the same one for each of my siblings if when they turn eighteen they get the foolish notion to find me. I do not want to be found, the only other information in the letters is to warn them their parents are a waste of space not worth the bother of seeing them. Having packed my stuff ready for departure the following morning to begin my University studies I feel restless, my inside is churning with anger, I tremble and shiver with something, a mixture of anger, aggression and the need for a violent act. I put my coat on and step out.

A typical early October evening I walk towards New Eltham train station turning right to walk past the library I see Stuart my old boss is locking up for the night, I stand for a moment as the voice quietly but clearly tells me to start crying, standing where I was I let the tears flow as Stuart finally finishes what he is doing and walks towards me where I stand on the footpath, my instructions are clear let him comfort you, lead him into the park beyond the children's playground.

Recognising me Stuart is all concerned switching into gear I babble about meeting my birth parents and how badly it's gone all the while moving in the direction of the park. Stuart falls into step with me, the park is quiet as I talk and he makes all the right noises, once past the kiddie area I keep to the left ignoring the open field as instructed by the voice still talking and crying.

I walk towards the rail track area I seat down by the embankment, Stuart is suggesting he takes me for a coffee while I talk, assuring him I just need some fresh air, could we remain for a few minutes I listen attentively to the voice who is telling me to move round and angle myself in a certain manner to Stuart.

Stuart a tiny build man who time left behind, his youth spent trying to avoid being bullied, his adult life spent looking after his parents never having left home nor left the shores of England, the yearly holiday destination of Bude in Devon, his specialist trade looking after books, with his balding hair and inability to relax from nerves he is a target whether you are looking for him or not, Stuart is surplus to requirement in the world.

Bending down as if to adjust my shoes secure in the knowledge the voice promised me immense strength I picked Stuart up and fling him high and in the foliage direction indicated by the voice and stroll away, Stuart never made a noise too surprised to react. As I walk away I hear the low rumble of the train and the swish as it passes back. I walk up to five ways down the road to Mottingham train station up back to the high street and home. Stuart's body was discovered in the morning by the track maintenance men, his death was recorded as suicide and a story recounting his sorry life made page six of the local news.

Me... I felt awesome, unstoppable, I had picked up a man and tossed him like a sack of spuds, the train driver hadn't realised it hit a human assuming it was the usual urban fox on the track. I am beginning to like the special treats the voice brings. For a brief moment I toyed with the idea of going to Bermondsey getting rid of another spud bag, the voice quietly tells me unlike the park there is close circuit tv at the entrance of the block of flats. I briefly wondered what Stuart had done to deserve being killed, the voice explained Stuart is a substitute for my father and that was that, chapter closed, wow, I love voice.

ADAM

Closing Susan's file I pull up Adam's details. Adam is what is called calculating, a young man who went looking for older women who had what he wanted, money, money and power in abundance is Adam's only interest. A product of ardent poverty where meat meant spam and a treat is a knob of butter in the mashed potato. Adam the only one able to read and write in his family left Ireland as soon as he was able with money in his pocket given to him when he threatened to expose what goes on in the church, plus a larger amount stolen over the years strapped safely to his body, at the time he headed to mainland England and the bright lights of London he already had one adult murder under his belt having killed more souls than he cared to consider and knew he would end up a mass murderer of fathers and nuns if he didn't migrate.

Adam hated being Irish and worked hard like a man driven to tone down his accent, in later years paying good money to a voice coach. Adam's biggest fear in life was that a member of his family would show up on his doorstep if they managed to find their way off the island to ensure he was never found he took on the surname of his wife effectively making it impossible to find him, still for a while he insisted they moved accommodation every few years.

Adam's earliest memories are of him feeling miserable and cold with a permanent hungry belly and being handled roughly, every year a new addition joined the squalid mess called home, a harp hazard lean-to that gave the appearance it would be swept away by the wind at any moment, stifling hot in summer, cold arctic conditions in the winter with the steady constant unchanging diet of gammon, cabbage and spuds. Many a night he laid there as a young boy listening to his father's drunken return and the pained words of his mother hushing him trying to delay the demand for sex pleading the children might still be awake feel on deaf ears.

Adam's hatred for his father knew no bounds as he dipped into a world of fantasy centred around the atrocities he would commit if he could get away with it. All the children bore the brunt of their father's uselessness while their mother scrapped to put the never ending potato cabbage and gammon boil on the table. The discomfort at night of two adults and eleven children sleeping in the same room farting and coughing throughout the night kept Adam awake, as he grew older listening to the nightly tussles of his parents he took an early interest in female anatomy.

No local lass his age was safe from him, his show me yours I'll show you mine game with the end threat of if you tell anyone I'll kill you stopped the young girls from speaking out. As time went on Adam realised that it is the male genitalia that excited him because something about it made him feel powerful, comparing sizes cupping the balls and weighing the size became normal, while his friends all participated they soon lost interest and moved on, not Adam, his non resistance to the hugs from the reverend fathers soon lead to him becoming a favourite child, after confessions he was given the task of helping to tidy up followed by a meal, all the time hugged and fondled to the contentment of both parties.

The beatings at home and lack of nourishment meant Adam was happy to spend his days in the church environment bringing him in contact with books, helping to count the offerings that led to his love for accountancy, money meant power, shelter, food and water. Adams presence in the church fold did not go unnoticed by the nuns and they wanted their equal share. There is clearly something that takes the excitement to new heights when the act is prohibited. By the age of fifteen Adam has the body of an Adonis, heavy, slim and hung in all the right places, when not studying or being pleased by the Fathers he is satisfying the Nuns.

Adam is unsure when his murderous rage begins to build but at the age of sixteen he was chosen to escort a group of Nuns for a trip to London, believing it was for a church attendance he is unprepared when the coach stops. A total of thirty three nuns got off the coach and filed into the building which consists of three floors high with a basement. There are no religious artefacts to indicate it's a Christian hostel but there are a lot of Italian's not sure if they are nuns also. Each nun came with a small bag of clothing essentials and were quickly assigned six to a room. Called down to the basement where he suddenly realised is a clinic, walking down the corridor lined with trolleys of women in various states of stupor. Handing over the letter the Padre gave me, the door swings open and Adam catches a glimpse of legs wide open in stirrups with a man standing between the legs and nurses doing various things.

Taken into a side room, quick wash and dress in a loose top and trousers. Directed into the large room there are four cubicles each with a black hard narrow leather bed with a female on it her back legs spread with someone busy between each leg and nurses helping quietly. Taking a closer look, I see a female private part for the first time in broad daylight. I am disgusted by this quite ugly feature, it reminded me of the rats we see in the rat catchers bucket. I am positioned and focused to observe closely. Trying to keep the bile down I make an effort to pay attention picking up a tub like metal contraption I watch as it's inserted and then widened, faced with the pink inside of a female, I retch.

What am I doing here in a hospital, why is it okay for me to be in a room with women whose insides are being displayed unceremoniously, I am spoken to harshly and told to concentrate on what I was there to learn, I was unaware I was on a learning trip. Looking down the tube like structure in place I see a closed up opening that looked like a tube opening, taking what looked like a crochet needle handed to him by the nurse the man gently inserts it into the opening, each time rotating it slightly as the flesh separated and widened the slow trickle of blood began, at this point I must have passed out having never come into contact with female related blood.

Opening my eyes I get off the floor, I have been ignored when I slumped. Straightening up I see the man remove the instrument and shove a wad of cotton wool in place under the woman, I am shocked to see she is awake, crying softly without making a noise, I will never forget her face, gracias she said, gracias and then began to recite Hail Mary. I don't understand my emotions, I feel fear, anger, the need to break something or someone but I keep myself in check what will become of me if the Fathers and Nuns ban me, I have been sent to learn something important, hopefully it might be something I can use as leverage one day.

The two days spent in the nameless and addressless clinic in London was spent watching and learning to familiarise myself with the tube like instrument and the crochet needle, my feet ached and my brain numbed itself as I lost count of the number of women who came spread their legs had a crochet needle used on them. When told to step in and do what I had been shown I was so desensitised I repeated what I had seen done more than seventeen times and was praised for my ability. I was shown how to feel the lower part of the stomach and as long as I couldn't feel a lump near the belly button I was told to go ahead with the clear instructions anytime I could feel a lump the person had to come to the mainland.

Thus I was trained over a four day period to become an abortionist, a minor, no medical background, couldn't even pronounce the name of the tube like instrument but I could duplicate what I had being shown without any difficulties, on that trip was born a child killer a readymade way out for wayward female or victims like me who were not allowed or couldn't keep their pants on. If there is hell I am surely going there.

With nil experience of the world I was unable to interpret the other things I saw thinking the sisters and nuns were there for medical check up, years later when I understood the church frowned on abortions and it was not available unless the mothers health is in danger I realised that on that trip at least some of the terminations done on that trip were my creation. Yet from that Thursday to Sunday when we departed back for Ireland I knew I was coming back to London, walking around mindful to go straight and then cross the road to walk back the same way I marvelled at the availability of food and drinks, but I could also see the signs above the pub doors, no Irish no blacks no dogs. Unless I spoke you couldn't tell I was Irish but better safe than sorry I simply walked and looked.

This was a different world to my world of hunger, cold, probing tugging hands that wanted their needs met and the mouth odour of the fathers and nuns, that unique bad breath will stay with me for life. It was while I was in London that I realised I had become dependent on the fine wine the fathers drank and shared with me. Eating without the wine I was unable to get comfortable afterwards with cramps waking me up repeatedly. Walking to the bay window I looked at the building across the road, an innocent building blending in yet with hoards of young women from Italy and Ireland, there must be anything up to seventy people in that building with minibuses arriving and picking up throughout the day.

Standing at the window in the building opposite where I was housed I try to make sense of my life so far, finding nothing meaningful except the achievement of literacy, nothing much to celebrate between the age of one to five, by age six I am an altar boy, correction the favourite altar boy by the age of seven I am staying between the vicarage and the convent, during the day while learning I am at the mercy of the fathers and at night meeting the needs of the eager nuns, meals were accompanied with fine wines.

While Ireland starved the church was our equivalent of a royal family, they ate the best dressed the best and wore jewellery such chains and rings with precious stones that took your breath away all done under the guise of religion. I was introduced to speed at the age of 9, rub a little in your gum and energy abounds. An off white colour powder with a bitter taste encouraged me, explaining without the small amount each morning they wouldn't have the stamina to get through their chores or days, try sleeping at night I thought.

The fall from grace with the fathers was a slow progression. By the age of eleven I was spending more time with the nuns than them, with the rush of hormones' and the overnight changes to my body I thought the fathers would appreciate me more but no they preferred me young. They couldn't get rid of me totally so occasionally I would be tolerated to ensure I remained in the loop I made sure they observed me play their play with the younger boys and participate fully in the seat on my lap scenarios, befriending and encouraging the favourite boys of the fathers so that they would want me around. Age sixteen I got my London training. Between that age and turning eighteen I crochet an average of sixteen women a month, significantly reducing the costs and need for mainland travel.

The anger that started to build up close to nine years suddenly surfaced one afternoon while crocheting a woman I deliberately poked round and severed the large blood vessels I had been warned to stay clear of. It was a nun who was holier than thou and had often been cruel and demanding of me, never a kind word and using me like I was put on earth for her pleasure at night, smelly breathe with a beard I used to pray for a quick end to any encounter I had with her, well that prayer like many went unanswered.

What a nation an entire body of people who made you go to confession and make up for sins you hadn't committed, who had more children than they could care for turning a blind eye to the cruelty going on in the church. That month I deliberately caused three deaths, each bleeding to death during the night and were buried before sunrise just like they never existed.

My first abuser was next, by now the most reverend holy father was in his late years and there was talk of him retiring and going to live some place. I knew he would simply find new little lads to take my place, yet not sure when I made the decision he had to die. Getting a small supply of speed was not a problem. Joining him one night without being asked I rubbed his legs not interfering with his activity with the latest little chap, when the little chap feel asleep I moved him to the small cot bed across the room, taking out the small paper wrap of speed I stand looking with disgust at the father his mouth gaping open he snores softly, his thin hair white as snow but it's his teeth that fascinate me, yellow with age and years of red wine consumption.

Tipping the powder into the side of his mouth rather than on the tongue he doesn't stir, getting a thin pillow with my left hand I shove my hand under his neck while bring my right hand over his neck from the opposite direction, I lean in and use all my strength to pull backwards in one swift movement breaking his neck without a whimper from him, opening a bottle of wine I shove the bottle down his throat, holding him upright slightly to ensure the as much of the wine went down I gently lower him down on the floor, pour a generous amount of wine on his lower face and neck, arranging the bottle goblet I leave the room, the little lad has not once stirred.

What a tragedy, the whole of Ireland is in mourning, his grace has died peacefully in his sleep, non spoke of finding him dead on the floor or the obvious drunken state which may have led to a fall during the night. All the important people came to Ireland for the burial. You could easily believe it was a saint that had died, not a dirty old man who for years subjected a generation to his vile appetite. The next death was my father's, nothing drastic. I simply waited one night as he rolled home drunk as a fart, all I did was step out of the dark, trip him up and disappear as quickly to the sound of his skull bouncing off the cobblestones.

I had been stealing from the collection for a long time, little sums that over a five year period had added up. Counting up I put a Two hundred and eighty pounds in a cloth tied it up and while giving the impression I was making sure the house was secure as we left for the funeral I looped back and put the money under the mattress. The haggard drained woman called mother would use it wisely to improve her lot if only for a short while. Outwardly I am calm, present as an intelligent, reliable, amiable friendly young man, inside I feel cold, emotionless and totally conditioned from years of living at the whim of others.

Two days after the funeral of my father I visited the house under the guise of wanting my birth certificate and health care card while my siblings look at me like I am an alien my mother surrounded by the usual collection of women that descend on your home following a death we look in the bedroom, my mother cannot read or write but showed me where father keep any paper he feels is important which simply is under the mattress. Ensuring we are alone together I find the document I need. First surprise, I am a year older than I thought. I was also born in March, not May as I believed. Anyway I made a show of finding the money and cautioned my mother not to reveal it to anyone, not even the children.

I encouraged her to move to Cork where she has an older sister married to a farmer who I am sure would not only accept her but welcome the large sum of money mother would contribute. As my aunt was visiting I made it clear to her I supported the move which she immediately began to plan. Exactly five days after father was buried the entire clan went home with my aunt. Promising to visit soon I heave a sigh of relief as I watch the raggedy lot disappear from my life.

It is time to leave for London with the rest of my hoard rolled and tucked into my butt cheek then strapped down. My departure coincides with the latest escort of those who I couldn't crochet as I was taught. I felt for a lump and could feel a hardness. Packing my bag for the four night five day visit I take all things good, helping myself to a pair of shoes that belonged to his new grace worn only when travelling so will not be noticed for a while. I show a complete disinterest to ensure I draw no attention to myself. I accepted God doesn't answer prayers a long time ago but still I pray during the drive to the coast during the crossing changing to a thank you prayer once on English soil.

Once the ladies are checked in and I am put across the road I leave and walk briskly to the High street, within moments I find what I want in the corner shop windows, rooms to let, single is twelve pounds a week, I am spoilt for choice but decide quickly on the building owned by Asians on the corner of the high street, they do not mind Irish just pay your rent, keep down the noise and alcohol, no police problem thus ends the screening.

I don't know anything about Asians but I was sure the name Tony is not Asian. There in that corner shop I paid the fifty pounds deposit and returned with four months' rent, giving the impression I had gone to the bank. I am reminded I need to buy gas which is sold through the landlord, at three pounds the canister should last a fortnight. I will be taking up residency on Sunday. I plan to sleep for free in my usual room for the next four nights, bringing me to Sunday when my tenancy starts. I am left with the grand sum of two thousand and sixty-two pounds I have done well over the years stealing sums so small you wouldn't notice but now I must find a job and know exactly where I want to work.

The ability to read and write and have actual paper qualifications is a massive bonus, I make inquiries at the local college. Yes, I have the maths and English basic requirement for studying bookkeeping, my goal is to be an accountant to the wealthy. My education is free, I am also entitled to various benefits as a student and with DWP as I fall in the category of minority ethnic group.

Returning to clinic I approach the senior nurse who showed me how to open closed cervix explain to him I have now moved to England will be attending college locally and need a job, they need people to work alongside the nurses as they have major difficulties retaining staff once they realise the true purpose of the building, I begin work as an orderly using an emergency tax number awaiting the arrival of an NI number. I throw myself into the mix of life in London, making friends easily and in no time have a steady stream of knocked up female visiting me for the knitting pin, over the years did I cause deaths, I have no doubt I did but my fault, no I don't think so, folks just need to learn how to keep their legs together.

I made good money asking no more than fifty pounds. I got involved with so many different stuff I just went with the flow, the real money started to roll in by the barrow full when I made friends with Africans over Guinness consumption. I learnt two things quickly, do not take your eye off the target and whatever you do academically you must achieve.

I met Sule while purchasing liquid gold as I referred to the favourite Irish tipple. He was buying in bulk, chatted easily and invited me to the gathering round his flat, we both had college in common. It was a gathering of African Nations, beautiful women with bodies to die for and perfume smells like I had never imagined in my life, the men were dressed smart casual but you could see all their clothes were top gear. These people did not know about poverty.

We chatted easily and I knew there and then I would do anything to stick with these guys, I need their energy levels and focus to stay on track. I will emulate them, study hard and party often. Have you ever dated a black woman? Oh man ! try to imagine, they were nothing like the nuns and their filthy pretensions habits. The African woman delighted in what she wants, celebrates herself and had no problems being seen with me, I was adopted by a whole Nation.

Where is Adam? not that they wanted anything but I was their white brother and like they checked in with each other they checked in with me. Their unpredictable pattern of turning up at all hours to say hello or goodnight meant my crochet needle business tapered down very quickly particularly as several of the girls had needed hospitalisation in the past few months, I put this down to nerves as I was always listening out for the door. Financially I am okay, an African woman says we, without living with me, it is when is our rent due, have we got food in the house, do we need to get any shopping, a quick call from the phone box, several bags of shopping and not a word about how much I owe, dawn I love these people they love me back and time flies by.

When I am not in lectures, working at the clinic I am with my second family. Within two years my diet changed completely and so did my accent. Academically I am on par with the top student in my friendship group so nil jokes about stupid Irish, another fact I have never drunk enough to get drunk for fear of loose tongue. With the whole African nation behind me I flourish academically, these guys don't joke with their education but neither can they say no to a quick buck.

My encounter with the Afro-Caribbean hard nuts of Peckham high street came about via one of those come on guys it can be done Nigerian brothers, it was after final exams hanging around anxiously to see if I got the grades needed for Accountancy at Lincoln University, now I am aware of the awful tension between these two black groups with the Africans loathing the perceived lazy life style of their Jamo relatives as they referred to anyone from the West Indian Isle. Casual relations are a no no.

The men kept a distance from each other but occasionally the girls will clash with the Africans looking down their noses at girls who at the time appeared to have at least one child by the age of fifteen, these clashes usually took place at hairdressers when the girls realised they were the topic of scorn, it's fearful to watch the screaming and threats while the African just sat and looked with that smug look of I'm educated my level is different to yours.

We gradually ventured into seeking out food namely curry goat and patties, we had two places we frequented a small shop behind the shopping centre in Lewisham and a shop opposite the bus stop in Peckham, it was outside here while munching to our hearts content that we were approached by Eddy, he was matter of fact, had apparently been watching us for several months and had a business proposition, making it clear he was looking for finance. He had two and a half grand and needed the same amount, we would split fifty-fifty if successful.

A lady was to go and bring a package from Gambia. He was told we would get back to him. At five hundred pounds each we could raise the money for an investment that would only tie our money down for less than a fortnight, we all agreed we would give it a go.

Eddy asked that we meet him at the indoor market once we said yes. Handing over our money I am excited, anything to do with money excites me, Kola drops out on the day and I jump in handing over a thousand pounds. Eddy gives us one warning: don't talk to me unless I approach you and start a conversation, even if you are standing next to me in the shop don't engage me. All over the top I thought. Leaving him we tease each other mercilessly that we've been duped. Our weekly visit to Peckham continued the same as usual that very week Eddy called us to the back of the shop. The four of us minus Kola who Eddy made clear was not to follow.

Two thousand five hundred pounds each and five thousand pounds to me, he cut us short when we started to gush at him. Do we want to do more business? If we do, come and see him on Thursday, every Thursday he holds an audience at the back of the shop. We had all doubled our money in eight days.

Thus we funded the trade, only we didn't know what the trade was, the cutlass on the table and a glimpse of the hand gun in the open draw was enough to correct our head as the Nigerians say. When the others eventually stopped I continued Eddy and I wary of each other but making good money. For over four years I funded goodness knows what, made good money, occasionally something would happen to Gambia and it would change to Ghana, Kenya and so on. I listened attentively to Eddy in his Cashmere coat not doubting for one moment he is a Kingpin in something. My Naija brother warned me again and again, their attitude is if it's too sweet it won't last, well it lasted a good bit, the day it came crashing down clashed with landing my first job in the Financial district of Moorgate.

Leaving the shop with a bag of food and my latest return of thirty thousand pounds rolled tight and stuck between by dick and balls I cross the road to catch a bus to Victoria where Kola stays, munching absentmindedly on a festival a rich fried sweet dough ball everything happens at once, police vans and cars screech to a stop and mayhem ensues, men in bullet proof gear dog handlers and all sorts pour forth, storming into the shop where a few moments earlier I was collecting food after having met with Eddy in the back office. I follow the lead of those at the bus stop.

We walk away quickly, a strange mixture cursing the Police, the Africans cursing their Jamaicans brethren and the white British saying nothing but body language saying plenty. I stay with the people moving to the next bus stop. Thankfully that Eddy is not the chatty type or I might have been caught up in the raid, thus ending my easy money that had enabled me to let the knitting needles rest.

Kola is a joke, despite all the brouhaha he is dating Jamaican. He insists she is one of a few, daughter of a Pastor and is at medical school like him; he has never introduced her to a family member or friends outside the college four. Such is the way both parties have been brainwashed to see each other as opposition, citing lots of examples told and believed but none witnessed.

Keisha is an unassuming girl who knows the score, she makes herself scarce when Kola's very wealthy parents are around but makes full use of the palatial house a stone throw from Victoria train station an easy ride to St Thomas's Hospital where they are both based.

Keisha cooks cleans and moans about Nigerians and their loud volume, Kola teases her of her people's lack of drive and baby mama's and fathers, if there are two people who can build a bridge to draw the two nations close it is Keisha and Kola.

Unfortunately this is not to be, arriving unannounced one evening, Kola's mum sights Keisha in the front room, standing outside she gets the black carriage cab that brought her from Heathrow to call the police, there is a thief in the house. You can imagine the chaos and high expressed emotions that followed with Kola's mum stating Keisha will return to rob the property when they break up, is Kola unaware of these people and the way they operate, turning on Keisha she demands to know how many children Keisha has and if their fathers are in touch, if it wasn't such a tragedy it would have been a great play.

Keisha kept a dignified silence until Kola's rapid return from the hospital. Wishing him well, Keisha made it clear she doesn't expect further contact from Kola; she makes her exit to the clear instructions of Kola's mother, summoning the locksmith and the crushing words, Kola has a wife, Kola will be marrying the girl we have chosen for him!

That evening I go and see my friend knowing I am deliberately cutting ties, telling him about my new job I leave out the fact I have moved to Angel. We reminisce a lot on the years of friendship, the mad escapade of his mum arriving unannounced, I am curious about the woman he is going to marry. Kola is resigned and casual, she will be moneyed like me. These families don't want their wealth falling into the hands of the common man. I have learnt a lot, my confidence and positivity comes from the rich mad Nigerians who took me under their wings, I know I speak like them, dress like them, walk like them, talk like them, taking my time, pronouncing words properly and commanding respect when I open my mouth, the Irish accent a memory locked and key thrown away.

Getting the first job I applied for is a testimony to that, they comment on my polished presentation. Mixing with black people I have been able to reinvent the Irish boy, learnt good and bad, loyalty, steadfastness but most importantly the value of self, financial independence plus moving in the right circles and marrying well. With this I Adam plunged into the money making world of finance specialising in index trading.

SAM

Sam the Surveyor in reality Sam the man is a butcher and disposer, a product of the East End. Sam understood the rules and ethics of living in the East end long before his gullible peers. He spent many hours looking out the window of their fourth floor council flat, from this vantage point he gathered intelligence the police would envy, moving quietly and casually from window to window, he watched money, goods and drug exchange, beatings, punishments and hits carried out. He knew who belonged to which gang, who was snitching.

Another one from a dirt poor family background with nil appreciation for education Sam is the only one who remained in school with the support of a head who saw the possibility of a brilliant future for a boy who was often called away to help with the rag and bone trade his father ran. Sam's home while not free of the usual pain, hunger and neglect was settled compared to others of his age.

Sam knew the streets like the back of his hand, by the age of nine he had acquired a reputation for keeping a tight trap. His first job was being asked to get rid of a small package where no one would find it, Sam simply stuck the package in a broken down washing machine destined for the crusher. Age twelve Sam began to get a name for himself amongst men old enough to know better. He shunned his age mates, working quietly and diligently, moving money, goods, even live objects for all top notch people who wanted it done. Sam knew exactly what he was doing unlike boys his age who daydreamed.

His head teacher did not recognise criminal intelligence but took it that Sam was a sharp boy who just needed someone to invest in him and took him under his wings. Speaking to Sam's parents and asking permission to let the school help by applying for various grants to enable Sam to remain in education. Sam's father would have preferred his son helping him in his trade but with a wife he feared he quickly warmed to the idea of their son getting an education so that 'he can decipher and no one can cheat us with reading and writing'

By the age of thirteen Sam was a fixture around his college, no one questioned his coming and going. He would be seen tidying cupboards and arranging storage while peers played football or lolled around. Had anyone kept an eye on Sam they would have realised the school premises was Sam's depot for the various gang lords he worked for. Opening a post office passbook account. Sam ensured he didn't deposit money at the same branch, frequently rotating branches.

Guns, evidence, money, packages small and not so small were all hidden within the school storage premises courtesy of the lazy school keeper who was happy to have Sam do a large chunk of his work. Not once did Sam mix items up or fail to deliver them when needed. Whenever Sam was found working with his father then an item needed to disappear forever, Sam never looked at the items he was asked to get rid of, wet or dry hard or soft he could guess when it was a man made object or a piece of man himself.

A not unattractive young man, Sam was seen as a good catch as he had remained in education. Keeping to himself gave Sam the greatest protection, he avoided pubs as he knew most of the landlords were snitches working for both sides and often caught in the crossfire be it arms or fighting, knuckle dusters were the tool of the trade.

Sam was a walking A-Z of the East end with a hatred for Asians that would scare those around him if they knew what was going on behind his thoughts. Most of his Asian schoolmates suffered falls and trips when he was around but none could make sense of it and often thought they had genuinely tripped over.

During the day Sam could touch no one but under cover of the night Sam dealt it out good. He moved alone and never struck in the same place twice, leaving enough time and space between incident but mash up he did when he got going, he only hurt men ensuring a good battering to the eyes so that identification was impossible, Sam also never spoke, he simply picked his victim got close to them and bashed away.

As with psychopathic personalities Sam excelled at his studies to the delight of his uneducated family who all turned up proper East end style to attend his graduation, he had tried to explain what a Surveyor did until he simply assured them he would make good money, that was all that mattered. With access to buildings finished and unfinished Sam pretty much continued his contact with the east end gang families except now whole bodies could be got rid off in the twinkle of an eye becoming a part of the buildings being erected at an astonishing rate.

Many pillars in and around London hold at the very least body parts. Sam gradually became a mini information centre for most thieves of calibre like himself, a respectable man during the day, to be found drinking good wine in the various posh wine bars springing up, Sam would nurse a glass of wine all evening while those around him will believe he is matching them glass for glass. Thus he picked up valuable information on politics, trading, property and anything else that was worth knowing.

Sam chose to find a home close to Custom's House on the Thames, the massive Sunday market acting as cover for delivery and exchange of goods on a scale that would give the tax man a coronary. If the law knew it looked the other way, the East enders are a unique breed. Sam did not do drugs but did just about everything else, no one knew where he lived, not even his family. Sam has a flat a few minutes from his parents, his mother delighted in letting herself in to clean and sit in the simple tastily furnished in masculine black and white flat. She complained endlessly that Sam was never in and simply assumed he was with a lady friend.

If there is one thing that doesn't interest Sam it is the opposite sex. Sam knew he is gay before he knew his times table. Sam loved the male anatomy, he thought of nothing else all day but knew to disclose that would earn him the label faggot.

Recognising money was to be made in the building trade Sam invested in his first property as soon as he landed his first job, keeping all his purchases to under thirty thousand pounds mostly two bed roomed properties, which once done up he rented out to the local council wherever the property is guaranteeing lifelong tenants if he so wished and money rolling in without holdup every month. By the age of thirty five Sam has twenty two properties. He has a good estate management team, he doesn't mind the tax and warned the company he uses not to cut corners as he doesn't want the taxman's headache.

From his properties Sam chooses a corner house tucked under the A13 route, here he brings back his liaisons, most of whom when able to get away from Sam move addresses immediately to other cities rather than remain in London.

Sam is not a violent lover. It always starts out well, the fine young men are wined and dined, taken on exotic holidays, credit card bills paid off, gifts, cars then taken to shop in exclusive areas they've only heard about. Tickets to top film premier and shows become a norm, nothing is too much trouble. Initially the fools think they have landed the jackpot with Sam. Sam reels them into a world they previously peeped in the window at, for months it's just kisses and cuddles, with Sam enjoying dressing up in his favourite silk pants and Chinese dragon emblem dressing gown, nothing feminine just the feel of silk exciting him no end.

The build up is slow, with Sam hating himself for wanting a same sex person. An expressionless guy, the innocent victims have no idea what awaits them. Suddenly they are pounced on and passion they had never imagined is unleashed, cries and pledges of I'm okay, I'm tired fall on deaf ears, yet Sam is careful not to hurt, like time he just keeps going. First they cry then they beg then they threaten finally they try to escape, this is their first mistake.

Sam is not violent but knows how to immobilise, you see when others had chosen to join gyms Sam went to train as a security expert, so the guy trying to get away from Sam didn't make it out of Sam's arm reach. Now Sam starts reminding them of the ridiculous amounts he spent on them all the while banging away, but with a clear head for figures he recites the various amount spent pointing at no time did he say he was giving the money but is a loan to a friend and could the friend now not do this little thing for him, most gave in when they realised the staggering amounts mentioned, when the ordeal is over none ever returned but Sam expects that. He gets laid a handful of times a year and finds total satisfaction whenever the opportunity surfaces.

Making waves and meeting milestones at work a nonsense Sam comes to the attention of the CEO, his well meaning boss introduces Sam to his daughter Cindy, a blond blue eyed beauty who makes Sam's skin crawl but he swallowed the bile and hid his revolution well, within a year they are married, Sam seeing it as an investment realising later to his dismay this time he is the one on the receiving end when his wife and her family hid the small fact she was diagnosed with Bi-Poplar Affective Disorder while studying for her Masters.

Their honeymoon was spent trying to understand dosages and relapse signatures. Between sharing the crisis plan with Sam they apologised profusely having assumed Cindy had told Sam about her difficulties. Cindy on the other hand spent the time doing what she does best, painting and photographing, Sam had never heard of honeymooning with the in-laws but such was the fear Sam would abandon Cindy her parents went along on the two weeks trip to the island of Bali.

That let's wait until we are married, the reason became clear when Cindy kept to herself not that Sam wanted conjugal rights. Cindy as far as Sam knew remained a virgin unless she managed to get laid before they met. Life wasn't so bad, Cindy was flown to Switzerland yearly suffering crisis periods just before each new year, despite this Sam was supportive, he made a decision if she was his cat or dog, he would take care of it so she would be his It! and take care of her he did. Visiting her in hospital until she stabilised, reassuring her parents their only child is in good hands.

Cindy came in danger of being killed shortly after one of her returns from the Swiss clinic, in deep sleep she rolls over and begins to fondle Sam, Sam who was exhausted from a long flight back from a meeting in Hong Kong came awake slowly having been dreaming about the discreet liaison he made with the Japanese first engineer of his flight into Hong Kong. A guy who had matched Sam in appetite, lasting power and needs, for the first time Sam felt accomplished like one who had been looking for a destination and found it.

Coming awake his member that had been hardening deflated and with the realisation he was home, with a woman he didn't want tugging at him, bringing his knee up he stuck his foot into her stomach lifted and kicked in the same moment, Cindy landed in a nasty heap on the floor her head striking the Japanese footstool brought back for her as a gift. Her scream had Sam jumping awake looking scattered and in shock to see his wife on the floor blood pouring out of the back of her head, Ensuring he got her to consider herself having a nightmare then trying to get away and falling out of the bed caught in the bed cover tripping falling backwards, Cindy in her agitated state would have believed anything, with a compression applied Sam drove her to the nearby Chelsea Hospital. If Cindy knew she never gave it away, but that night she asked Sam if she could sleep in the second bedroom, Sam volunteered to move out of the main bedroom, Cindy never again laid her hand on her husband apart from the necessary public display.

Sam's life is back on track, this suits him just fine and he has to work hard not to display any emotion when his in-laws apologies over and over about Cindy not wanting to share a room with him. Not much to Sam really. He stayed away from the East end of his youth, kept his flat for the few times a year he was able to get sex, Sam the man has plans and it's not to be caught in a honey trap scandal.

As an only child Cindy is close to her cousin, asked to be the maid of honour Sam making an appearance is essential. On a blustery spring day in April they troop to Eltham Palace where the wedding and reception is held. Secure in the life he's built for himself Sam has no concerns or care in the world as he walks in and takes a seat on the bride's side of the family, looking up to he finds himself staring into the smouldering brown green eyes of one of his conquests at his corner flat, dressed in top hat and tails Sam cannot break eye contact.

For the first time in his life Sam feels fear, there is a whooshing noise in his ears and the room darkens then brightens in sequences, Sam realises he is a panicking, but years of self discipline kicks in, drawing all his strength he looks down his nose and raises an eyebrow at Paul who is the groom, he gets an immediate reaction and knows he is safe they both have something to lose. Paul too is clearly marrying money rather than love.

The ceremony goes without a hitch, when Sam manages to get to the bride and groom he invites them over for a meal before they fly out for their honeymoon, this delights Cindy no end. Paul smiles miserably, sure Sam has more of the same in mind for him, his mind plays back the scene of when he met Sam. Paul was studying and had been told by a friend about an App to link you to mature adults wanting companionship for activities they are interested in.

The first couple of outings Paul had was to nice Michelin star restaurants before he met Sam. With Sam he flew first class to Beijing, while Sam concluded his meetings and business, Paul slept, ate, shopped and generally marvelled at the world of the rich. On return to England he was given an envelope with five grand. It was Paul himself who contacted Sam to say he is at Sam's disposal should he require his company in the future thus the stage was set.

Trips of a weekend in Madrid to a week in far flung places followed, Sam never made a pass at him, thanked him for his time and gave him generous amounts. Despite writing his thesis at University Paul was at the beck and call of Sam, he knew it meant a good time and always obliged. Five months of living above and beyond his means via Sam's generosity had Paul looking at Sam in a compassionate way, never imagining himself paying for other people's company, nor did it occur to him that pay day is always a day away.

That evening they had a meal at some restaurant that had a three month waiting list, returning to the flat was routine with Paul catching the train from Canning town to head back home in the morning.

If Sam had given any indication he was interested in Paul would have obliged but no, one minute Paul was asleep then a heavy weight that spread his legs wide open and kept them open for pretty much the next three hours, screaming was out of the question Sam is not a stranger and kept up soothing dialogue throughout his act of non-stop pounding sex.

When he finished he pulled Paul into his arms and cuddled him further confusing Paul and desensitising him, the conversation never stopped how attractive he found Paul how in love with Paul he is, what does Paul want he would support him in all areas Paul only had to say and on and on it went for the rest of the night, Paul raw and in severe pain had the common sense not to let on how disgusted and frightened he was, also made reassuring noise back about really liking Sam but felt overwhelmed by the passion, now he knew Sam thought he was fine with it.

Paul expected to be ravished again but it seemed thankfully Sam was done. Now seven years on they find themselves standing toe to toe married to cousins, at this thought Paul felt faint and tugged at his cravat without realising it. Dinner was agreed for the night before they flew out.

Like the predator he is Sam had thought through and planned the perfect evening, he felt incredibly turned on at seeing Paul again, he particularly liked Paul's small dainty like figure and his soft quiet voice, Sam remembers the softness of Paul's skin where he's never met a white guy who shaved below Paul had stuck in his mind because of this, a pleasant surprise when he had slept with him. Sam realised he liked a groomer, clean body manicure nails and smart haircut. If hell froze over he was going to sleep with Paul and knew the perfect place, while Cindy chatted away happily beside him and Paul looked pale enough to warrant his new bride to ask if he was okay.

Sam happily drank in Paul noting the cleanliness and sharpness in his manner, feeling himself stir Sam positions himself so Paul has no choice but to follow the direction of Sam's gaze and hand as he brushed the crotch for a brief second outlining the bulge, mercifully for Paul some friends came up and he was able to turn his back on Sam.

Paul's new bride put the lack of erection and fatigue down to tiredness, reassuring him to get plenty of rest; she cuddles him, spooning herself into his back. Paul lay there in the dark scenario after scenario played in his mind, how to get away from Sam, nothing looked remotely possible without raising questions. Cindy had mentioned in passing that the wealthy Londoners did not like Sam as he had a habit of buying their businesses and home when the chips were down for them, this only added to Paul's sleeplessness, recognition he is dealing with a ruthless individual. As it is with nature when awaiting bad news the hours fly while dragging when impatiently waiting for positive things to happen. Paul finally dropped asleep from sheer exhaustion at dawn.

Seven pm found him at Paul and Cindy's door, thankfully the home help opened the door, a tour of the house had Paul wondering why two people would need so much space, it escaped Paul there was a door they didn't look in. Returning upstairs they are joined by Sam, kisses and handshakes exchanged they sit down to dinner. Paul forces himself to eat, feeling a mixture of terror tumbling in the pit of his stomach unchecked as Sam tries again and again to touch him with his foot under the table, a feat made possible by the intimate dining plan.

What they ate, drank and talked about Paul has no idea, feeling the sweat well up under his armpit each time he remembers his night with Sam. For a wild moment he wondered what would happen if he was to blurt out the facts. Taking strength from the fact he is no longer the same kid seven years ago he looks Sam straight in the eyes as a form of warning, Sam smiles back giving him a long stare, on queue the ladies start talking fashion, Sam asks Paul to come and catch the rest of the football match with him.

Leading Paul down to the basement level each cradling a glass of Remi Martins Paul finds himself in a typical man den, done in bold black and white contrast, picking up the controls Sam switched on the large screen turns the volume down low and plunks himself down, Paul continues to stand where he is just inside the door, he wants to speak but his throat is stuck together, he looks at Sam like a deer caught in headlights he remains rooted. Sam walks over to him, taking his glass out his hand, he sets it aside.

Taking a motionless Paul into his arms he holds him close and begins his spill, talking in a low soothing tone, Paul doesn't realise when Sam turns him round to face the door but snaps out of his paralyses when pressed against the door he feels Sam undo his belt and move his trousers down pulling one shoe off and easing just one leg out, in a moment Sam has his legs spread and begins the relentless drive, with his face squashed against the door, mindful of the low volume of the TV Paul prays for a quick release, if forty minutes is quick then he doesn't want to think what would happen to him if left alone with Sam.

Taking the tissue Sam hands him, Paul finally finds the strength, 'this is the last time you touch me, I will tell everyone and would rather walk away from my marriage than you ever touching me again. I am not gay, I did what some students do to get through Uni. You have a lot to lose Sam. I haven't got your business image. I find you totally repulsive, if you think I'm kidding, come near me again.

With that last statement Sam finally reactions a loud long unnecessary laugh picking up the control he increases the volume, keeping his back to Paul he waves in a dismissive manner making a point of taking a satisfying pull of his brandy, he hears the click of the door and Paul's receding steps only then does Sam breath properly, if Paul had been brave enough to walk over to Sam he would have seen the sheer terror in Sam's eyes of being outed as the closet man he is. Suddenly the smell of Paul no longer brings pleasure, switching the TV off he heads to his room, the irony of others having frantic showers to get rid of his smell not lost on him.

Heading back down in a linen shirt and pants he finds the trio making a move to wrap up the evening. Bye-bye's said, Cindy states to Sam in the coldest voice with deadpan eyes and expression if you ever bother Paul again I will kill you and give my illness as the reason. I have a condition Sam not a diagnosis of stupidity. Anyone can see at the wedding that you and Paul knew each other but more importantly he wasn't happy to see you, that got me thinking and your behaviour tonight at the dinner table explained it all. Cutting Sam off as he attempted to speak, Cindy continued. I dropped my hankie a few times to make sure I saw what I saw, you trying to play footsies with Paul while he did his best to avoid you.

If you go back to your man den you'll see a small phone positioned by the tv, if you had watched any tv and I was wrong you would have spotted the phone, it's on a wide angle so anything that took place in that room would have been captured. Listening to Paul trying to be as quiet as possible while throwing up meant I didn't need to go and retrieve my phone. You leave him alone the way you've left me alone.
Continue to use your corner flat if you're lucky none of your unwilling conquests will report you for rape, rape is not when you are violent its cohesion forcing someone against their will not giving them a choice or say Sam, rape is what you do whatever you prefer to convince yourself it is, but leave Paul alone Sam. I actually told Paul I know and it will never happen again, why do you think he was more relaxed when you came back. Check out your antics then tell yourself it's consensual, goodnight Sam.
If Cindy had known the monster she unleashed that night she would have held onto her words, every single chap that Sam took to the flat after that suffered the fate of being drugged and roughed up to wake with scanty memory of acts that took place or knowledge and complete disorientation of time and place. Each person paying for the perceived insult and frustration of a man couldn't be himself.
Thus the years passed with Cindy painting and drawing in between spells in hospital while Sam the man continues to build his mini empire having successfully reduced any chance of anyone from his past finding him out, honouring his father in law by taking his surname, not that anyone from Bethnal Green would recognise the polished man as one of their own.

JW Wilson

JW takes a lot of reading where does one begin with him, making myself comfortable. I begin to read about a man who is not who he says he is but then he is. The American who headed a multibillion empire. Born to Marylou-beth and taken casually like a bag of groceries the stolen baby Billy incident made headlines and was regularly brought up as a cold case investigation on TV, eventually as it was pre DNA dates it was concluded the boy had been stolen by a female who wanted to be a mother but couldn't. As the young college mother of the child eventually moved away with her family following the distressing events it soon faded from people's minds, moving on to the next juicy occurrences that were taking place up and down the country. When questioned about the identity of the child's father the young woman Marylou-Beth refused to answer, stating it was her child she had given birth to and taken care of him without anyone's help, the father and I are not together.

Billy's new mother Lucy-May, a real roughneck hillbilly, had given birth five days early to a stillborn child, stopping long enough to bury the little one they had continued their drive. Lucy slightly crazy with the fever of loss and milk that would not stop flowing with no newborn to give it to had simply picked up a watermelon, scooped up the child and put the watermelon under the baby blanket, opening her blouse in the back of the truck she watched with contentment as the child fed without even opening his eyes, by the time the mother realised she had been pushing a watermelon round Lucy-May and Bobby-Joe were long gone. Back in their community no one batted an eyelid at the appearance of the baby.

Named Billy by his dirt poor farming parents he settled down into the wanderer life they lead just outside Royal. Billy's early days were unremarkable, on the move with the season to where they were needed the one consistency was they were referred to as trash by fellow Americans, yet Billy regularly showed knowledge and wisdom beyond his age you only had to explain or show him anything once.

Despite the two mile hike his mother ensured he got an education, there was something very special about Billy, Lucy just knew. Supported by his mother to attend school Billy soon took the lead when it came to handling correspondents for the family once he could read and write, at home he showed no interest in corn but regularly gave farming and innovative advice to his father which bore fruit until eventually his father stopped asking him to get involved in hands on planting and farm matters.

Billy could be found hanging around town, clean clothes and the one black pair of trainers that he kept immaculate, never got into trouble or anyone's way but soaked in the knowledge and modern approach around him. Billy wanted to belong amongst people he admired. He repeated words spoken until he was happy with his pronunciation. Like a sponge he soaked up the knowledge and skills in town filed away for the right occasion. Home life apart from their lowly status was fine, his five other siblings on the other hand were like cheese to his chalk, they spoke like their father, walked like him, spat tobacco like him and dreamt in farmland. Dirty and crude they ran wild but knew from the beatings they got from their mother to leave Billy be.

During school then college Billy didn't try to befriend the popular boys knowing they wouldn't accept him but stayed close enough to observe them and their mannerism. With an indulgent mother Billy dressed well for a trash farmer's son. The more versed and experienced adults who came across him in those days remarked that he would go places but there was something calculating about Billy.

By the age of fourteen like others his age and in view of the largeness of area Billy had access to a small car. The person Billy most wanted to be was Jefferson, a lad who bore an uncanny resemblance to him but not enough to remark on as he was polished to the point of shining in manners, character and the manner he carried himself. Jefferson and his posse of rich male kids were popular beyond the news. Billy watched him, listened to him and learnt what he could of life in the bigger towns and cities outside college that he never got to see. Jefferson came from the richest corn producing family and hung out in town a lot for the girls who flocked to speak to him. To ensure no comment was ever made about him Billy dressed and groomed himself in a manner that minimised the resemblance.

Age seventeen late one evening the conversation is about heading to a casino upstate before driving back down highway fifty-seven then changing to seventy-four for the drive back to Indianapolis where the Jefferson spread is. Well if I can't go with them I will see them returning Billy decided.
This decision finds Billy parked at the intersection of railroad and county road twenty some hours later. The screech of tires and almighty bang woke him up in the early hours, jumping out of his car he runs to where Jefferson's car has come to rest Jefferson has been thrown clear and is dead, Ted and the other three who are still strapped in their seat are covered in blood unconscious.

Running back to his car Billy goes to Jefferson working quickly he changes all apparels with him then drags him into his own car seat leaving the handbrake off rolls the car down the same embankment ensuring it crashes into Jefferson's car that had started to smoke, he sticks his hand under the car and gets handfuls of petrol which he rubs lightly over his clothing and his face, going back to his car he pushes it first then comes back for the Jefferson car, knowing the impact would set both cars on fire, Billy pushes knowing success means a new life, the impact bares the results he wants, it is this double explosion and the resulting fire that draws attention to the area.
What Billy had not anticipated was the intensity of the explosion and his petrol rubbed clothing, when he caught fire from one of the embers flying past Billy was convinced he was going to die, engulfed in fire and pain he managed to roll himself a couple of times before passing out.
This was how his body was recovered as the only survivor of the two car crash with Jefferson's family accepting responsibility and paying the grieving families without the matter going to court.

Billy now Jefferson was flown to Mount Sinai Hospital the leading and the best, put in a coma for the first ten days, then he was slowly allowed to wake, mirrors were banned and his mother took up residence at the hospital which Billy found hilarious, a woman who couldn't tell her son apart from a stranger. Thus began a two year period of rehabilitation, learning to speak, then walk as plastic surgery after surgery followed.

The SALT input ensured he lost any pronunciation that could connect him to his previous life, the trauma to the head explained the gaps in memory. No one could explain the disappearance of his asthma or borderline diabetes, it was assumed the time in hospital aided the recovery of the conditions. Skin graft to his arm and leg and face ensured his old yet new face was accepted.

Nothing but the best was okay, when he got names and places wrong it was excused. JW only got something wrong once, name person or item.

The one regret his parents had was following his accident he wouldn't ride his favourite horse who seemed to know his owner couldn't ride and shielded away from him any time he came to the stables.

Eating food he had previously disliked took his parents by surprise but delighted them. On his nineteenth birthday his father gave him thirty percent of the family fortune when after two years of intensive rehab and private tuitions he got into Yale no less. Here JW really started to reinvent himself, presented with a clean slate as Jefferson not once did he waste his time with thoughts of the life he left behind, Billy died a long time back.

An uneventful life to some but a prayer answered JW threw himself into life at Yale University, doing all the right things he excelled and was respected by all who knew him, but behind his back the same statement was repeated, there is something about Jefferson! such was the intensity in approach to anything he had to do, eventually people accepted it's just Jefferson. In his third year he was drawn to a senior like himself, like him Mai came from an affluent background, the friendship was not discouraged but the tension between the fathers did not go unnoticed. This was not a meeting of the flesh rather a coming together of two brilliant minds, their attraction for each other as academia.

Mai was fair and good on the eye, well mannered hardworking she had a no nonsense attitude to life, JW was drawn to her brain, there was no physical attraction just a mutual recognition of 'I will step over anything that stands in my way' Chatting after a lecture she dropped a piece of paper as she picked it up her blouse rose up and for a few seconds JW caught sight of something familiar that he couldn't really place, just a slight skin patch. Inviting Mai over to continue their chat, five of them pile into his car and head home.

Hearing his parents' car arrive JW goes through to welcome them and to let them know he's got friends over, if he hadn't been looking at his mum he would have missed the look, venom so terrifying but so quickly masked, his parents say hello and leave them to it. Giving them a moment Billy excuses himself to use the bathroom, he hears them as soon as he gets to the door of his father's office 'he brought your bastard home, your indiscretion is sitting in my lounge, you said I would never have to see any child, you promised me' well she's here in my living room'

Christ of all the people he could make friends with why her for goodness sake why her, she has to go, you have to tell Jefferson we don't want friendship with that family, tell him it's trade tell him anything just make sure I never have to see her again. At that moment JW realised he got a glimpse of the birthmark on the edge of her armpit same as his. One of the reasons no one had doubted he is JW, thinking this was a stroke of luck he realises he is also one of JW's bastards. Mai is his sister, no wonder he is drawn to her.

Having softened towards his mother he waits for her to leave fathers office, following her up the stairs he goes into her room and without a word gathers her into his arms. I heard everything Mum, I promise her I will have nothing to do with her in the future. I'm sorry I had no idea, crying gently as taught she tells her son, there are a few children up and down the Country wherever they have investments, she has not met any, did not realise Mai was one of that product until a summer trip she saw the then child in a swimsuit and noticed the birthmark.

Give me a moment mum, I'll be back. Downstairs his visitors are informed mother is not feeling well, all depart. Returning upstairs JW settles on the chaise longue in his mothers room.

Talk to me, he says to a mother who is more than happy to offload. Half a dozen children from his liaison with women from the top tier of society to a school teacher. I've lived in fear of them turning up, she shares.

Just curious do you know where the other five are. Yes mother responded I got a detective to get me details on each, it was easy your father sends monthly allowance to all, the worst is the teacher even after her son went missing he continued to take care of her thankfully she did not have another child. I love Daddy but he sure has put me through a lot. How old is the file ? JW I tell you such is my fear I have made sure I know where they are, the details are checked every summer and updated.

Let me have the file mother, a problem shared and all, more important you've protected me so far, I need to have knowledge of all to continue to protect myself and the family fortune in the future. Handing the file over my mother looked like she was about to pass out, lying down she asked me to leave her. It was a terrible shock coming home to see Mai, having just received the latest report a mere three weeks ago to find the same girl coincidentally wearing the same dress sitting in her front room had been too much. I kiss her on the forehead and repeat I love her after all it costs me nothing.

Settling down in my part of the house, I read. These young people are literally pointers for each place of investment for my father. If we had a plant there he had a child, if there was a production line there was a child there, in fairness if you got us together you will see we are sired by the same man. Suddenly the desire to laze around in Europe for the summer goes out the window. I study each file like an exam then go and find my father. I request to visit our investments, something he's been trying to get me interested in for a while. A tour! He says great stuff. Had JW senior had an inkling of the elimination of his five children he certainly wouldn't have supported the trip. The dutiful father quickly ensures arrangements are made for his son's comfort, putting the refusal to take someone along as a sign of maturity in the young JW.

To ensure he is close home JW junior asks for the schedule to be in the following order, New Albany, Columbus, Richmond,

Marion and Kokomo. He shares his plan with no one, prior to setting off spends as much time picking his mothers brain about the other children to ensure nil child left out. His mother marvelled at sons patience, listening to her recite all the facts she knew several times, she practically knew the content of the files off head.

By the time JW set off not only did he know content of the file back to front he could also pick his siblings out in a crowd, the nonstop study of the file content making him feel feverish, no way is he going to sit around waiting for one of them to show. Their age similar it would appear all were born within a three year period, daddy has been a busy man. The next few weeks are going to be interesting. The plan is to keep it simple, make friends, reveal who I am to ensure I get them on their own. Unlike me who lives at home all five lives away independently in their own way, whoever it is Mum used to keep tabs is the best in the business, all details needed right down to the minute details. Locations, work, home address, you name it nothing was left out.

My movement is thus, simple Carotid Sinus, if you don't know it is that spot structure that when pressed on one side of the neck can cause a person to faint, known as a pressure sensitive area located within the Carotid artery that major blood vessel that supplies our brain with blood, so if know where to press, cut the blood supply off and lights out keep the pressure on and snuff out. My plan is simple and foolproof and without boosting the best way to get to any human born of casual relationship is to give a waterfall of positive self identity and the 'I am' biscuit for a perfect bite. Keeping it simple is what brings success and safety.

I will introduce myself to each sibling, ask them to join me and get rid of them between each destination. No bastard child can resist when identity and validation comes knocking. With father having called ahead I insist on going on my own secure in the knowledge of my ability to return home the only child of JW snr. New Albany first to visit the lumber and ironwork factories. Columbus power solutions-energy. Richmond..Quaker controlled region I wonder how father managed to access some of the fertile land for crop production. Marion quilt factory. Kokomo Automobile assembly plant.

I will not bore you with the details, it was the same reaction, like a plant desperate for water. Each of my siblings took one look at me and wanted my lifestyle, telling them about the other sibling at my next destination and making contact when I am ready to leave town. I was able to leave town with each, not even giving time for a call, all the time in the world for that, making sure lots of glimpses of the hundred dollar bills stacked neatly just for that purpose, always late evening departure.

Mapping out each journey I chose my locations before making contact having previously visited the place to avoid any surprises.

Each contact was the same, introducing myself, creation of excitement, encouragement to come and meet the other siblings, the usual line that father couldn't wait to have us under the same roof. He sent me, and wants all his children together. Life is going to be wonderful. I'm glad I met you. I can't wait for you to come and enjoy all that I have access to, let's go and each followed me, after all what did they have to wait behind for. Each male sibling died exactly halfway to our destination and from the departure destination where I picked them up. I simply pulled over and said I needed to take a leak, encourage them to do the same and went straight for the appropriate Carotid Sinus.

They went out like a light. I ensured I kept pressing, putting all my strength in to ensure that there was no more life and simply tossed them down the foliage. It would take a miracle for anyone to find them. Someone would have to stop at that very same spot to take a leak and be looking down the Valley to spot a body. Thus went Noah, Oliver and Theodore. More difficult where the two females seemed to be more alert and didn't just up and follow me. It was difficult to end Mai's life but she had to go, she put up a hell of a struggle.

In the process not only was I pressing down on the Carotid Sinus to ensure that the blood supply was cut off I also had to rough Mai up a little bit more from irritation that the girl I was looking forward to dating turned out to be one of my dad's five seconds of enjoyment somewhere but more her refusal to come out of the car to stretch our legs, with her offering to continue the driving, fussing she hadn't told her mother where she was or who she was with.

With Mai I felt a connection but Marion there was no such thing. It was worse, this girl is fat with annoying bouncy curls, she sure as hell did not take after father. Her mother must be big bones, since the last photo she has spread in all directions but still recognisable. Initially she thought I was trying to chat her up. Once she realised who I was she seemed not only disappointed but reluctant to speak to me, some nonsense about loyalty to her mother. Not aware of the rage behind my eyes, she talked a lot of nonsense while I listened patiently. Because of this she got a violent end. Once agreed she remained highly strung. When I did stop there were no lets get out and stretch our legs, I simply reached across behind her and pressing her head forward against the dashboard I put my entire weight behind the pressure.

Fright and surprise being the main element she died quickly, dragging her out of the car was no mean feat, I was pouring with sweat by the time I had her out and over the edge of the ridge, I ensured I used a branch to sweep the area to ensure nil curious highway police driver with sharp eyes stopping to see why curbside has so much disturbance. God I hated that girl, she reminded me of all I was and no longer am. Such was my fury I pounded her with both fists and booted her several times for good measure.

So here I am as far as I know I am now the only surviving child of JW senior and that's the way it's going to stay, those who are ruthless don't broadcast it they take care of matters, they don't waste time with emotions they're only interested in the facts and the effects plus the outcomes and if it's not favorable for them they do something about it, that's the meaning of ruthless. When they heard the news about Mai's disappearance, father was terribly upset.

On arrival back home I was out of the country within a fortnight. I can't remember the last time I remembered that I killed my half siblings, it's such an irrelevant information it has no place in my everyday life, they are obstacles that needed to be removed so that everything that I sacrifice by the roadside that day when I rubbed petrol on my body and was set alight is not jeopardized. I've come a long long way. I am not going back to that way of life where I was looking in on the rich. I myself am now looked at, people want to be with me, they want to be my friend, they want to enjoy the wealth that surrounds me, they want to experience the kind of life that is at my beck and call, plus fingertips. I am finally no longer the looker.

All this JW jr thinks is a secret. Unknown to him not once was he on his own. The precious son of his father his entire journey had a tail sitting on him. A clever ex-Nam veteran, each stop he double checked to ensure the bodies are never found. Each death photographed and a detailed report given to his mother rather than JW snr. For the rest of his life the man was quietly given an allowance by the old girl. Grateful but scared of her murderous son. These documents like others found their way to the holding area once JW made his mark in the UK and curiosity regarding the calibre of man heading a hydrogene supply to seventy-two percent of the nation at the time when things were good. Interestingly he didn't once show any interest in returning to his country of origin.

Sector Matters

Expressing my condolences to the group in front of me I get straight to the point. None of them pretended to be overly distressed by their loss. It is what it is. I begin to share the intel we have.

Sector 8 issues, the formation of new leadership, Sector 8 is terrorising the neighbouring sectorsImpacting the lives of those there. Broken away from the agreed council rules and structures that enabled us to live alongside each other peacefully. While not racially motivated it is clearly power driven. Complete domination of the people in Sector eight. Restricting movements and ensuring a percentage of the sector entitlement is made available for them,

Information about shortage of food and compiling of various ammunition, control of people's everyday life, ignoring Sector one directives their numbers quickly swell with the discontent braving the terrain to make their way to sector 8 collecting others as they make their way inland for what is called 'freedom of living' to do what they please when they please with a total disregard for what has helped us to survive so far.

As experts in your various fields I realise if anything is going to change and change quickly before things get out of hand and we implode the five of you in this room have the expertise, tools, brains, the decision making power and skills needed to make a difference. We, the Council, are asking for your help. Looking round the room I face each as I speak. The plan is simple, you will make your way inland some will require face to face others just the presence to carry instruction through. There will be a need to take some people out. I will meet with you individually to let you know what I know about you if you are in doubt, but as a blanket statement there is not one person in this room who is not a killing machine, so please let's keep it real. Be who you are, use this talent you have to quash the nonsense going on in Sector eight.

JW you will need to withdraw electricity supply to Sector 8, you will need to be there physically otherwise there will be question on the authenticity of the order, 'should you need to you have the Councils backing to take out anyone that stands in your way, you all do' I say knowing JW is the least significant of the group other than his holdings and the need to have him give orders and keep doing so for light as needed for the mission ahead.

Sam surveyor and security expert you will take the lead on the mission inland to sector 8, Matt will be working in tandem with you regarding disarming electric supply and making sure the supply stays off once JW has made his presence known at the Sector

Adam and Betty will journey inwards as a couple, never far behind Sam and Matt but not connectable unless their expertise is needed.

Susan IT expert and Medic will always be a short reachable distance from the others in case of any medical intervention requirement, I continue hoping her mental state holds.

In the middle of the meeting as I made my way to the essential map, the latest of the terrain that lies ahead chaos, we are under attack, my brain freezes for a moment, this is impossible the sector headquarter is so rigid up no one can approach without being seen non can certainly get in without being let, coming alive my brain screams, internal breach.... Rosie, no one can get to you without the aid of those close to you, the real enemy is always under your roof or in the backyard, rarely is it an outsider.

Nil alarm on approach so Rosie must have let them in the building the night before. It was quick and swift, what troubles me more is the language. Restrained, I struggle to understand this strange conversation. I look at Adam Susan Sam Matt and Betty, as each is lifted off the floor , what are they doing on the floor ? Once they are taken away I am left, asking me if I am calm and can be trusted to sit up and in the chair I nod affirmation, I am lifted up and sat in a chair, the circle of chairs remain, instead of the team I gathered sit Sector 8 terrors. My thoughts are murderous but hard to do much with a room full of people who will kill you without a second thought, their leader speaks.

Can you hear me James, are you with me, can you hear me the leader's voice is insistence repeating itself, looking up from where I had been resting my chin on my chest concerned about the latest messages and instructions that are distorted, the moss code missing vital bits the covert messages jumbled like written in a hurry information and directives not concise. I pick up the urgency of the content that forecasts and warns of looming disaster regarding sector one, it does not say if it is nature or man finally the persistent irritating voice finally makes me snap...what ? I yell what the hell is so important? You interrupt me? Looking up I see Adam and the other four have joined the enemy, all present seated and waiting for me. I did not call this meeting, why have they left their sectors to come down to sector one.

We really need you on board with this James Sector 8 leader Liam Williams starts, I stare at them in shock, at a mutiny no less ? I am Sector One leader. I shout, I call the shots, I say when, who where what and how many. I make the decisions, do the talking, not the listening, something is clearly very wrong here. Reverting to my military training I sat quietly watching, listening and waiting for a chance to take Liam out so they will remember who is boss.

James, do you know where you are.? Has Liam and the entire sector leaders lost the plot and their mind in the process. Do I know where I am? I roared, what do you think, sector 8?

If you can try and remember to address me as your named nurse and care coordinator, Liam response, you know everyone in the room for good record keeping. We will all say who we are and what we do. Care what! I watch all the sector leaders as they speak. Has there been a mass incident of hysteria? Why is Adam calling himself Liam, this guy singlehanded stole enough money via such sophisticated electronic fraud, it fucked up index trading enough for them to make a decision not to release the information to the public. My head throbs from the knocks received during the struggle to overpower me.

I'm Dr Samuel Francis, this is JW electricity controller but amongst other things in the past was a drug baron with the facade of total respectability but on off file best friend with the Colombians nil hesitation in taking out killing contracts on business opponents, up to his eyeballs with any corrupt foreign government that turned a blind eye to his drugs, fraudulent business moves as long as he deposits their 20 percent in the appropriate Swiss or Cayman account, now introduces himself as a Responsible Medical Officer.

Matt the electronic genius killer of two wives and two business partners states he is Paul Lardner Junior Doctor and ECT something or the other. This sadomasochist who took part in three murders in the space of ten days and is possibly responsible for countless other murders but with no bodies and the world population drifting all over the place there are no true statistics for missing people in the major cities he's lived in.

Sector two leader Susan introduces herself as Hannah Sky, ward manager, Susan the trained medic who used to live off internet drug purchases, medicating herself to keep the illness she wrestles with at bay, fantastic IT skills and record keeping of events and documentation she pops strong painkillers when the voices get so loud they hurt her head, I have evidence of her giving herself an injection in the thigh following our last meeting and her use of the toilet before leaving, so I know what I'm talking about but for now I'll listen to the drama that's unfolding in front of me.

Sam, my closet gay re-con expert, no terrain stumps him, he uses nature to his advantage and is the best security expert who sells information to the thieves that can afford his asking price now says he's Jack Dean a social worker. Betty, an ex-call girl alcohol dependent and bi-sexual to boot, insists she is Sharon Tills Occupational Therapist, when I raised my eyebrow she nodded her head then gave herself away by saying 'trust me'.

Yeah right trust a bunch of lying toe-rag sector leaders who are up to no good. This explains why there has been a distortion in recent days. Well the mission will go ahead at all cost even if lives have to be lost this rag tail collection in front of me will not be allowed to jeopardise the future.

JW Wilson saving the best to last like fine wine no one can rush JW.

'James, you have been very ill. This is your twenty-sixth day here with us, as you are not getting any better we are unable to take you off the section of mental health act and will be converting it to a section 3 to keep you in hospital and treat you, your consent is not needed. It's not the first time we have needed to use the mental health act to ensure you receive the treatment you need while unwell. We can see how unwell you are and will do our best to keep your distress to a minimum. He rambles on and on while I let my survival training kick in I lower my breathing and refocus my mind, where is my next instruction, as words like psychosis, delusions of grandeur, hallucinations wash over my head I see the formation take place in amongst the black scribble on the whiteboard.

This is part of the training, you are going to lead the expedition to the North yourself, just not now, relax and go with the flow, comply with everything, tell them what they want to hear, we need to get you ready for the mission ahead which will be grueling, what you have experienced today is a run of what can happen if you and your crew are caught. Get ready, the date is exactly six months from today, we remain on track.

Looking away I turn to those in the room and respond ' I understand, I am willing to stay and receive the treatment, the section 3 is for six months isn't it, yes comes the response. Fine let's get started I smile, getting up I walk quietly and majestically from the room, power and all senses restored, ahead lies a period of quiet. Six months is nothing, in no time I will be back managing the sectors and following instructions, for now sleep calls as the Diazepam takes effect. I am on special watch, turning my back I sigh and handover to sleep. Six months from today the mission resumes.

As I drift off the conversation being had is amplified. 'It's incredible how James took each healthcare professional and built a horrendous history around them. His conversation and beliefs got worse with the risk mounting each session I heard Paul Lardner's voice or Matt. We will have a low threshold for moving James to PQ....I smile as I drift off, PQ is the signature of my handler and has been since day one, I am in safe hands, these fools wouldn't know mental illness if it knocked and introduced itself. I am Sector One leader Richard Monice.

Incident form:
01-04-2025
Waterfront Ward
Time:09:02 hrs
Patient: James Perry-Kay
Diagnosis: Paranoid Schizophrenia

At 09:02 hrs, James barged into the wardround room, he locked and barricaded the team in the room. The entire incident lasted for 1 hour and 4 minutes. None of the staff was hurt.

In that period James was loud, grandiose and delusional about the environment and staff, he shared lots of conspiratorial theories and was clearly in the grip of a psychotic episode, calling himself Sector one leader Richard Monice.

While distracted, the Clinical Psychologist whom James referred to as his child was able to open the side door connecting the room to the staff office, in this way the team that had gathered to respond to the crisis were able to go in and get everyone out while restraining James. To note at no point was James violent.

Action:
The team reconvened shortly after James had been given intramuscular Lorazepam. Brief conversation with James and reassurance given he will be taken good care of, Section 3 explained, James offered to stay in hospital for six months as a voluntary patient. James' family have been informed.

Currently on two to one observation, asleep at time of report.
Staff debrief and support to take place at the end of the shift

Section 3 MHA papers prepared, Consultants recommendation completed.
Uploaded at 15:00 hrs.

www.ingramcontent.com/pod-product-compliance
Lightning Source LLC
Chambersburg PA
CBHW052209090526
44584CB00016BA/1784